FISHING
the Great Lakes
of New York

T0127608

FISHING
the Great Lakes
of New York

A Guide to Lakes
Erie and Ontario,
their Tributaries,
and the
Thousand Islands

SPIDER RYBAAK

BURFORD BOOKS

DEDICATION

To Susan for 30 years of . . . you name it!

CONTENTS

ACKNOWLEDGMENTS

COMPLETING A WORK this ambitious all by myself would have taken more years than I have left—not to mention gas, money, and time away from Susan, the cats, and my favorite fishing spots. Adding to the burden was Governor Cuomo's directive forbidding New York State Department of Environmental Conservation personnel from talking spontaneously to the media. Surprisingly, some DEC employees obeyed the order and wouldn't talk to me, forcing me to clear questions through the press office in Albany, a lengthy process complicating matters by involving way more people than was necessary, and often resulting in dull statistics. Fortunately, some of my old DEC contacts ignored the order, and their help, combined with the NYSDEC website and numerous private sources, provided everything from local fishing tips and techniques to secret fishing spots and charter trips, helping me complete the work. So here's a list of those I bugged most of all, at all hours: Marc Arena, Ron Bierstine, Sue Bookout, Captain Frank Campbell, Corky Cansdale, Raymond Chittenden, Janet Clerkin, Susan Douglass, Gary Fisher, Frank Flack, Todd Frank, Captain Ryan "Tiny" Gilbert, Captain George Haskin, Captain Matt Heath, Bill Hilts Jr., Mike Kelly, Chris Kenyon, Roger Klindt, Fred Kucharski, Captain Nick Lee, Captain Mark Lewis, Captain Tom Marks, Captain Dick McDonald, Mike McGrath, Captain Rick Miick, Mark Moskal, Larry Muroski, Stan Ouellette, Captain Darryl Raate, cousin Staash Rybaak, Captain Dick Stanton, Mike Todd, Dave Turner, Scott VanderWater, Harvey VanDewalker, Fran Verdoliva, Captain Bob Walters, Captain Mike Waterhouse, Migell Wedderburn.

INTRODUCTION

BEING RELATED TO Niagara Falls, a Natural Wonder of the World, is a hard act to follow. But Lakes Erie and Ontario, their tributaries, and outlet, the St. Lawrence River, give it the old college try. Indeed, each casts a spell on us. Whether we're humbled by the lakes reaching beyond our field of vision, mildly disturbed witnessing the roaring rapids of their major tributaries, delighted watching their skinny creeks wind over the countryside, or pleased by the intimacy of the Thousand Islands, merely being in their presence is enough to etch the experience into our fondest memories.

Unfortunately, most people are superficial and don't see the whole picture. If you look deeply, it becomes obvious that the water endlessly chiseling the mighty cataract and its spectacular gorge into the world's imagination is as productive as it is destructive. Running above the falls or below it, filling the lakes or pouring down the St. Lawrence River, the magical flow of New York's north shore boasts the greatest freshwater fishery on the planet.

But don't take my word for it. At press time, the world-record coho salmon—a species indigenous to the Pacific Ocean, no less—was wrenched from Lake Ontario. Arthur Lawton's 69-pound, 15-ounce muskellunge, a former world record, came out of the St. Lawrence River. The New York State record smallie (8 pounds, 4 ounces) and yellow perch (3 pounds, 8 ounces) were pulled out of Lake Erie. Thirty-pound Chinook salmon, smallmouths over 5 pounds, 20-something-pound northerns, 30-inch walleye, steelhead, brown trout, and lake trout stretching over 3 feet long, 4-foot muskies, and trophy landlocked Atlantic salmon are all available in sufficient quantities to make catching one a reasonable goal every time you head out.

Regardless of how you cut it, the Great Lakes, their tributaries, and their outlet offer a fish for every dream. And while there's no guarantee you'll catch one the size of the monster swimming through your imagination, this book can lead you to a critter that comes close.

NEW YORK'S WILDLIFE

While puma sightings have been reported all over upstate New York in the past couple of decades, their numbers are so small you've got a better chance of catching a meowing catfish than seeing a mountain lion.

About the most dangerous critter you are likely to encounter is a black bear. These can show up just about anywhere in rural New York; I've run into two of them in 50-something years of fishing, and both snuck away. Still, if you see one clumsily lumbering down the trail or splashing up creek toward you, make enough noise to be noticed, then make yourself as big as you can.

And then there are coyotes, thousands of 'em. Corrupted by timber wolf genes, they are fully 30 percent larger than the western variety. And though their howls have probably cut some camping trips short, there is no record of one hurting a human. Several have crossed my path over the years, but when they caught wind of me, they split so fast, I was left wondering if I ever saw one in the first place.

Besides dump ducks (gulls), the friendly skies over the Great Lakes are loaded with kingfishers, blue herons, cormorants, wild ducks, and geese. Loons can be seen in wildlife management area ponds and swampy areas of the St. Lawrence River. Bald eagles are making a comeback, and you can expect to see them on popular streams like the Salmon River.

Insects are so ubiquitous and plentiful, they can really bug you. Yellow jackets and bald-faced hornets have sent more than one angler diving for cover. In late spring, blackflies rule the air over backcountry creeks. Some are so aggressive, an old-timer tells me he's seen them chase trout. While that's stretching things a bit, they can swarm in such numbers from mid-May through June, especially in the Salmon River drainage, they'll drive an unprotected fly fisher off a stream in the middle of a mayfly hatch. What's more, not all insect repellents discourage them—indeed, some actually seem to sound the dinner bell. Those containing DEET work best. Most roadside streams and lakes are sprayed to keep blackflies in check, but waters in wild forests and wilderness areas are not.

Finally, we have a lot of mosquitoes, attempts at eradication notwithstanding. They've become particularly troublesome lately because some carry the West Nile virus, a pathogen known to be fatal to crows and humans. These tiny vampires are especially active at dusk and dawn, near shore around ponds, lakes, canals, and slow-moving rivers. They don't cotton to insect repellents. Those who are allergic to harsh chemicals, or simply wish to avoid them, should wear mesh garments over their regular clothes.

NEW YORK'S WEATHER

New York has a temperate climate with an average temperature of about 48 degrees Fahrenheit. But that doesn't mean we don't get wild swings. Most winters see thermometer readings drop below zero. Indeed, several years this century saw record-breaking snowfall and temperatures so cold, they turned weak followers of the global warming crowd into believing the earth was facing an ice age instead, causing some to burn their copies of Al Gore's *Earth in the Balance* for kindling. Syracuse, in the heart of the state, averages 120 inches of snow annually, a statistic that earns it the distinction of being the snowiest city in the country. The Tug Hill Plateau region, stretching from the north shore of Oneida Lake to about Watertown, is blessed with a meteorological phenomenon known as lake effect, in which cold winds blowing over the warmer waters of Lake Ontario generate enough snow to blanket the countryside from the tiniest Great Lake's east shore to the Adirondack foothills with an average of 200 inches each winter. While Lake Erie freezes enough most winters for anglers to walk out and drill for perch and walleye, and Lake Ontario's bays and ponds develop ice caps thick enough to support pickup trucks, Lake "O" seldom freezes over entirely; and even on those rare years when ice spreads out for several miles from shore, it's so thin, only the careless and suicidal dare to tread on it.

Summer is very humid and hot. Temperatures vary with sea level. The Finger Lakes region sees a lot of days in the high 70s and 80s. The St. Lawrence River lowlands are normally 5 degrees cooler, and the Tug Hill Plateau can be as much as 10 degrees cooler.

Spring and fall are the reason many New Yorkers put up with winter and summer. Temperatures range from 55 to 65. And while many complain that it is always cloudy or raining, the truth is, the sun shines about half the time.

CATCH-AND-RELEASE

One thing all competent anglers with average luck can expect to do in New York is catch fish. So many, in fact, that some will have to be released eventually for reasons ranging from the fish being out of season or too small, to catching more than you feel like cleaning, to simply not feeling like killing anymore. Of course, there are also those who practice catch-and-release religiously. Whatever the reason, it is in the best interest of all concerned for the critter to be released unharmed. Here are some simple pointers to ensure you release a fish with a future instead of a dead fish swimming.

- Avoid going after big fish with ultralight tackle. The cruel, frustrating struggle for freedom can exhaust them beyond recovery.
- Only use a net when absolutely necessary. Nets tear mouths, rip gills, break fins and teeth, scratch eyes, and remove slime, an important barrier against harmful bacteria.
- Keep the fish submerged in water, even when unhooking it.
- If you must remove a fish from the water, always wet your hands before touching it, and place it on something wet.
- If the fish is hooked deep in the tongue, guts, or gills, cut the line. Fish are bleeders, and an internal wound as small as a pinhole can be fatal. By leaving the hook in place, healing will occur around it as it rusts away. No hook is worth a life.
- Never lift a pike by squeezing its eyes with your fingers.
- Keep fingers out of a fish's gills.

PERSONAL FLOTATION DEVICES

Cousin Staash calls Brookfield Renewable Power Inc.'s mandate requiring anglers to wear PFDs while fishing the Oswego River between the power plant tailrace and Varick Dam in the city of Oswego "an exercise in a fishy form of nannyism." His position is shared by many anglers who feel wearing a PFD should be a personal choice, and don't cotton to in-your-face signs posted up and down the river reminding them rising water can be dangerous to their health. Still, when you're fishing on private property, you have to abide by the owner's rules, and at press time the power company was evicting anglers fishing the Enforcement Zone mentioned above without being properly dressed. At press time, the urge to pass similar feel-good legislation on the fishing and boating communities hasn't contaminated a majority in Albany yet—but, hey, you never know.

PREVENTING THE SPREAD OF INVASIVE SPECIES

Spiny water fleas, zebra mussels, water chestnut, round goby . . . it seems every year introduces a new critter into the Great Lakes anglers' lexicon. Unfortunately, exotic species hurt: They hurt fish by destroying habitat and competing for scarce food sources; they hurt anglers by fouling fishing spots and equipment; and they hurt the outdoors by altering the environment. Anglers can help prevent the spread of invasive species by following these simple steps posted on the "Stop Aquatic Hitchhikers" website:

- Remove all visible mud, plants, fish, or animals before transporting equipment.

- Eliminate water from equipment like live wells and bait buckets before transporting.
- Clean and dry boats, trailers, pets: anything that has come into contact with the water.
- Never release a fish or discard a plant into a body of water unless it came from there.
- Stream anglers should wear metal traction devices on their boots instead of carpet or felt.

STURGEON ALERT

The state's attempt to restore lake sturgeon into the Great Lakes system is bearing fruit. Anglers are catching increasing numbers of 4-something-footers, particularly in the large tributaries in spring. Although its size, shark-like appearance, and bony plates make it look tough, it's still a fish and shouldn't be handled. Females can take up to 26 years to reach reproductive age—males mature in half that time—and they only spawn about every 6 years. Lake sturgeon are totally protected, and it is illegal to target them or possess them. If you catch one and just gotta photograph it, take its picture while it's in the water, then release it immediately.

FISH CONSUMPTION ADVISORY

While eating fish is generally considered good for you, the Great Lakes and their tributaries have been corrupted to some degree by pollution and the state recommends eating only one meal (8 oz.) per month of most game fish and no more than four meals per month of most panfish. What's more, the "Health Advisories" section of the "New York Freshwater Fishing: . . . Regulations Guide" advises that women under 50 and kids under 15 eat no fish from these waters, and places additional restrictions on spots like the Lower Niagara River. For a printed copy of the state's detailed "Health Advice on Eating Sportfish and Game," or electronic updates on the health advisory, go to www.health.ny.gov/fish.

REGULATIONS

This state has so many fishing regulations, it takes the *New York Freshwater Fishing Official Regulations Guide* over 30 pages to list them all. Pick up a copy wherever licenses are sold and study the "Great Lakes and Tributary Regulations" section before fishing the sites listed in this book.

PUBLIC FISHING RIGHTS

The state has purchased easements along hundreds of miles of streams. These sites are normally posted with yellow signs announcing PUBLIC FISHING STREAM. Access is limited to the stream and the band of land 33 feet from the bank. Activities other than fishing are prohibited.

CAMPING

Many lakeside parks have campgrounds, and some even rent rustic cabins. Contact the park directly (see the appendix for addresses and phone numbers) for informational brochures. Camping in wildlife management areas is prohibited.

HOW TO USE THIS GUIDE

Numerous books have been written about fishing New York's Great Lakes region. However, none has covered every spot because many of the smaller tributaries run through private land and are inaccessible. This book is also limited in scope, including only those waters that are open to the public and easily accessible. The book covers 63 sites, detailing each in the following way:

KEY SPECIES: This section will include all the fish commonly sought in the spot.

DESCRIPTION: The site's physical characteristics will be given: stuff like the square mileage of the lakes and their rank on the list of the world's greatest bodies of fresh water. Stream descriptions will contain information on their sources, the distance lake-run fish can travel, and the locations of their mouths.

TIPS: Site-specific tips will be given.

THE FISHING: This section will provide details on the fishery: typical sizes you can expect to catch, bait and habitat preferences, seasonal variations, and stocking statistics.

DIRECTIONS: How to get there from the nearest major town or highway. Since one of the main focuses of this book is to introduce traveling anglers to this fabulous fishery's numerous opportunities, the directions will be the easiest way to go—not the shortest. For streams, the major routes paralleling them will be given.

ADDITIONAL INFORMATION: This section will contain on-site camping information, boat launches, bank-fishing access, and other site-specific information.

CONTACT: State and local agencies to contact for information on the site; phone numbers, addresses, and websites are listed in the appendix.

Lettered sites below numbered ones include additional features like access points, boat launches, and camping opportunities.

TO BEAD OR NOT TO BEAD

To those unfamiliar with ceramic beads, they're one of the hottest baits for steelhead. But the way you have to fish them is the subject of controversy. You see, they're rock-hard, just like baubles on a cheap necklace. If the hook is in the bead, all a fish does is breaks its teeth trying to bite it. So you have to fish one by hanging the hook anywhere from 0.5 to 3 inches below it. When the fish hits, you floss it with the line until the hook is stopped by its jaw, often on the outside. Purists claim this amounts to lining, a form of snagging, which is illegal. In their corner are trophy anglers who complain many of the fish they're catching are deformed by injuries caused by hooks snagging the hinge on the side of the fish's mouth, damaging it or tearing it right off. The fish not only looks unsightly, but can't close its mouth properly. A state fisheries biologist I spoke with under condition of anonymity says he doesn't feel the department will totally ban beads, but he does expect to see regulations on hook placement in the near future.

BEST TIMES TO FISH

All fish feed most actively around dusk and dawn. Some biologists and successful anglers claim the moon influences feeding, and commercial calendars such as Rick Taylor's "Prime Times" list the best days and most productive hours. Still, some fish like catfish and walleye feed best at night—especially when there's no moon, according to some—while yellow perch and northern pike feed best during daylight. The rest—from trout, salmon, and bass to muskies, crappies, and sunfish—feed whenever they feel like it.

SECURITY NOTICE

The terrorist incidents of September 11, 2001, commonly referred to as 9/11, have taken a big bite out of fishing opportunities. In the name of national security, the government has slapped a security zone around all nuclear power plants. Restricted areas are clearly marked with buoys.

DEFINITIONS (GLOSSARY)

BERGER KING RIG: This rig, generally used for muskies, allows a large plug like a Swim Whizz and a spoon to be run off the same line, giving the impression of a really large bait, or one fish chasing another. The spoon is attached to the screw eye of the plug's rear hook with an 18- to 24-inch steel leader. In cases where a three-jointed lure is used, the center hook is removed and the leader attached to its screw eye.

BONY WATER: Shallows over rocky bottoms.

BREAKLINE OR BREAK: Transition from a shallow flat to deep water.

CADILLAC FISHING: Angling from a driftboat.

CENTERPIN: A single-action reel in which the spool revolves on a centerpin and spins so smoothly that your offering moves effortlessly, in perfect time with the current, allowing the bait to remain at the desired depth throughout the cast. Popularly used in float-fishing.

CHUCK-N-DUCK: Generally practiced on fast streams, split shots are used with fly-fishing equipment to weigh down the bait and whip it to the target, while ducking to avoid getting hit in the head.

CHEATER: A lure on a leader is pinned into position on the main line above the rigger weight so it runs above the main lure. See *slider*.

CHUTE: Outlet to a bay or harbor lined with breakwalls.

COMBAT FISHING: Shoulder-to-shoulder fishing conditions found at all tributary hot spots during the salmon runs.

CONTROLLED DRIFT: Using a motor to control a drift affected by factors like heavy winds, strong current, and high water.

COWBELLS OR LAKE TROLLS: A string of spinner blades used as an attractor during trolling.

CRANKING: Casting crankbaits.

CURLY-TAIL GRUB: Aka twister tail and jigging grub.

DARTER: A cigar-shaped floating lure used for walking-the-dog (jerked so its head swings from side to side).

DEAD DRIFT: Allowing your bait to drift naturally with the current.

DIVER: Aka Dipsy, a portable trolling device attached to the line, allowing you to run a lure at greater depths than would by possible by itself, and off to port or starboard.

DODGER: An attractor used while trolling for salmonids, it swings back and forth like a pendulum.

DROPBACK: A spawned-out steelie heading back to the lake.

EGG SAC: Several trout or salmon eggs wrapped in mesh to resemble a clump of roe.

FISHING ON THE FLY: Casting from a moving driftboat while the guide rows to keep the boat in line on skinny water, the heat, and other white-water situations.

FISHING THE HEAT: Fishing in rapids.

FLASHER: An attractor popularly used while trolling for salmonids, it's set a short distance ahead of the bait and run at speeds fast enough to make it spin.

FLATLINING: Trolling a lure freely, without additional weight.

FLAT WATER: Aka smooth water and slack water; a slow spot in a fast-moving stream, usually in the middle of a pool.

FLEA-FLICKING: A derogatory term for fly fishing coined by average Salmon River anglers.

FREE-LINING: Fishing a minnow without weight or a bobber so it swims naturally.

HEAT: Rapids.

JUNKLINE: A trolling term referring to any line not on downriggers; a flatline.

LEAD CORE: A line consisting of a core of lead wrapped in braid, generally used to get a lure deep while flatlining.

MINNOWBAIT: Minnow-imitating crankbait; aka stickbait.

NYSDEC OR DEC: New York State Department of Environmental Conservation.

PIN-HEAD: Angler using a centerpin.

PFR: Public fishing rights.

POCKET: The hydraulic found below a rock, windfall, or other structure breaking the surface of rapids.

PROP BAIT: A long, floating lure with a propeller (generally in back) or two (one in front and one in back) so it creates commotion when retrieved.

ROPE LURE: Made from a strip of soft nylon rope exploded at the back end so it'll ensnare a fish's teeth, this lure is mostly used for catching gar.

SCUM LINE: A transition caused by factors ranging from clashing currents and colliding winds to upwellings and temperature breaks, where waters of differing densities slam into one another but don't mix, creating edges where floating debris gathers in a long line, often on a seam of seemingly calm water.

SHOT SET (SHOT PATTERN): A string of split shots staggered 2 to 6 inches apart; used primarily while float fishing and in combat fishing when it's essential to get a glo bug or other bait deep quickly.

SKEIN: Salmon or trout eggs still attached to the ovarian membrane.

SKINNY WATER: Bottlenecks, sharp curves, and other narrow spots in white water.

SLIDER: A lure on a leader clipped onto the main line with a swivel and allowed to run the belly (bow) of the line.

SLOW DEATH: A hook with a kink or bend that causes the bait, usually a worm, to spin as it is pulled through the water. Normally fished with a bottom bouncer behind a 4-foot leader.

SNAP-JIGGING: Working a jig forcefully and rapidly so it jumps wildly along bottom.

SPOON-FEEDING: Casting spoons.

STICKWORM OR SOFT STICKBAIT: A fat-bodied plastic worm like a YUM Dinger, Yamamoto Senko, or Bass Pro Stik-O Worm.

SWIMBAIT: A soft plastic minnow imitation generally rigged on a jighead and swimmed or jigged.

SWIMMING: Retrieving a lure at a steady pace.

SWINGING: In fly fishing, casting a fly, usually a streamer, across the current and letting it swing back to your side of the stream.

WACKY RIG: Hooking a soft stickbait or plastic worm in the middle and letting it simply flutter to bottom without any weight.

WALK-THE-DOG: Twitching the rod tip while fishing a cigar-shaped, topwater lure like a Zara Spook so it walks from side to side.

WEIGHT-FORWARD SPINNER: A rig in which a metal head rides before a spinner blade followed by a hook.

YO-YO: Jigging a lure in long, yo-yo-like sweeps.

ZOMBIES: Spawned-out Pacific salmon, usually disfigured and discolored, milling around in pools, waiting to die.

FISH SPECIES OF THE GREAT LAKES DRAINAGE

BROOK TROUT OR SQUARETAIL (*SALVELINUS FONTINALIS*)

GENERAL DESCRIPTION: This beautiful fish normally has a deep olive back decorated with a labyrinth of worm-like markings. Spots on its sides are red and blue, and a white line traces its reddish lower fins. A member of the char family, its mouth and appetite are bigger than your average trout's.

DISTRIBUTION: The state's official fish, brookies are also called natives, speckled trout, and squaretails. Found in clear, cold brooks feeding Great Lakes tributaries, they are the fish of choice for anglers hiking to remote sections of streams pouring out of the Tug Hill Plateau.

ADDITIONAL INFORMATION: Brookies assume their most striking colors in autumn when they're ready to spawn. Males often have bright red bellies and large hooked jaws. Their propensity for eagerly striking any bite-sized creature that crosses their paths earns them the distinction of being the easiest trout to catch. The state's smallest trout, most range from 4 to 10 inches long, but fish around 20 inches are possible. The state record, caught on May 5, 2012, in the West Canada Wilderness Area of the Adirondack Mountains, is 5 pounds, 14 ounces.

LAKE TROUT (*SALVELINUS NAMAYCUSH*)

GENERAL DESCRIPTION: Like the brookie, this delicious member of the char family isn't exactly the brightest fish in the tank. It has a relatively big mouth and an appetite to match. Its back is generally gray or green; the sides are silvery or gray and speckled with light spots. The belly is white, and its tail is forked.

DISTRIBUTION: Another native New Yorker, this species prefers cold, deep water and is often found near bottom, in depths exceeding 100 feet. While Lake Ontario has a greater population than Lake Erie, New York's biggest specimens come out of the latter because it has far less of the deep habitat they require, so they're concentrated in a smaller area.

ADDITIONAL INFORMATION: One of the larger Great Lakes species, lakers easily reach 20 inches, and 30-plus-inch fish are common. They spawn in autumn in shallow water over gravel. The state record, caught in Lake Erie (site 1) on August 9, 2003, is 41 pounds, 8 ounces.

BROWN TROUT (*SALMO TRUTTA*)

GENERAL DESCRIPTION: Sporting deep brown backs, this species' color lightens into golden sides splashed with red and brown spots surrounded by light halos. Sometimes the red spots are so bright, they look like burning embers. Mature males sport kypes (curved lower jaws) that are often so extremely hooked, they seem deformed.

DISTRIBUTION: Imported back in the 1830s from Germany, browns found America to their liking and have prospered. Far more tolerant of warm water than are brookies or lakers, they do well in every kind of clean, oxygenated water, and prefer to hang out near bottom, inshore.

ADDITIONAL INFORMATION: Purist fly fishers consider the brown the savviest of trout. Its propensity for hitting a well-presented dry fly has endeared the species to some of the world's most famous authors—Dame Juliana Berners, Izaak Walton, William Butler Yeats, and Ernest Hemingway, to name a few. Especially colorful when they spawn in autumn, browns assume a brilliance that perfectly complements Earth's most colorful season. The state record, caught in Lake Ontario (site 11) on June 10, 1997, by Tony Brown (no relation), is 33 pounds, 2 ounces.

RAINBOW TROUT, STEELHEAD, CHROMER, AND IRONHEAD (*ONCORHYNCHUS MYKISS*)

GENERAL DESCRIPTION: This species has a deep green back that melts into silvery sides. A pink stripe stretching from the corner of the fish's jaw to the base of its tail is what gives it its name. The upper half of its body, upper fins, and entire tail are splattered with black spots.

DISTRIBUTION: Native to the West Coast, rainbows were introduced to New York in the 19th century and have been here ever since. Although they're found in deep, cool lakes and cold streams throughout the state, they enjoy a wide variety of foods, including insects, and feed in warmer water, often above the thermocline.

ADDITIONAL INFORMATION: Anadromous rainbows are called steelhead, ironheads, and chromers. Lake-dwelling domestic rainbows and steelhead run up Lake Ontario's tributaries in autumn to feast on brown trout and salmon eggs, and may spend the entire winter. Come spring, they run upstream en masse to spawn, providing some of the year's most exciting fishing action. The state record, caught in Lake Ontario (site 11) on August 14, 2004, is 31 pounds, 3 ounces.

ATLANTIC SALMON OR LANDLOCKED SALMON (*SALMO SALAR*)

GENERAL DESCRIPTION: The only salmon native to the state, Atlantic salmon generally have deep brown backs that quickly dissolve to silvery sides splattered with irregularly shaped spots, which are often crossed.

DISTRIBUTION: At one time Lake Ontario boasted the greatest population of landlocked Atlantic salmon in the world. A combination of pollution, dam building on natal streams, and sterility caused by a thiamine deficiency linked to eating exotic forage (alewives and smelt) wiped them out. Currently a token presence is maintained in Lake Ontario by stocking. The state releases over 365,000 fingerlings in the lake annually. In addition, local, state, and federal agencies chip in by unloading surplus fish from hatcheries and research laboratories.

COMEBACK KIDS: Recently, naturally bred young-of-the-year Atlantics have been caught in research nets set in various Lake Ontario tributaries. Biologists believe round gobies may be responsible. Gobies are rich in thiamine, a vitamin essential for salmon reproduction; contact with the exotics, even for short periods, replenishes this vitamin. Salmon otherwise lose it by feeding on alewives and smelt—forage rich in thiaminase, an enzyme that breaks down thiamine.

ADDITIONAL INFORMATION: Atlantics are the only salmon that survive the spawning ordeal, often returning to spawn a second and sometimes even a third time. They're considered the classiest salmon; catching one, especially on a fly, is many a fly-fishing purist's greatest dream. Atlantic salmon spawn in autumn. The state record, caught in Lake Ontario (site 11) on April 5, 1997, is 24 pounds, 15 ounces.

CHINOOK SALMON OR KING SALMON (*ONCORHYNCHUS TSHAWYTSCHA*)

GENERAL DESCRIPTION: A silvery fish with a green back, it has black spots along the upper half of its body, including the fins and the entire tail. When chinooks are ready to spawn, they become a dark olive-brown, and the males develop a kype (hooked jaw). The inside of the mouth is entirely black.

DISTRIBUTION: The largest of Lake Ontario's Pacific salmon, chinooks were introduced in the late 1960s. Currently upward of 1.5 million are stocked annually by the state. Individuals can reach 40 pounds—even better—and the species has become one of the lake's most important gamefish.

ADDITIONAL INFORMATION: The most exciting fishing occurs roughly from mid-September through mid-November, when mature three-and-a-half-year-olds averaging 25 pounds run tributaries to spawn; a few precocious one-and-a-half-year-olds (females are called jennies and males are called jacks), averaging 8 pounds, also run. Kings die soon after spawning, littering the floors of streams with cadavers. Fortunately, these carpets of death only last until high water sweeps the carcasses back into the lake or decomposition quickly breaks them down (most start rotting while still alive). The state record, caught in the Salmon River (site 41) on September 7, 1991, is 47 pounds, 13 ounces.

COHO SALMON OR SILVER SALMON (*ONCORHYNCHUS KISUTCH*)

GENERAL DESCRIPTION: Lake O's other Pacific salmon, introduced about the same time as the chinook, the coho is a silvery fish when actively feeding in the lake but develops red sides when it stops eating and heads upstream to spawn. The upper half of its body has black spots, but only the upper quarter of its tail and the lower half of its dorsal fin are spotted. Another identifying factor is that its mouth is black but not its gums.

DISTRIBUTION: The state maintains their presence in Lake Ontario by stocking upward of 225,000 annually.

ADDITIONAL INFORMATION: Cohos spawn between mid-September and mid-November in the same streams as chinooks. While they're only about a third the size of kings, their sizzling runs, spectacular leaps, and incredible stamina endear them to legions of anglers. For some strange reason, Lake Ontario's cohos grow larger than those in the Pacific Ocean, and 30-pounders are caught in the Salmon River each year. The fish spawn in autumn and then die. The state record—and the International Game Fish Association's all-tackle world record—was caught in the Salmon River (site 41) on August 13, 1998, and weighs 33 pounds, 7 ounces.

LAKE WHITEFISH (*COREGONUS CLUPEAFORMIS*)

GENERAL DESCRIPTION: These fish generally have brown or blue backs that fade into silvery sides and white bellies.

DISTRIBUTION: Although lake whitefish were once distributed widely throughout the state, pollution has run them out of most of their range. However, they are still found in cool, deep places like Lake Ontario.

ADDITIONAL INFORMATION: Zebra mussels feed on the same phytoplankton that lake whitefish eat, prompting some experts to warn they will wipe out the whitefish in waters occupied by both. Others counter that zebra mussels simply redistribute the biomass by laying their waste on the floor, causing explosions in populations of bottom-feeding invertebrates, which whitefish also eat. While the jury is still out on the zebra mussel question, most scientists agree that alewives are definitely a threat: They feed heavily on whitefish fry and can send the population into a nosedive. The state record, caught in Lake Pleasant on August 29, 1995, is 10 pounds, 8 ounces.

LAKE STURGEON (*ACIPENSER FULVESCENS*)

GENERAL DESCRIPTION: Ranging in color from dark gray to brown, this ancient fish is long and relatively slender. Its mouth is located on the underside of its shovel-shaped snout (ventrally) and has barbels. It has rows of bony plates (scutes), one running the length of its back and two along each side. The largest fish swimming the fresh waters of the state, lake sturgeon generally run 3 to 5 feet long but can reach up to 9 feet and weigh over 300 pounds.

DISTRIBUTION: Great Lakes and their major tributaries.

ADDITIONAL INFORMATION: Listed as threatened, sturgeon are completely protected in New York. Attempts by the authorities to restore them to their former range are bearing fruit and anglers are catching them with increasing frequency, especially in the spring when they run rivers like the Oswego to spawn.

LARGEMOUTH BASS OR BUCKETMOUTH (*MICROPTERUS SALMOIDES*)

GENERAL DESCRIPTION: The largest bass in New York's Great Lakes, this species is dark green on the back, with the color lightening as it approaches the white belly. A horizontal row of large black splotches runs along the middle of the side, from the gill plate to the base of the tail. Its trademark is its huge head and mouth. The ends of the mouth reach past the eyes. Largemouths and smallmouths are listed as black bass in *New York Freshwater Fishing Official Regulations Guide*.

DISTRIBUTION: Found in bays, barrier ponds, and the estuaries of the lakes' large tributaries.

ADDITIONAL INFORMATION: Found in all the lower 48 states and inclined to hit artificial lures of every description, the largemouth bass is one of America's favorite gamefish. It'll hit just about anything that moves and is notorious for its explosive, heart-stopping strikes on surface lures. This species spawns in the spring when water temperatures range from 62 to 65 degrees Fahrenheit. The state record, caught in Buckhorn Lake on September 11, 1987, is 11 pounds, 4 ounces.

SMALLMOUTH BASS OR BRONZEBACK (*MICROPTERUS DOLOMIEU*)

GENERAL DESCRIPTION: Brownish in color, it is easily differentiated from the largemouth because the ends of the mouth occur below the eyes. One of America's most popular fish, it is granted equal status with the bucketmouth in most bass tournaments. Largemouths and smallmouths are listed as black bass in *New York Freshwater Fishing Official Regulations Guide*.

DISTRIBUTION: Found in the open lakes and their large tributaries.

ADDITIONAL INFORMATION: Bronzebacks spawn in late spring and early summer when water temperatures range from 61 to 65 degrees Fahrenheit. The state record, caught in Lake Erie (site 1) on June 4, 1995, is 8 pounds, 4 ounces.

MUSKELLUNGE OR MUSKIE (*ESOX MASQUINONGY*)

GENERAL DESCRIPTION: The largest member of the pike family, this long, sleek species commonly reaches 35 pounds. The back is a light green to brownish yellow, and the sides can have dark bars or blotches. Its most prominent feature is its duck-billed mouth filled with razor-sharp teeth. Only the upper halves of the gill covers and cheeks have scales, a fact normally used to differentiate muskies from northern pike and pickerel.

DISTRIBUTION: Found throughout the Great Lakes, and in the Niagara and St. Lawrence Rivers.

ADDITIONAL INFORMATION: New York boasts two strains, the Great Lakes and Ohio strains. Muskies spawn in late April through early May when water temperatures range from 49 to 59 degrees Fahrenheit. The state record, caught in the St. Lawrence (site 62) in 1957, is 69 pounds, 15 ounces.

CAUTION: Keep your fingers out of the gill rakers; they are sharp enough to shred human flesh.

TIGER MUSKIE OR NORLUNGE (*ESOX MASQUINONGY*)

GENERAL DESCRIPTION: This species is a cross between a male northern pike and a muskie. Its body is shaped the same as a true muskie, but its colors are more vivid, and its sides have wavy, tiger-like stripes. Its teeth are razor-sharp.

DISTRIBUTION: Although tigers occur naturally in some places like the St. Lawrence River, the vast majority of their distribution is man-made—they're stocked in lakes and rivers to provide trophy fishing and to control runaway populations of hardy panfish like white perch.

ADDITIONAL INFORMATION: These strikingly beautiful hybrids are sterile. The state record, caught in the Tioughnioga River on May 25, 1990, is 35 pounds, 8 ounces.

CAUTION: Keep your fingers out of the gill rakers; they are sharp enough to shred human flesh.

NORTHERN PIKE OR PIKEASAURUS (*ESOX LUCIUS*)

GENERAL DESCRIPTION: A medium-sized member of the pike family, this long, slender fish is named after a spear popular during the Middle Ages. Its body is the same as the muskie's, but its color is almost invariably green, and it has large, oblong white spots on its sides. Its cheeks are fully scaled, along with the top half (only) of its gill plates. Its teeth are razor-sharp.

DISTRIBUTION: Great Lakes bays and large tributaries.

ADDITIONAL INFORMATION: Spawns from late March through early May in water temperatures ranging from 40 to 52 degrees Fahrenheit. The state record, caught in Great Sacandaga Lake on September 15, 1940, is 46 pounds, 2 ounces.

CAUTION: Keep your fingers out of the gill rakers; they are sharp enough to shred human flesh.

CHAIN PICKEREL (*ESOX NIGER*)

GENERAL DESCRIPTION: The smallest member of the pike family, the pickerel is shaped exactly like its larger cousins, but its green sides are overlaid in a yellow, chain-mail-like pattern. Its teeth are razor-sharp.

DISTRIBUTION: Great Lakes bays and rivers.

ADDITIONAL INFORMATION: Spawns in early spring in water temperatures ranging from 47 to 52 degrees Fahrenheit. The state record, caught in Toronto Reservoir in 1965, is 8 pounds, 1 ounce.

CAUTION: Keep your fingers out of the gill rakers; they are sharp enough to shred human flesh.

WALLEYE (*STIZOSTEDION VITREUM*)

GENERAL DESCRIPTION: The largest member of the perch family, it gets its name from its big opaque eyes. The walleye's back is dark gray to black and fades as it slips down the sides, which are often streaked in gold. It has two dorsal fins; the front one's last few spines have a black blotch at their base. Its teeth are pointed and can puncture but won't slice. Nocturnal critters, walleye often enter shallow areas to feed. If the moon is out, their eyes catch and hold the beams, spawning stories of ghost and extraterrestrial sightings by folks who see the eerie lights moving around in the water.

DISTRIBUTION: Found in Great Lakes and their large tributaries.

ADDITIONAL INFORMATION: Walleye spawn in early spring when water temperatures range from 44 to 48 degrees Fahrenheit. The state record, caught in Mystic Lake on January 20, 2009, is 16 pounds, 9 ounces.

YELLOW PERCH (*PERCA FLAVESCENS*)

GENERAL DESCRIPTION: This popular panfish has a dark back that fades to golden-yellow sides overlaid with five to eight dark vertical bands. Sometimes its lower fins are traced in bright orange.

DISTRIBUTION: Found in every type of water, in every type of habitat, in the Great Lakes system.

ADDITIONAL INFORMATION: Spawns from mid-April through May when water temperatures range from 44 to 54 degrees Fahrenheit. The state record, caught in Lake Erie (site 1) in April 1982, is 3 pounds, 8 ounces.

BLACK CRAPPIE (*POMOXIS NIGROMACULATUS*)

GENERAL DESCRIPTION: Arguably the most delicious of the state's panfish, this member of the bass family has a dark olive or black back and silver sides streaked with gold and overlaid with black spots and blotches. The front of its dorsal fin has seven or eight sharp spines followed by a soft fan.

DISTRIBUTION: The state's most common crappie, it occurs in Great Lakes bays and ponds, and the still to slow-moving waters of the system's large tributaries.

ADDITIONAL INFORMATION: Spawns in late spring when water temperatures range from 57 to 73 degrees Fahrenheit. The state record, caught in Duck Lake on April 17, 1998, is 3 pounds, 12 ounces.

WHITE CRAPPIE (*POMOXIS ANNULARIS*)

GENERAL DESCRIPTION: This species looks pretty much the same as its black cousin, but it is generally lighter and only has six spines on its dorsal fin.

DISTRIBUTION: Great Lakes bays and ponds, and the still to slow-moving waters of the system's large tributaries.

ADDITIONAL INFORMATION: Spawns late spring and early summer when water temperatures range from 57 to 73 degrees Fahrenheit. The state record, caught in Sleepy Hollow Lake on June 9, 2001, is 3 pounds, 13 ounces.

ROCK BASS OR REDEYE OR GOOGLEYE (*AMBLOPLITES RUPESTRIS*)

GENERAL DESCRIPTION: This popular member of the bass family resembles bass more closely than do pumpkinseeds and bluegills. It's dark brown to deep bronze in color, is heavily spotted in black, and has big red eyes.

DISTRIBUTION: Found in the shallow, rocky areas of the lakes and their major tributaries.

ADDITIONAL INFORMATION: Spawns over rocky areas in late spring and early summer. The state record, caught in the Ramapo River on May 26, 1984, is 1 pound, 15 ounces.

BLUEGILL (*LEPOMIS MACROCHIRUS*)

GENERAL DESCRIPTION: One of the most popular sunfishes, its color varies. It has anywhere from five to eight vertical bars running down its sides, a deep orange breast, and a dark blue, rounded gill flap.

DISTRIBUTION: Found in the shallow, weedy areas of the lakes and their major tributaries.

ADDITIONAL INFORMATION: Ounce for ounce, bluegills are the sportiest fish. Fly fishing for them with wet flies and poppers is very popular. The species spawns in shallow, muddy areas near vegetation in summer. The state record, caught in Kohlbach Pond on August 3, 1992, is 2 pounds, 8 ounces.

PUMPKINSEED (*LEPOMIS GIBBOSUS*)

GENERAL DESCRIPTION: This popular sunfish is the most widespread in the state. Its color ranges from bronze to dark green, and the end of its gill flap is traced in orange/red.

DISTRIBUTION: Found in the shallow, weedy areas of the lakes and their major tributaries.

ADDITIONAL INFORMATION: Spawns in shallow, muddy areas near vegetation in early summer. The state record, caught in Indian Lake on July 19, 1994, is 1 pound, 9 ounces.

CHANNEL CATFISH (*ICTALURUS PUNCTATUS*)

GENERAL DESCRIPTION: The state's largest catfish, it has a dark brown back, a white belly, a forked tail, and barbels around its mouth. Juveniles up to 24 inches have black spots on their sides. Spines on the dorsal and pectoral fins can inflict a nasty wound.

DISTRIBUTION: Found in deep water in the open lakes; the deep channels of major tributaries, often in fast current; and the deep holes at the mouths of small tributaries.

ADDITIONAL INFORMATION: Spawning takes place in summer when water temperatures reach 75 to 85 degrees Fahrenheit. The state record, caught in Brant Lake on June 21, 2002, is 32 pounds, 12 ounces.

BROWN BULLHEAD (*AMEIURUS NEBULOSUS*)

GENERAL DESCRIPTION: With a dark brown back and white belly, this small member of the catfish family can be distinguished from the catfish by its square tail.

DISTRIBUTION: The bullhead's tolerance for high temperatures and low oxygen levels allows it to live in muddy, shallow areas where other species of fish don't dare to tread. It is found in every type of habitat except extremely deep water.

ADDITIONAL INFORMATION: Spawns in muddy areas from late June through July. Both parents guard the schooling fry for the first few weeks of life. The state record, caught in Lake Mahopac on August 1, 2009, is 7 pounds, 6 ounces.

WHITE PERCH OR SILVER BASS (*MORONE AMERICANA*)

GENERAL DESCRIPTION: A member of the temperate bass family Perchthyidae, this species' back can range in color from olive to silvery gray. Its sides are pale olive or silver.

DISTRIBUTION: Throughout the Great Lakes drainage, in all kinds of open habitat, but especially in the rapids of large tributaries.

ADDITIONAL INFORMATION: Most locals don't differentiate between these and white bass, simply calling both silver bass. White perch spawn from mid-May through mid-June when the water temperature reaches 52 to 59 degrees Fahrenheit. The state record, caught in Lake Oscaletta on September 21, 1991, is 3 pounds, 1 ounce.

WHITE BASS OR SILVER BASS (*MORONE CHRYSOPS*)

GENERAL DESCRIPTION: As with the white perch, this species' back can range in color from olive to silvery gray. Its sides are pale olive or silver. It differs in its bold lateral stripes.

DISTRIBUTION: Mainly found in the inshore waters of the big lakes and in major tributaries. Populations have boom and bust cycles: One year, huge rafts can be seen feeding on the surface; the next year, they're as rare as hen's teeth.

ADDITIONAL INFORMATION: Most locals don't differentiate between these and white perch, simply calling both silver bass. They spawn in late spring. The state record, caught in Furnace Brook on May 2, 1992, is 3 pounds, 6 ounces.

BURBOT, LING, OR LAWYER (*LOTA LOTA*)

GENERAL DESCRIPTION: Looking like a cross between a bullhead and an eel, colored yellow-brown overlaid with a dark mottled pattern, it has a single barbel on its chin and deeply embedded scales that are so tiny, they are almost invisible.

DISTRIBUTION: Cold, deep lakes and rivers.

ADDITIONAL INFORMATION: Found in water up to 700 feet deep, individuals range from 12 to 20 inches. They are the only freshwater fish in the state that spawn in winter. Females lay up to one million eggs at a time. The state record, caught in Black River Bay (site 56) on February 14, 1991, is 16 pounds, 12 ounces. The strange appearance of this freshwater cod, coupled with its relative rarity (the only folks who catch it regularly are ice fishermen), results in its being confused with everything from snakeheads to aliens, causing this delicacy to be treated with extreme prejudice by ignorant anglers.

FRESHWATER DRUM OR SHEEPSHEAD (*APLODINOTUS GRUNNIENS*)

GENERAL DESCRIPTION: Overall color is silvery with a blue to olive-brown back and a white belly.

DISTRIBUTION: Inshore waters of the Great Lakes and their major tributaries.

ADDITIONAL INFORMATION: Sheepshead have small round teeth for crushing shells and have a taste for snails and zebra mussels. They use muscles around their swimming bladders to produce drumming sounds. Spawning takes place from July through September. The state record, caught in Chaumont Bay (site 59) on June 8, 2005, is 24 pounds, 8 ounces.

COMMON CARP (*CYPRINUS CARPIO*)

GENERAL DESCRIPTION: A brown-colored, large-scaled fish with orange fins, it has two barbels on each side of its upper jaw. Some are leathery with no scales, or leathery and spotted with disproportionately large scales.

DISTRIBUTION: Native to Eurasia, the species was introduced into American waters around 1830 and found the habitat good. Carp thrive in warm water and can be found in the weedy shallows of the Great Lakes, their ponds, and tributaries.

ADDITIONAL INFORMATION: Like many introduced species, carp suffer an image problem. Recently, however, traveling European anglers have discovered the state's tremendous carp fishery, and the species is gaining cult status. A good way to catch them is to find a spot that looks fishy and still-fish with a piece of baked potato about the size of a bouillon cube, a marble-sized piece of white bread, or several kernels of canned corn. They will also hit worms. One of the most exciting ways to catch them is to sight-fish in a sluggish creek, slowly working the bait to the fish. They spawn in late spring when the water temperature reaches 62 degrees Fahrenheit. The state record, caught in Tomhannock Reservoir on May 12, 1995, is 50 pounds, 4 ounces.

AMERICAN EEL (*ANGUILLA ROSTRATA*)

GENERAL DESCRIPTION: A snake-like fish with a pointed head, the eel has a dorsal fin that starts midway down its back, wraps around the end, and becomes continuous with the caudal and anal fins, reaching halfway up the belly.

DISTRIBUTION: These fish are found throughout the Great Lakes and their large tributaries.

ADDITIONAL INFORMATION: Nocturnal by nature, eels are often caught at night on worms by bullhead anglers fishing in swamps and marshes and by walleye anglers fishing large minnows on the bottom in canals or in holes below dams. After hatching in the Atlantic Ocean, the larvae migrate to fresh water, where individuals live for varying lengths of time before maturing and returning to the Sargasso Sea to spawn and die, a life cycle known as catadromous. Mature adults migrate back to sea in autumn. The eel's life span is unknown, but one was kept in captivity for 88 years. Females migrate for great distances inland, while males stay close to the sea. The state record, caught in Cayuga Lake on July 25, 1984, is 7 pounds, 14 ounces.

Lately American eel numbers are way down, causing some experts to fear they're facing extinction. As a result, they are totally protected in the waters covered in this book, and their possession is prohibited.

BOWFIN OR DOG FISH (*AMIA CALVA*)

GENERAL DESCRIPTION: Easily recognized by its primitive appearance, this native New Yorker has a long flat head, a large mouth full of sharp teeth, a dorsal fin running along most of its back, and a rounded tail. It is able to breathe air, using its swim bladder as a lung. Males have a large spot at the upper corner of the base of the tail. It is often confused with the snakehead, an exotic species.

DISTRIBUTION: Found in the weedy ponds and bays of the Great Lakes and their major tributaries, often in swamps and edge habitats inaccessible to other piscivorous fish.

ADDITIONAL INFORMATION: The sole surviving member of the Amiiformes family, a group of species that was around when dinosaurs roamed the countryside, bowfin spawn in the spring. The state record, caught in Bashakill Marsh on June 5, 2000, is 12 pounds, 8 ounces.

LONGNOSE GAR OR GAR PIKE (*LEPISOSTEUS OSSEUS*)

GENERAL DESCRIPTION: Its long, narrow snout makes this fish easily identifiable. Spotted, brown, or olive in color, it is often called gar pike because of its pike-like appearance: toothy snout (up to twice as long as its head) and short dorsal fin located far on its back, almost at the tail. Its flesh is edible but tastes too funky for most palates; its roe is toxic.

DISTRIBUTION: Found in the Great Lakes and their major river systems.

ADDITIONAL INFORMATION: Gars have been around for about 100 million years. Like the bowfin, this living fossil's appearance hasn't changed since the days of the dinosaurs. They can tolerate waters with low oxygen levels because their swim bladder allows them to breathe air. The state record, caught in Lake Champlain, is 13 pounds, 3 ounces.

SHORTHEAD REDHORSE, FRENCH TROUT, OR RUBBER LIPS (*MOXOSTOMA MACROLEPIDOTUM*)

GENERAL DESCRIPTION: A large-scaled, cylindrically shaped fish, it has a dark streak along its back, large, golden scales on its sides, a white belly, golden fins, and a red tail. It normally ranges from 10 to 20 inches.

DISTRIBUTION: Throughout the Great Lakes, in just about every kind of water, from tiny brooks to the open blue.

ADDITIONAL INFORMATION: Although their flesh is sweet in the early spring, it gets funky as the water warms up. About the only use most anglers have for these suckers is as bait. Their young are among the hardiest minnows, capable of living for hours while hooked through the back. Many anglers snag spawning adults while fishing for steelhead and kill them needlessly. This is a terrible waste because suckers are valuable forage for everything from pike and bass to muskies, walleye, and trout. The state record, caught in the Salmon River (site 41) on May 26, 1996, is 11 pounds, 11 ounces.

RAINBOW SMELT (*OSMERUS MORDAX*)

GENERAL DESCRIPTION: A cylindrically shaped silver fish with an olive back, it generally sports a noticeable silver stripe and a pink or blue iridescence along its sides. It has a large mouth for a small fish, with two large canine teeth on the roof. Smelt normally range from 6 to 9 inches but can reach 13 inches.

DISTRIBUTION: Throughout the Great Lakes.

ADDITIONAL INFORMATION: Smelt are considered a delicacy wherever they are found. They ascend streams in the spring to spawn and are often taken with dip nets. There is no state record.

ROUND GOBY (*NEOGOBIUS MELANOSTOMUS*)

GENERAL DESCRIPTION: Typically measuring less than 6 inches long, gray and mottled with dark spots, this slope-headed bottom dweller has big frog-like eyes high atop its head, a large black spot at the rear of its first dorsal fin, and a single, fan-shaped pelvic fin.

DISTRIBUTION: Native to Central Eurasia, this species was first discovered in America in the St. Clare River in 1990, and has spread throughout the Great Lakes watershed.

ADDITIONAL INFORMATION: Highly aggressive, gobies feed on just about anything they can fit in their mouths, but are especially fond of zebra mussels, worms, and fish eggs or fry. Prolific breeders, they reproduce multiple times each year, providing a constant supply of bite-sized minnows for every piscivorous species in the drink, from yellow perch and crappies to landlocked Atlantic salmon and black bass. There is no state record.

FALLFISH (*SEMOTILUS CORPORALIS*)

GENERAL DESCRIPTION: Fairly long, big-eyed, and plated with large silvery scales, this chub typically runs 6 to 18 inches and is the largest minnow native to eastern North America.

DISTRIBUTION: Partial to fast water, they occur in most Great Lakes tributaries and the St. Lawrence River.

ADDITIONAL INFORMATION: Although they taste terrible, fallfish are notorious for their savage strikes and spirited fight when hooked. They'll hit just about anything from worms and minnows to lures and flies. They've saved many fly-fishing trips by being the only fish to bite, and the vast majority of anglers release them in appreciation. They're so feisty and aggressive, in fact, they're enjoying growing popularity among catch-and-release sport anglers. It's only a matter of time before they gain the respect they richly deserve.

LAKE ERIE

1. LAKE ERIE

KEY SPECIES: Smallmouth bass, largemouth bass, walleye, muskellunge, steelhead, brown trout, lake trout, yellow perch, channel catfish, and sheepshead.

DESCRIPTION: The 4th largest Great Lake and, according to the National Oceanic and Atmospheric Administration, the 13th largest freshwater body in the world, Lake Erie is relatively shallow, averaging about 60 feet deep. Lacking the great depths of its sister lakes makes it one of the most productive warm-water fisheries on the planet, all 9,910 square miles of it.

TIPS: Work Gulp! 3-inch leeches on drop-shot rigs.

THE FISHING: Ever since being brought back from the dead in the 1970s, Lake Erie has been famous for smallmouth bass. Averaging 2 pounds, you can expect to catch a heap of 'em up to 3 pounds; at least one 4-pounder per trip; and a giant over 5 pounds if you're lucky. Fifty-fish days—and then some—are possible. The easiest way to get them is to drift live bait like golden shiner minnows and crayfish on bottom. Still, bronzebacks are notorious for striking lures and love soft plastics—everything from jig-rigged craws, curly-tail grubs, and tubes to 3-inch Berkley minnows on drop-shot rigs and Carolina-rigged 4-inch finesse worms dragged slowly on bottom. If they're on top chasing minnows, go for 'em by ripping a Jerk Shad or walk-the-dog with a Zara Spook. Suspended smallies will take a minnowbait, bladebait, or wide-bodied crankbait like Bass Pro Shops XPS Square Bill. Captain Tom Marks says, "The eastern end of the lake is sand- or muddy-bottomed so search for humps and rock piles, and work baits over and around the structure."

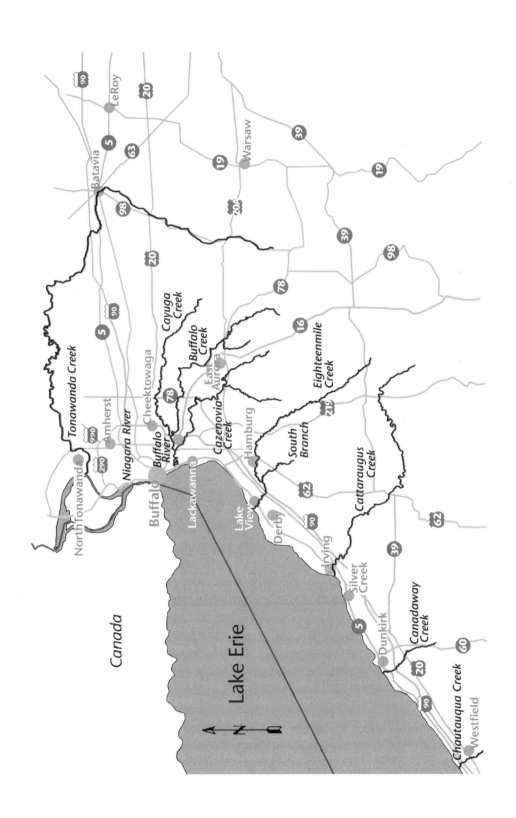

Largemouth bass are nowhere near as plentiful as smallmouths, and are all but impossible to find in the open lake. However, a few can be found in marinas, weedy bays, and the mouths of streams, where they'll hit wacky-rigged Bass Pro Stik-O Worms cast into weed openings, under docks, and around timber, and XPS Minnows twitched across the surface around dawn.

Walleyes generally go anywhere from 3 to 8 pounds, but so many 10-something-pounders have been caught, no one gets excited about it anymore. While the greatest schools are found in the western basin most of the year, they follow the bait into the cooler, eastern basin starting in June, joining the resident fish, earning the area around Dunkirk a reputation as the lake's hottest summer walleye bite. They're inclined to suspend offshore and respond to flatlined deep-diving crankbaits like Thundersticks, or shallow divers like ChatterSticks and Bombers trolled behind divers or flatlined off planer boards; or even run directly in the motor's wake behind 8 to 10 colors of lead core. If you're the type who likes live bait, troll a night crawler on a Northland spinner attached to a bottom bouncer.

Susan Rybaak snowshoeing on early pack ice ringing Lake Erie.

Yellow perch ranging from too small to 15 inches roam the open lake in anywhere from 40 to 70 feet of water, sometimes even deeper. And there's a lot of 'em. Indeed, schools can stretch over a mile long, half a mile wide, and 30 feet deep. Marks calls fishing these groups "a perch a minute," explaining, "It takes several seconds for the bait to drop to bottom, get hit, and for you to reel the fish in. Don't wait too long to set the hook after your sinker hits bottom," he warns, "because perch in the upper layer often hit the minnow as it drops through the school and the heavy sinker can prevent you from feeling the bite on the way down." They respond best to emerald shiners (buckeyes). Marks uses two Eagle Claw crappie rigs, each baited with a minnow, and set 1 foot and 2 feet, respectively, above a heavy sinker. "In spring and summer perch of all sizes hang out together; in fall they group up in year classes," he adds.

Huge muskies up to 50 pounds can show up anytime and are often caught on crankbaits intended for bass. They're seldom targeted in the open lake because it's so vast, and their numbers so few, that it would amount to an exercise in saintly patience—and that's very rare nowadays. However, when autumn cools the lake's inshore waters to comfortable levels, muskies follow the bait in close, especially in Buffalo Harbor where serious muskie hunters target them by trolling large crankbaits. Indeed, so many muskies are taken under the shadow of downtown Buffalo's waterfront late in the year, the DEC has raised the minimum length for the species in Lake Erie and its tributaries to 54 inches.

Steelhead ranging from 3 to 20 pounds are caught offshore by trolling spoons and plugs late spring through early autumn; and off piers with worms and egg sacs in late fall and for several weeks after ice-out. In addition, many anglers target chromers while downrigging for walleyes by running spoons and minnowbaits on cheaters and sliders.

Over the past 10 years or so the state has been stocking brown trout and they've prospered, running anywhere from 2 to 15 pounds. Quite a few are taken in winter by guys trolling for steelies in Barcelona Harbor (the local power plant's discharge keeps the place ice-free), and by bank anglers casting lures, egg sacs, and live bait from the Central Avenue Pier. In spring, they follow the bait in close and respond to crankbaits and spoons cast from shore, especially from the piers and breakwalls in Barcelona, Dunkirk, and Sturgeon Point. In summer, some are taken by trolling spoons in the deep water just off Brocton Shoals, north of Lake Erie State Park.

This is one of the best bets in the lower 48 for catching a huge lake trout. In fact, the state record, a 41-pound, 8-ounce brute came from here, as have several others weighing 40-something pounds. And they're relatively easy to get because the lake is so shallow that they're concentrated in the only decent lake trout habitat, all located in New York's part of the pond. They'll hit spoons, crankbaits, peanuts, and even streamers fished just off bottom in deep water behind flashers, dodgers, and, especially, cowbells.

Monster channel catfish up to 30 pounds are targeted in stream mouths with cutbait and chicken liver. Sheepshead running from 2 to 15 pounds can be taken just about anytime from breakwalls, from piers, and in Buffalo Harbor. These powerful fighters respond best to crayfish and worms but will take a jig and crankbait. (See One Worm George in site 1F.)

DIRECTIONS: NY 5 (aka the Seaway Trail) parallels the lake, coming so close to the water half the time, motorists can see it.

ADDITIONAL INFORMATION: The lake boasts a special season for trophy bass: from the first Saturday in May until the regular season opener, anglers are entitled to keep one bass daily at least 20 inches long. The minimum length for muskies is 54 inches. If you are going to fish offshore and aren't sure where the international border is, carry a Canadian fishing license. The local visitors bureaus offer a free Greater Niagara Hot Spot Fishing Map: Erie and Niagara County Fishing Guide.

CONTACT: New York State Department of Environmental Conservation Region 9, Chautauqua County Visitors Bureau, and Buffalo Niagara Convention & Visitors Bureau.

1A. Barcelona Harbor Boat Launch/Dan Reed Memorial Pier

DESCRIPTION: This facility offers multiple paved ramps, parking for 75 rigs, and shore-fishing access. A launch fee is charged during peak season, from around a week before Memorial Day through a week after Labor Day.

THE FISHING: Ice-out finds loads of steelhead and browns within casting range of the west breakwall and the Dan Reid Memorial Pier. They take spoons like Little Cleos and minnowbaits like Challengers. Walleyes hang out at the base of the breakwaters and pier for a couple of weeks after their opener and respond to vertically jigged bucktails tipped with worms, and to crankbaits worked parallel to shore, particularly around dawn and dusk and on cloudy days.

DIRECTIONS: At the US 20/NY 394 intersection in the village of Westfield, head north on NY 394 for almost 2 miles to NY 5 and turn east.

1B. Lake Erie State Park

DESCRIPTION: This 355-acre fee area offers 102 campsites (19 are non-electric), 10 cabins, hot showers, a picnic area, and a 0.75-mile beach at the base of a spectacular bluff.

THE FISHING: In spring and autumn a smattering of locals surf-cast spoons and minnowbaits for browns, steelhead, and walleyes.

DIRECTIONS: From Dunkirk, take NY 5 west for about 5 miles.

Brown trout caught by the author on a Smithwick Rogue at Lake Erie State Park.

1C. Dunkirk Harbor Ramp/City Pier Park

DESCRIPTION: A large pier with a parking strip down the middle, bait shop, double-lane concrete ramp, parking for 50 rigs, and shore-fishing access.

THE FISHING: The lake around the harbor is a great spot for catching smallmouth bass ranging from 2 to 7 pounds. In spring, they come within range of guys casting crankbaits, jigs, and tubes from the pier. Early in the season, boat anglers drag rubber worms, tubes, curly-tail grubs, and just about any other soft plastic on bottom in 15 to 25 feet of water. By mid-July the bass move out to water from 25 to 35 feet deep. Toward season's end they're even deeper, up to 40 feet. Catfish ranging from 6 to 18 pounds are partial to this area and respond to cutbait, strips of salmon milt, and gobs of salmon skein. Sheepshead get huge and respond to crayfish still-fished on bottom.

DIRECTIONS: On Central Avenue in the heart of Dunkirk.

1D. Cattaraugus Creek Harbor Public Access

DESCRIPTION: This site has parking for about 10 cars.

THE FISHING: The mouth of Cattaraugus Creek is protected by a long, tall breakwall. Anglers stand at its base and target steelhead averaging 5 pounds with spinners, crankbaits, and egg sacs in autumn and spring. This is also a popular spot for trophy channel catfish up to 25 pounds. They like meat (big minnows, chicken liver, cutbait, and shrimp) fished on bottom in deep holes.

DIRECTIONS: From the hamlet of Silver Creek, take NY 5 east for about 2 miles, turn north onto Allegheny Avenue, and continue to its end.

1E. Evangola State Park

DESCRIPTION: Sprawling over 700 scenic acres, this fee area offers 80 campsites, one cabin, a natural sandy beach, a snack bar, and showers. The campground is open mid-April through mid-October; free day use off season.

DIRECTIONS: From Buffalo, take NY 5 west for about 15 miles.

1F. Sturgeon Point Marina Public Access

DESCRIPTION: This fee area offers paved launch ramps, parking for over 100 rigs, additional parking for over 100 cars, and shore-fishing access. A launch fee is charged in summer.

THE FISHING: The breakwall is a productive bank-fishing spot. Steelhead are targeted in autumn and spring with egg sacs and spinners; browns in fall on spoons and crankbaits; walleyes in spring and fall with jig-rigged curly-tail grubs and bucktail jigs tipped with worms; and perch and smallmouth bass in spring and summer with minnows, crayfish, and plugs. Additionally, the lake off Sturgeon Point is famed for post-spawn smallmouths ranging from 1 to 5 pounds. They can be taken from June through mid-July in 15 to 25 feet of water with scented tubes, Carolina-rigged 4-inch finesse worms, or bucktail jigs. Huge resident walleyes are also available out here and can be taken by trolling minnow-imitating crankbaits like Smithwick Rogues. From fall through spring, fish the 40- to 60-foot depths about 3 miles offshore for yellow perch up to 15 inches.

Monument to One Worm George at Sturgeon Point Marina.

DIRECTIONS: Head west on NY 5 for about 2.5 miles from Highland-on-the-Lake and turn right onto Sturgeon Point Road.

ADDITIONAL INFORMATION: Marina Park is protected by a wraparound breakwall that has been a popular shore-fishing spot for as long as it's been there, spawning characters like One Worm George. In his last days, he used to sit on the breakwall, watch freighters go by off in the distance, and give anglers advice like: "If you wanta catch walleyes, cast your worm toward Buffalo."

Captain Tom Marks recalls a story One Worm told him about the Chinese cook at the old Sturgeon Point Hotel:

One day the chef asked One Worm: "You catchy sheepshead?"

"Yup."

"I pay 25 cents each sheepshead you gimmee."

It was the beginning of a lucrative relationship, until the cook quit after a disagreement with Mr. Weiss, the hotel's owner. Ms. Weiss took over kitchen duties and served the customary haddock dinner that Friday. Customers complained it didn't taste like the haddock they'd been eating all summer long.

One Worm ended the story with characteristic understatement: "That Chinaman could make any fish taste good."

Memorials to One Worm and Lackawanna Joe, another local legend, have been placed on site.

1G. Buffalo Harbor

DESCRIPTION: Averaging 30 feet deep, the harbor's waves break against downtown Buffalo's west bank. Five miles of breakwall protect it from the worst Lake Erie can dish out.

THE FISHING: Compared with the rest of the lake, the smallmouth bass and walleye fisheries are poor here. However, trophy muskies and huge walleyes move into the area in November, lured by schools of bait seeking refuge in the harbor's warmer waters. Most are targeted by trolling large crankbaits. The minimum length for muskies is 54 inches.

ADDITIONAL INFORMATION: Formerly heavily industrialized, the harbor has a lot of shore-fishing access but is best fished from a boat. The NFTA Small Boat Harbor and Marina, the country's largest freshwater marina, boasts 14 concrete ramps, loading docks, parking for 1,000 rigs, shuttle service to the parking lot, modern restrooms, and a restaurant. Open May 15 through November 30; a launch fee is charged during peak periods.

DIRECTIONS: Off Fuhrmann Boulevard in Buffalo.

2. CHAUTAUQUA CREEK

KEY SPECIES: Steelhead, brown trout, and smallmouth bass.

DESCRIPTION: Powered by a drop in the landscape geologists call the Erie Scarp, this fast-paced stream slices a 15-mile-long swath along the northwestern edge of the Allegheny Plateau, much of it through a spectacular gorge, offering anglers a full menu of whitewater habitats few world class trout streams can match. But its exuberance doesn't last. Tumbling through the fish passage at the Westfield Waterworks dam knocks the creative juices out of it and it grows wider and lazier. At the NY 5 bridge, it rumbles over its last waterfall, reaches the same gradient as Lake Erie, and becomes flat water punctuated with deep spots.

TIPS: Float-fish a pink, 3-inch Berkley Floating Trout Worm.

THE FISHING: A combination of human intervention (the state stocks roughly 45,000 steelies annually) and natural reproduction makes this stream New York's second most productive Lake Erie tributary for steelhead (Cattaraugus Creek, site 4, is numero uno). From autumn through spring, ironheads ranging from 3 to 15 pounds storm in from the lake, staging the kind of heart-pounding runs anglers dream about. In addition, they're joined in autumn and spring by lake-run browns weighing up to 15 pounds. In May and June, the creek's plume invites lake smallies upstream to spawn. Mark Moskal, a Finger Lakes guide who loves fly-fishing Lake Erie's tributaries for trout, suggests fishing "small beadheads and nymphs in riffles and seams in spring; and swinging Zonkers and Egg-Sucking Leeches in deeper pools in October and November." The bronzebacks take streamers, too, but also like swimbaits and crayfish patterns dipped in scent.

DIRECTIONS: NY 394 parallels the stream.

ADDITIONAL INFORMATION: The state owns roughly 8.5 miles of public fishing rights easements, including both sides of the stream from NY 5 to the mouth. One of the most popular access sites is the NY 5 bridge; park at the shoulder. The creek has a section set aside for catch-and-release fishing with artificial lures only (see site 2B).

CONTACT: New York State Department of Environmental Conservation Region 9 and Chautauqua County Visitors Bureau.

2A. Public Access

DESCRIPTION: There's parking for about five cars at an abandoned bridge; PFR on the right bank (looking downstream) all the way to the mouth, and on the left bank from the access site downstream for about 500 yards.

THE FISHING: This stretch is wide and slow, so the meandering channel holds most of the fish. This area is ideal for swinging streamers and float fishing.

DIRECTIONS: From the west side of Barcelona, head south on North Gale Street for 0.2 mile.

2B. Public Access

DESCRIPTION: This site offers parking for about 10 cars.

THE FISHING: This site sits on the 1.3-mile-long catch-and-release/artificial-lures-only section stretching from the South Gale Street Bridge to the Westfield Waterworks dam. The state owns PFR easements on both banks for a few hundred feet around the parking area, and upstream, on the right bank (looking downstream), for almost a mile. There's a short break in the PFR just below the dam, but it continues on the right bank, from the dam upstream for about a 0.5 mile.

DIRECTIONS: From its intersection with US 20 on the west side of Westfield, head south on Chestnut Street (CR 21) for 2 miles.

2C. Public Access

DESCRIPTION: Parking and access to over 3 miles of PFR.

THE FISHING: Running through the gorge, fed by several tributaries, this scenic area is steeped in rugged scenery in early spring and splashed in brilliant color in fall. The fishing is extraordinary during the spring thaw when runoff raises and discolors the water slightly. Autumn sees massive runs of salmonids after a rain. Chuck-n-duck glo bugs and nymphs, weighed down with split-shot sets, into pockets, seams, and eddies for lake-run trout. Use an indicator to help detect subtle strikes.

DIRECTIONS: From site 2B, continue on CR 21 for a little over 2 miles, bear left on Ogden Road, then make another left onto Taylor Road a mile later. Continue about 0.75 mile to where the road loops and the blacktop ends. Park in the area on the left, and follow the access trail down to the creek; the hike is about 300 yards.

2D. Chautauqua Gorge State Forest

DESCRIPTION: Located a little upstream and on the other side of the gorge from 2C, this site offers parking and access to over 3 miles of PFR.

DIRECTIONS: From its intersection with NY 394 in the Chautauqua Lake village of Mayville, head south on Sherman Mayville Road (NY 430) for about 1.5 miles, turn right onto Hannum Road, follow it to the end, and park. On the left, you'll see a couple of trails. Take the one to the right—it's blocked by a pile of gravel—to the creek. Although this road is on private property, it wasn't posted at press time, and should remain that way so long as people don't abuse the place.

3. CANADAWAY CREEK

KEY SPECIES: Steelhead and brown trout.

DESCRIPTION: This medium-sized stream offers 6 miles of excellent steelhead and brown trout fishing in spring and fall, from its mouth to Laona Falls.

TIPS: Work a ⅛- to ¹⁄₁₆-ounce white spinner through the hydraulics below the wing dams in high water.

THE FISHING: Spending most of its lower reach running over a relatively smooth riverbed on comparatively level ground, this stream's timid rapids and deep pools are ideal for bouncing egg sacs on bottom with spinning tackle, and casting spinners and plugs, especially around transitions where smooth bottom is fractured or littered with rocks. Below the NY 5 bridge, several wing dams speed the flow a bit during high water, punctuating the last leg of the stream with pockets and rapids.

DIRECTIONS: Temple Road parallels the creek on the village of Dunkirk's east side.

ADDITIONAL INFORMATION: The state owns 0.6 mile of PFR easements off NY 5. Popular—but informal—access sites are the railroad tracks crossing Temple Road about 0.5 mile south of NY 5; and Laona Falls off Webster Road.

CONTACT: New York State Department of Environmental Conservation Region 9 and Chautauqua County Visitors Bureau.

4. CATTARAUGUS CREEK

KEY SPECIES: Steelhead, brown trout, smallmouth bass, and channel catfish.

DESCRIPTION: Roughly half of the Catt's 65 miles, from the Springville Dam to its mouth, hosts lake-run fish. Narrow and shallow at the barrier, the stream grows steadily, reaching the size of a small river by the time it pours into Lake Erie. Along the way, its character changes often, from exuberant white water tumbling over a boulder-strewn floor snaking 300 feet below the cliffs of the Zoar Valley, to the pools and riffs of Gowanda's urban landscape and the wide swaths of flat water at its end on Seneca Nation of Indians Cattaraugus territory.

TIPS: After a summer rain, fish cutbait or large minnows on bottom, near the mouth, for channel catfish.

THE FISHING: Steelhead, including a good number of wild fish, are the Catt's bread-and-butter. From October through March, they run inland all the way to the Springville Dam—water levels permitting. Mark Moskal, a Finger Lakes guide who takes breaks from his daily routine by fishing Lake Erie tributaries, advises, "Use individual egg patterns in peach, pink, and orange under normal water conditions, and work black and olive Woolly Buggers when the water's high and discolored." Large browns come in from the lake to spawn in autumn, and respond to Egg-Sucking Leeches, sacs made of trout eggs, and single plastic eggs. Smallmouths storm the lower leg in May and June to spawn, and many stick around a week or two afterward. They'll hit streamers swung through the current, crayfish, minnows, and all the other usual suspects. Channel catfish stage spawning runs in May and June and will hits worms, minnows, and Berkley's Catfish Bait Chunks bounced on bottom in deep rapids and pools at night. Come autumn, some of the biggest cats in the lake enter the mouth and will take cutbait, gobs of raw skein, and other fish parts.

DIRECTIONS: NY 438 parallels the creek from Irving to Gowanda, and Zoar Valley Road follows it from Gowanda to Springville.

ADDITIONAL INFORMATION: Most of the creek's last 14 miles, from the mouth to a few hundred yards downstream of the US 62 bridge, runs through Seneca Nation of Indians Cattaraugus Territory where all a New York State fishing license gets you is in trouble; you'll need to pack a license issued by the sovereign nation or face getting busted. The natives and the state offer maps of the area.

CONTACT: New York State Department of Environmental Conservation Region 9, Cattaraugus Indian Reservation, and Buffalo Niagara Convention & Visitors Bureau.

4A. Public Access

DESCRIPTION: Parking for 10 cars and a steep, 0.25-mile-long trail to a spectacularly scenic section of the Zoar Valley.

DIRECTIONS: In Gowanda, head south on Jamestown Street (US 62), turn left onto East Hill Street, travel 0.6 mile, turn right onto Broadway, continue 0.7 mile, turn left onto Point Peter Road, travel for 0.9 mile, turn left onto Valentine Flats Road, and continue to the end, about a mile.

ADDITIONAL INFORMATION: This site is a favorite of sun worshipers; expect nudity.

4B. Public Access

DESCRIPTION: Located at the bottom of a hill, this site has parking for 10 cars and a short trail to the stream.

DIRECTIONS: From site 4A, head back to Point Peter Road, turn left, travel 0.7 mile, bear left at the fork onto Forty Road, and continue for 0.5 mile.

4C. Public Access

DESCRIPTION: Located at the bridge, this site offers parking for about 10 cars.

THE FISHING: After heavy autumn rains and during winter thaws and spring runoff, steelhead up to 15 pounds run into the gorge.

DIRECTIONS: Take Gowanda Zoar Road for about 6 miles east from Gowanda and turn south onto North Otto Road (CR 11).

ADDITIONAL INFORMATION: This spot is a little upstream of the Zoar Valley State Multiple Use Area. Adventurous anglers launch canoes here and float through the scenic gorge.

5. EIGHTEENMILE CREEK (ERIE COUNTY)

KEY SPECIES: Steelhead, brown trout, and channel catfish.

DESCRIPTION: Named for its distance from the source of the Niagara River, this creek meanders for about 30 miles as the crow flies, and assumes all the personalities you'd expect from a stream that slices through a gorge: plunge pools fed by sheets of water gently sliding over slanted bedrock, low waterfalls, trout-friendly pocket water, smooth-bottomed pools punctuated with fractured seams, and cliffside drops. The state boasts 1.4 miles of public fishing rights, all of it west of I-90; and an additional 2.5 miles of public access is available in Eighteen Mile Creek County Park, a remote and undeveloped wedge of forest deep in Erie County's farm country.

TIPS: Use yellow Woolly Buggers for autumn browns.

THE FISHING: Fly-fishing guide Mark Moskal claims, "This is where I take my clients when the water's too high or muddy on the bigger streams." Chromers start trickling in around mid-October and continue entering all winter long. Come spring, their numbers increase significantly when the lake sends its ripe steelies upstream to spawn. Lake-run browns begin appearing in late October and stick around until December. Both species take small minnowbaits, spinners, and sacs made of trout or salmon eggs. Monster channel catfish up to 25 pounds hang out in the holes at the creek's mouth, and take chicken livers, cut bait, Berkley Catfish Bait Chunks, and large minnows fished on bottom.

DIRECTIONS: North and South Creek Roads parallel the stream in both directions east and west of the hamlet of North Evans.

ADDITIONAL INFORMATION: The marshy area around the mouth of the creek is rich in fossils. This stream has a special catch-and-release, artificial-lures-only section (see site 5C).

CONTACT: New York State Department of Environmental Conservation Region 9 and Buffalo Niagara Convention & Visitors Bureau.

5A. Public Access

DESCRIPTION: Located below the Old Lake Shore Road Bridge, this site has a beach launch for car-toppers, and parking for about 10 cars.

THE FISHING: The water downstream is slow and holds smallmouths most of the time. Upstream the water picks up the pace a bit and offers mild rapids punctuated by pools; good holding water for browns in autumn, and steelhead from November through March. They'll hit egg sacs and 3-inch scented plastic worms chuck-n-ducked or float-fished, and in-line spinners.

DIRECTIONS: Head west on South Shore Road from North Evans for about 1.5 miles, turn right onto Old Lake Shore Road, and continue for a few hundred yards to the access point below the bridge.

5B. Hobuck Flats Public Access

DESCRIPTION: Parking for 10 cars and a pedestrian bridge crossing the creek.

DIRECTIONS: From South Creek Road in North Evans, turn left onto Versailles Road and travel a few hundred yards down a steep hill to the parking site at the bridge.

ADDITIONAL INFORMATION: The state owns public fishing rights easements stretching from a few hundred yards downstream of the access site, to a couple hundred yards upstream of the US 20 bridge.

5C. Eighteenmile Creek County Park Public Access

DESCRIPTION: Shoulder parking for about 10 cars. While the state's PFR map shows the official parking area off South Creek Road, this site's path down to the gorge is shorter and easier to walk.

DIRECTIONS: From its intersection with US 20, head east on North Creek Road for about 1.5 miles. When the road banks sharply to the left, continue for about another 0.5 mile and keep your eyes peeled for an unusually wide shoulder on the left side of the road. Park and take the old road on the other side of the street down to the creek. On the DEC's Eighteen Mile Creek Map 2, the box containing the catch-and-release notice points to this spot.

THE FISHING: This site takes you to the dynamite pool where the main stem of Eighteenmile Creek and the South Branch merge. A little farther downstream the creek crashes over a boulder field, offering some beautiful pocket water. Egg patterns, both flies and streamers, work well here.

ADDITIONAL INFORMATION: The stretch of Eighteenmile Creek within the county park is restricted to catch-and-release fishing with artificial lures only. The South Branch is open to all forms of legal angling, including catch-and-release.

6. CAZENOVIA CREEK

KEY SPECIES: Steelhead and brown trout.

DESCRIPTION: Formed by the confluence of the east and west branches outside of East Aurora, this stream flows west for about 11 miles and hooks up with Buffalo Creek, spawning the Buffalo River on the south side of the state's second largest city. A pool/riff stream, it runs along a moderate gradient, through a combination of rural, suburban, and urban wilderness; its water is relatively clear.

TIPS: Work tiny flatfish and in-line spinners through the flat water.

THE FISHING: Savvy locals have been catching salmonids in this stream for as long as they've been stocked in Lake Erie. Though their numbers aren't great, its lake-run trout can reach 10 pounds, even better. Browns are usually available from mid-October through the first of the year. Steelhead also move in as early as October and continue running until the end of April. They'll take single egg patterns and streamers like Egg-Sucking Leeches and Zonkers.

DIRECTIONS: Seneca Street (NY 16) parallels the creek from East Aurora to Buffalo.

ADDITIONAL INFORMATION: The state doesn't provide any formal fishing access sites. However, a popular spot is the Cazenovia Street Bridge at the head of Cazenovia Park in West Seneca; limited parking at the shoulder. The low waterfall just above the bridge is the creek's last set of rapids. Upstream from this point, the creek runs at a decent clip and is where you'll find the most active trout; downstream, it goes low and slow, ideal habitat for warm-water species, especially panfish and bottom feeders.

CONTACT: New York State Department of Environmental Conservation Region 9 and Buffalo Niagara Convention & Visitors Bureau.

7. BUFFALO CREEK

KEY SPECIES: Walleye, smallmouth bass, steelhead, and brown trout.

DESCRIPTION: The headwaters of the Buffalo River, this stream twists and turns every chance it gets, meandering for a dizzying 35 miles or so before joining Cazenovia Creek on the southern outskirts of Buffalo, just upstream of Harlem Road (NY 240), to form the Buffalo River.

TIPS: In autumn, work Woolly Worms at a dead drift or swing them through fast water for brown trout and steelhead.

THE FISHING: The mouth of this stream is a popular local hot spot for post-spawn walleyes and smallmouths. "Eyes" can go anywhere from 2 to 8 pounds, and respond to minnowbaits like Smithwick Rogues, bucktail jigs fished plain or tipped with a minnow, piece of worm, or scented curly-tail grub, and worms on spinner-rigged harnesses. Bronzebacks generally go from too small to about 2 pounds and hit spoons, bucktail jigs, and minnows. Lake-run browns tour the place in autumn and steelhead run fall through spring, making it as far as the Blossom Dam. They'll hit egg sacs, nymphs, streamers, and worms.

DIRECTIONS: Clinton Street (NY 354) parallels the creek.

ADDITIONAL INFORMATION: There are no formal public access sites, but posted signs are few. Most folks enter the stream anywhere it comes close to the road and at bridges. One of the most popular stretches is from the Borden Road Bridge to Transit Road Bridge (NY 78/US 20).

CONTACT: New York State Department of Environmental Conservation Region 9 and Buffalo Niagara Convention & Visitors Bureau.

7A. Cayuga Creek

DESCRIPTION: The second source of the Buffalo River, this stream offers decent fishing for lake-run trout from its convergence with Buffalo Creek upstream to the dam at Como Lake County Park, a distance of about 10 miles.

DIRECTIONS: Como Park Boulevard parallels the stream south of Cheektowaga.

ADDITIONAL INFORMATION: Public access is available at J. C. Stigmeier Park, Como Park Boulevard, Cheektowaga.

8. BUFFALO RIVER

KEY SPECIES: Walleye, smallmouth bass, steelhead, sheepshead, catfish, panfish, and carp.

DESCRIPTION: Flowing through Buffalo's industrial wilderness, this tributary got dumped on quite a bit in the past. Indeed, in the 1960s about all that plied its sticky waves were brown nasties—not trout, either. Currently the stuff flowing through it resembles water again, prompting some to proclaim it's one of the state's greatest environmental success stories. It is a popular canoe trail; signs along the bank mark areas of interest.

TIPS: Cast rattling crankbaits for post-spawn walleyes and smallmouths.

THE FISHING: This urban stream can cough up anything found in Lake Erie, including muskies and brown trout. Boasting a long history as a walleye fishery, good numbers of lake-run fish storm in each spring to spawn and many stick around for a couple weeks afterward; some males hang around all summer. "Eyes" generally range from 3 to 10 pounds and are taken by trolling minnowbaits and by drifting worms; plain, on spinner harnesses, or slow death rigs. Smallmouth bass also run the stream to spawn. In May, they're popular with anglers throwing every lure imaginable, from heavy metal like spoons, spinners, and bladebaits to softer fare like balsawood stickbaits and soft plastic swimbaits. Post-spawn bronzebacks are popularly targeted by subsistence anglers float-fishing and bottom-fishing with crayfish and minnows. Sheepshead up to 10 pounds are plentiful and enjoy a dedicated following of anglers who specifically target them with crayfish and worms. Steelies pass through on their autumn and winter forays, and spring spawning runs up Cayuga, Cazenovia, and Buffalo Creeks; they're often taken incidentally in the lower river by anglers targeting bass and walleye with crankbaits and spinnerbaits. Others are targeted specifically with egg-pattern flies and egg sacs in the fast water below the junction pool at the stream's head. Channel catfish ranging from 1 to 20 pounds find the moderate current in the deep pools of the industrialized area to their liking and respond to shrimp, clumps of worms, and cutbait still-fished on bottom. Panfish of every stripe, from yellow perch to white perch and sunfish to rock bass, are available. White and yellow perch can go a foot and are especially abundant in spring in deeper water of the harbor areas. They will take minnows, worms, and tiny lures. Sunfish and rock bass running from 5 to 8 inches are plentiful and also most active in spring but can be found in good numbers all summer long. They like it close to shore and hit worms fished around timber and pilings, on boulder fields, and along weed edges. They get pounded a lot by kids and meat anglers, often developing deep suspicion of a worm dropping by. If you're being teased by panfish you feel are spooked, try fly-fishing with tiny surface poppers or wet flies. Monster carp thrive in the slow-moving waters, too. Considered a thinking man's fish, their fans chum the waters with stuff like kernel corn or bread balls, bait up, cast out, prop their rods on rocks or forked sticks, then think about anything they want to . . . all the while watching their lines carefully, of course.

DIRECTIONS: The river meanders along Buffalo's south side and is paralleled by South Park Avenue and Ohio Street.

ADDITIONAL INFORMATION: An official public fishing access site on Harlem Road has parking for 25 cars; another popular site, designated for launching hand-carried craft, has parking for 15 cars and is located off Ohio Street, next to Great Lakes Paper.

CONTACT: New York State Department of Environmental Conservation Region 9 and Buffalo Niagara Convention & Visitors Bureau.

9. TONAWANDA CREEK

KEY SPECIES: Walleye, northern pike, largemouth bass, smallmouth bass, black crappies, and channel catfish.

DESCRIPTION: While the last 13 miles or so of the creek have been channeled and made into the New Erie Canal, the water upstream of Pendleton occupies the natural course and snakes east for about 40 scenic miles.

TIPS: Cast crankbaits like Bomber Long A's and Rat-L-Traps through deep pools upstream of Pendleton in May and June for walleyes.

THE FISHING: Walleyes from 18 to 25 inches are available year-round. However, the most productive time is the month of May, when the resident population is beefed up by Lake Erie fish that swarmed upcreek to spawn and stuck around afterward. One of the most popular spots is the bridge at South Transit Road in the village of Pendleton. Go for them with lipless crankbaits like Rat-L-Traps, bucktail jigs tipped with minnows or worms, scented curly-tail grubs (white and yellow), or by drifting and trolling night crawlers on spinner rigs. Northern pike in the 18- to 22-inch range are plentiful, and 10-pounders are available. They respond to live minnows and spinnerbaits. Largemouth bass ranging from 1½ to 4 pounds and bronzebacks up to a couple of pounds are plentiful. They pretty much share range, responding to swimbaits and jerkbaits worked along rip-rap and weed edges; and minnowbaits twitched on the surface near structure, especially around sunup and dusk. Still, bronzebacks are especially fond of drop-offs, where they respond to bucktail jigs and minnows on drop-shot rigs. Bucketmouths like slop, weeds, and emergent vegetation, where they'll hit just about anything swimming on the surface (frogs, snakes, deer hair bugs), along with big baits like jig-n-pigs and Texas-rigged 7- to 10-inch worms pitched into heavy cover. Black crappies typically range from 9 to 12 inches, but dream-sized 14-inchers and better are taken regularly. They like minnows, Beetle Spins, and wet flies worked around overhanging brush and windfalls. Channel catfish capable of torturing the scale to over 5 pounds are taken regularly; mostly they run 15 to 20 inches—perfect eating size. They like worms, shrimp, and minnows fished on bottom.

DIRECTIONS: Tonawanda Creek Road parallels the stream.

ADDITIONAL INFORMATION: The creek forms the Niagara–Erie County line.

CONTACT: New York State Department of Environmental Conservation Region 9 and the Niagara Tourism and Convention Corporation.

9A. North Tonawanda Botanical Gardens

DESCRIPTION: A paved two-lane ramp and parking for 25 rigs.

DIRECTIONS: From its intersection with Main Street (NY 384) in North Tonawanda, take Sweeney Street east for a little over 3 miles.

9B. West Canal County Park

DESCRIPTION: Paved four-lane ramp and parking for 20 rigs.

DIRECTIONS: From site 9A, continue on Sweeney Street (it turns into Old Falls Boulevard) for just under a mile, turn right onto Lockport Avenue, and continue for a little over 0.5 mile.

9C. Amherst Veterans Canal Park

DESCRIPTION: Paved ramp and parking for 20 rigs.

DIRECTIONS: From its intersection with US 62 on the east side of North Tonawanda, head east on Tonawanda Creek Road for about 1.25 miles.

10. NIAGARA RIVER

KEY SPECIES: Muskellunge, walleye, smallmouth bass, largemouth bass, northern pike, lake trout, steelhead, chinook salmon, coho salmon, brown trout, channel catfish, carp, sheepshead, and panfish.

DESCRIPTION: Carrying the weight of four Great Lakes, this stream starts out at a brisk pace on the west side of Buffalo, steadily accelerates into dangerous rapids, and ends up diving over Niagara Falls—all in the span of about 16 miles. But it doesn't take a break after the plunge. Indeed, the drop only riles it more, and it rages, spits, and foams through a steep gorge for about another 4 miles to just below the hydroelectric power plants clinging to both sides of the gorge like ancient temples to Poseidon. Downstream of the I-190 (Lewiston Heights–Queenston) bridge, it simmers down into a more dignified, mild-mannered stream and steadily, quickly flows an additional 8 miles through a splendid wooded gorge to its union with Lake Ontario. Anglers generally split this stream in two: the upper river (above the falls) and the lower river.

TIPS: "The Niagara River has a heavy current," says Captain Frank Campbell, one of the area's most respected guides, "and you should fish structure, above and below the surface, that breaks the current."

THE FISHING: This stream has been spitting out huge muskies since before white men even knew they existed. Indeed, Native Americans ranked them right up there with another animal they honored, the black bear. Twenty-five-pounders are plentiful, and going for a 40-pounder is a realistic goal. Bill Hilts Jr., outdoor sports specialist for Niagara County Tourism and Convention Corporation, says, "The upper river is well known in muskie circles nationwide for its fantastic autumn bite. But the lower river is virtually untapped—the biggest muskie secret in the Lower 48 States." He adds with the confidence and satisfaction

Niagara Tourism's Bill Hilts Jr. holding a nice smallie he took in the Lower Niagara River.

of someone in the know, "And it's starting to get a lot of attention." Traditionalists fish for them by drifting large minnows up to 18 inches long, casting huge bucktail spinners, and trolling large plugs like Legend Perch Baits, Swim Whizzes, Believers, and Depth Raiders, especially in "the Triangle": the area around Strawberry Island, the northern tip of Grand Island, and Frenchman Creek on the Canadian side. However, a new wave is sweeping in. "Since 2004, jigging with large tubes has revolutionized the fishing," claims Tony Scime, owner of Scime's Tackle and Variety. Local muskie expert and lure manufacturer Marc Arena agrees: "Now tubes catch more muskies on the Niagara River than any other lure." One of Arena's favorite techniques is drifting in 18 to 25 feet of water and snap-jigging a 7.5-inch Red October Monster Tube, a bait he manufactures.

Northerns average 5 pounds and love ambushing spinnerbaits and buzzbaits worked in marinas and over weeds cropping shelves along the bank. Pikeasaurus enthusiasts nail numerous fish in the 5- to 10-pound class by drifting alewives or shiners on bottom or suspending them below bobbers and fishing tight to weed edges.

Black bass aren't as plentiful or as big as they are in the Great Lakes, but there are enough trophies to make fishing for them worthwhile. Smallies are particularly abundant and respond to all the usual suspects and techniques: drifting crayfish, minnows, and tubes; jigging Gulp! minnows and bucktail jigs tipped with worms and minnows on bottom, along drop-offs or breaks, and around structure, including construction debris; and shaking 4-inch finesse worms and Gulp! Gobies in deep water on drop-shot rigs. An especially exciting way that those locals who are experienced in navigating dangerous heavy current use to take bronzebacks is drifting close to the bank in the lower river, downstream of the power plants, and casting spinnerbaits or jerkbaits into shore. Drifting tubes or drop-shotting Power Minnows or Gulp! Gobies while drifting from the Fort Niagara State Park Fishing Access Site to a little way beyond the mouth of the river are also techniques favored by locals. Lately, the largemouth bass fishery has been coming into its own in the upper river, particularly on the east side of Grand Island; an 8-pound, 4-ounce trophy was caught in 2001. They respond to jig-n-pigs pitched into slop, spinnerbaits run along weed edges in heavy current, and walking-the-dog with lures like Zara Spooks in quiet water, early in the morning and just before dark.

Walleyes are in the river year-round, but the greatest numbers move in from the Great Lakes in spring and fall. They're easiest to catch in low light or at night by drifting worms and minnows, or slow-trolling worms on spinner-rigged harnesses with the current—but slightly faster—off the mouth of the river, and in the eddies of places like Stella Niagara. In deep summer, bottom-bouncing juicy night crawlers on spinner harnesses, and jigging bladebaits, as well as bucktails tipped with worms, minnows, or leeches, along drop-offs work well. In spring and fall, walleyes come close to shore and hit crankbaits like Smithwick Rogues and Bass Pro XPS Minnows cast parallel to the bank.

Steelhead can be taken just about anytime, anywhere in the stream's rapids. They're particularly abundant in the lower river, especially from autumn through spring, and respond to egg sacs, worms, in-line spinners, and minnowbaits like Challengers. Float-fishing Berkley trout worms, egg sacs, or ceramic beads on centerpin equipment is also effective. Spey casters take them by swinging Woolly Buggers and Spey flies through the fast water.

Each fall sees massive numbers of chinook salmon, and a smattering of cohos and landlocked Atlantic salmon, ascend the lower river's rapids to spawn. Highly aggressive, these beasts will lash out at anything that comes in their way, including fresh and cured salmon skein, egg sacs, spinners, plugs, and streamers.

Mature browns run the stream in fall to spawn, too. Decked out in autumn colors that would make autumn foliage blush, these attractive beasts can reach 20 pounds. They'll hit the same lures salmon and steelies do.

Come fall, lake trout migrate up the rapids in the lower river. "The US Fish and Wildlife Service confirmed for the first time ever that natural reproduction is actually occurring in this river system," says Hilts, "a very rare situation, indeed. The last documented spawning of lake trout in a river system was in the 1940s in Wisconsin," adds the colorful Niagara County Tourism outdoor sports specialist. From April through May, back-trolling crankbaits, especially Flatfish and Kwikfish, just off bottom in the deep rapids between the Niagara Power Project and the first set of riverwide rapids about 0.25 mile upstream is effective in taking these fish.

Lesser but equally sporting fish also enjoy this stream's highly oxygenated flow. Huge catfish up to 20-something pounds prowl deep eddies and can be taken on live minnows and cutbait fished on bottom. White bass ranging from 6 inches to 2 pounds concentrate below the Niagara Power Project's turbines and hit worms, minnows, small spinners, crankbaits, and curly-tail grubs worked through the turbulence. Sheepshead the size of garbage can lids munch zebra mussels, crayfish, and just about any other organic tidbit they can find on bottom. These hard fighters have had more than one angler dreaming of glory thinking there was a new world-record smallmouth on the end of the line. They eagerly hit worms and crayfish, and have a habit of striking artificial lures targeting other species. Carp running from 5 to 35 pounds are so common, they've developed followings of anglers who fish for them with corn, bread balls, dough balls, pieces of baked potato, you name it, in extraordinarily scenic areas of the river like the Devil's Hole, or in kick-back-and-relax spots like the Fort Niagara State Park fishing access site.

DIRECTIONS: NY 266, NY 265, and NY 384, respectively, run along the river from Buffalo to Niagara Falls, and Robert Moses Parkway parallels the river from its intersection with I–190 to NY 104 in Lewiston, and NY 18F parallels it from there all the way to Fort Niagara State Park at the mouth.

ADDITIONAL INFORMATION: The international border between the United States and Canada runs down the middle of the river. Since the Canadian authorities have no sense of humor when it comes to folks fishing their territory without a license—and they expect you to notify customs when coming over, to boot—boat anglers have two options: staying on the American half of the stream or carrying a Canadian license. Boats are prohibited beyond the line of buoys stretching across the river north of Grand Island, to prevent folks from getting caught in the current and being swept over the falls. Niagara Tourism and Convention Corporation publishes a free fishing map: Greater Niagara Hot Spot Fishing Map: Erie and Niagara County Fishing Guide. There are no public campgrounds on the river, but numerous private ones are in the area. Niagara Falls, a Natural Wonder of the World, is popular with honeymooners and tourists. The cities on both sides of the cataract are loaded with motels and features ranging from theme parks and aquariums to gambling casinos.

CONTACT: New York State Department of Environmental Conservation Region 9, Buffalo Niagara Convention & Visitors Bureau, and Niagara County Tourism and Convention Corporation.

10A. Bird Island Pier

DESCRIPTION: Roughly 2 miles long, this pier separates the fast-flowing head of the Niagara River from the placid waters of the Black Rock Canal, which offers boaters smooth passage to Buffalo Harbor. Built around 1860, it's the city's most popular recreational trail, offering hikers spectacular views of Lake Erie and the Buffalo skyline, and anglers some of the best shore-fishing access on the Great Lakes. A long stretch was closed to the public several years ago after inspections revealed that the structure's decomposing concrete threatened to collapse. However, the fishing was so good and the view so beautiful on the other side of the fence, folks kept going over it, spurring the authorities to do a major restoration.

THE FISHING: Every species in the Great Lakes comes to within casting distance in the spring or fall—or both. Post-spawn smallies respond eagerly to all the usual suspects; they come in so close in June and early July, they're easily accessible to fly fishermen casting poppers (on windless days) and streamers. "Oops" northerns, walleyes, largemouths, and even muskies are often taken on crankbaits targeting bronzebacks. Locals dangle worms below bobbers just about anytime for perch, rock bass, sunfish, and small minnows in spring for crappies. Still-fishing worms or crayfish on bottom, from May through October, is dynamite for sheepshead, channel cats, and bullheads; be prepared to be pestered by round gobies.

DIRECTIONS: Access is at Broderick Park (take Ferry Street off Niagara Street) in Buffalo.

10B. The Riverwalk

DESCRIPTION: Some shoulder parking and several parks punctuate this 14-mile recreational trail hugging the Niagara River from downtown Buffalo to the mouth of the Erie Canal.

THE FISHING: This trail offers loads of shore fishing along a variety of habitats ranging from riprap and concrete walls to marsh edges, weed beds and docks. Like site 10A above, every species in the river comes within range of bank anglers in the spring or fall, and the same techniques can be used to take them. One major difference is the presence of numerous culverts and tributary mouths. These areas draw lots of bullheads and northern pike in the spring. The bullheads respond best to worms still-fished on bottom, especially at night and during periods of low light; the northerns take minnow-imitating crankbaits like Smithwick Rogues and fat-bodied baits like Bomber's Square A.

DIRECTIONS: Niagara Street (NY 266), which turns into River Road north of Buffalo, parallels the Riverwalk.

10C. Fishermen's Park

DESCRIPTION: This site offers parking for several cars, about 150 yards of great shore-fishing access, toilets, and a shelter.

THE FISHING: Most folks come here to leisurely bottom-fish with live bait for everything from catfish and sheepshead to white bass and sunfish. However, spin fishers do well casting crankbaits or swimming 3-inch scented curly-tail grubs for smallmouths ranging from 1 to 2½ pounds and an occasional walleye up to 8 pounds. Monster carp prowl the area and respond to bread balls and kernel corn fished on bottom.

ADDITIONAL INFORMATION: A US Marine Corps monument and a memorial to veterans of the US Navy Seabees are on site.

DIRECTIONS: Off River Road (NY 265), North Tonawanda.

10D. Gratwick Riverside Park

DESCRIPTION: This fee area offers a two-lane paved ramp, parking for 50 rigs, picnic tables, a shelter, hundreds of yards of shore-fishing access, and a fishing pier designed for the handicapped.

THE FISHING: A low, broken stone wall runs parallel to much of this park. Located several yards offshore, the inside channel is shallow and warms quickly, attracting loads of panfish in the spring. Sunfish and bullheads take worms; the perch, rock bass, and white perch will hit worms, too, but they, and a few crappies that come around, also take minnows. Northern pike are known to prowl the wall's openings and will hit large minnows and crankbaits. In summer, carp come into the shallow inside channel early in the morning and evening, and even in broad daylight when there aren't a lot of folks around to scare them. They hit bread balls and corn.

DIRECTIONS: On River Road (NY 265) in the city of North Tonawanda.

10E. Griffon Park Shore Public Access

DESCRIPTION: This tiny park offers a paved ramp, parking for 10 rigs, and shore-fishing access on the channel (called the Little River) flowing between Cayuga Island and the mainland.

THE FISHING: The main river off Cayuga Island to about 1 mile upstream is a muskie hot spot. The beasts have a taste for Red October Baits' Ninja, Monster Tubes, and Big Sexy Tubes, snap-jigged on bottom. At spawning time, the Little River draws massive quantities of mature bucketmouths to its gentle currents. After mating, many stick around to protect their young and fatten up on all the panfish that come into the warm shallows to spawn. The bass will take anything threatening their fry—a crankbait or swimbait—or resembling a dishy life-form, including a stickworm, a loud popper, and stuff like that.

DIRECTIONS: Off Buffalo Avenue on the south edge of the city of Niagara Falls.

10F. Niagara Falls State Park

DESCRIPTION: Besides boasting Niagara Falls, this state park, America's oldest, offers shore-fishing access—from a sidewalk, no less—to almost a mile of rapids above the world-famous cataract. Huge pay lots are at the falls, and a no-fee shoulder parking area for about five cars is about 1 mile upstream, off the southbound lane.

THE FISHING: Steelhead averaging 5 pounds move into this fast water (the nastiest rapids this side of the Colorado River) autumn through spring, and smallmouth bass up to 18 inches hang out in the pockets in summer and fall. Both species take crankbaits and streamers, and the chromers take egg sacs, too.

DIRECTIONS: Robert Moses Parkway parallels the park above Niagara Falls.

10G. Whirlpool State Park Gorge Access

DESCRIPTION: Located on the Niagara Gorge Rim Trail, Whirlpool State Park offers a 300-foot, environmentally friendly Civilian Conservation Corps–era stone stairway to an abandoned trolley grade that runs a few feet above the river in both directions. Numerous short paths strike off the main trail to hardened landings for bank fishing. Downstream about a mile, stairs lead back up to the rim, to Devil's Hole State Park (see site 10H).

THE FISHING: Trophy lake-run salmonids and resident smallmouths up to 18 inches hang out in the oxygenated water. The area is challenging to fish because of its monster rapids and huge boulders calved off the soaring cliffs. But the spectacular scenery and chance to catch a trophy salmonid just about any time of year make the effort worthwhile.

DIRECTIONS: This park is located about 2 miles north of Niagara Falls, off the southbound lane of Robert Moses Parkway. From the parking lot, follow the rim railing downstream (north) for about 0.25 mile to the stairs.

ADDITIONAL INFORMATION: During the evening the New York Power Authority draws water from the Upper Niagara River to fill its power reservoir. Come morning, it closes its intake pipes, and the river rises dramatically. If you're down there at first light and the water starts coming up, back off to higher ground immediately.

10H. Devil's Hole State Park Gorge Access

DESCRIPTION: An environmentally friendly Civilian Conservation Corps–era stone staircase winds down to a trail at the bottom of the gorge. An old trolley grade skirts the bottom. If you head upstream on the trail for about 1 mile, you'll find the stairs leading up to Whirlpool State Park.

THE FISHING: While salmonids draw the lion's share of anglers to the whitewater, lately it's become one of the hottest spots on the Great Lakes for sight fishing for monster carp.

DIRECTIONS: The park is about 3 miles north of the city of Niagara Falls, off the southbound lane of Robert Moses Parkway.

ADDITIONAL INFORMATION: See site 10G.

10I. New York Power Authority Fishing Platform

DESCRIPTION: Located at the foot of the NYPA Power Vista, this site boasts a handicapped-accessible fishing platform within casting distance of the turbines' discharges.

THE FISHING: After ice-out, lake trout and steelhead run the river to spawn and are targeted by anglers throwing everything from spoons, swimbaits, and spinners to worms and egg sacs and minnows. Come summer, massive schools of white perch, with some up to 2 pounds and better, invade the effervescence below the turbines and strike worms, minnows, small spinners, spoons, and curly-tail grubs. Monster sheepshead and some smallmouths also love the bubbly and strike crayfish and jigs. In autumn, king and coho salmon, brown trout, and steelhead are the main feature. Salmon strike raw skein and lures; the steelhead and browns like egg sacs, in-line spinners, and minnow-imitating crankbaits.

DIRECTIONS: The NYPA access road is off Hyde Park Boulevard (NY 61).

ADDITIONAL INFORMATION: Limited parking is available, primarily for the handicapped, at river level. There's additional parking at the top of the gorge.

10J. Earl W. Brydges Art Park

DESCRIPTION: Dedicated to the performing and visual arts, this 150-acre state park offers trails down gentle slopes to two fishing access landings on quiet stretches of the river. In addition, adventurous types can strike out on their own to fish the park's rugged mile-long shoreline stretching to the Niagara Power Project's Robert Moses Power Plant.

THE FISHING: This spot's deep water and strong current holds a litany of the river's most popular species year-round. In summer, it's especially popular with bank anglers still-fishing live bait for bottom feeders like carp, sheepshead, and catfish.

DIRECTIONS: Entrances on South 8th Street and South 4th Street in the village of Lewiston.

10K. Lewiston Landing Waterfront Park

DESCRIPTION: Stretching along several hundred feet of prime waterfront, this site offers a double-lane paved ramp, parking for 50 rigs, bank-fishing access, a fish-cleaning station, picnic tables, and toilets. A fee is charged to launch when an attendant is on duty, primarily on weekends in spring and fall, and all summer.

THE FISHING: Sitting at the end of town, boasting deep water near shore, this is a local hot spot for bottom feeders ranging from catfish and bullheads to smallmouth bass, sheepshead, carp, perch, rock bass, and even a few walleye. Each of these species will take worms. However, the bass and sheepshead are partial to crayfish; the carp are especially fond of vegetarian fare like kernel corn, baked potato, and bread balls; and the catfish like cutbait and shrimp.

DIRECTIONS: Located on Water Street, at the end of Center Street, on the western edge of Lewiston.

10L. Joseph Davis State Park

DESCRIPTION: Spread over more than 200 acres, this site offers parking for fifteen cars, a handicapped fishing platform, and about 300 yards of shore fishing on a quiet stretch of the Niagara River.

DIRECTIONS: Head north out of Lewiston on Lower River Road (NY 18F) for a little under 2 miles.

10M. Village of Youngstown Launch

DESCRIPTION: This no-fee site offers a paved ramp and parking for 20 rigs—the walk to the parking lot is a long one.

DIRECTIONS: On Water Street.

THE FISHING: This spot draws loads of panfish. They love worms, minnows, and small scented jigs like Makiplastic micro-fishing baits and Berkley's Atomic Teasers. Use a float to stay out of the weeds. Smallmouths always hang out in the deeper water just beyond the reach of anglers casting from shore, but move in at dawn and dusk and respond to floating lures and spinnerbaits. Bill Hilts Jr. says this is one of the best spots on the river for catching serendipitous muskies while targeting smallies.

10N. Fort Niagara State Park

DESCRIPTION: Sprawling over 240 acres, including a stretch of Lake Ontario Beach and the Niagara River, this fee area offers shore fishing, two paved boat launches on the Niagara River, parking for 100 rigs, and restrooms.

DIRECTIONS: Located on the northern edge of Youngstown, off NY 18F.

ADDITIONAL INFORMATION: Standing at the mouth of the Niagara River, the fort was built by the French during the French and Indian War, but they lost it to the British. It was ceded to America in 1796, and our troops used it to stage their unsuccessful invasion of Canada during the War of 1812, after which the British recaptured it briefly but returned it following the conflict. The United States stationed troops at the fort until 1963. Currently, it is staffed in summer by Revolutionary War reenactors.

100. Fourmile Creek State Park

DESCRIPTION: Spread over 248 acres, including a long stretch of Lake Ontario Beach, this fee area isn't on the Niagara River—but it's close, only about 3 miles east of the mouth. It offers more than 250 campsites (100 electric), showers, toilets, and access to Fourmile Creek. A day-use fee is charged non-campers in season, the third weekend of April through October.

THE FISHING: Fourmile Creek gets minor autumnal runs of salmonids, water levels permitting, and small groups of ripe, bragging-sized steelhead in the spring.

DIRECTIONS: From Youngstown, head east on NY 93 for about 2 miles, turn left onto NY 18 (Lake Road) and continue north for about 1.5 miles.

LAKE ONTARIO

11. LAKE ONTARIO

KEY SPECIES: Chinook salmon, coho salmon, lake trout, brown trout, rainbow trout, landlocked Atlantic salmon, smallmouth bass, walleye, sheepshead, channel catfish, and panfish.

DESCRIPTION: Big enough to fit the state of Hawaii and still have room left over for the current charter fleet to make a living, Lake Ontario is an exercise in relativity. The tiniest Great Lake, it measures 193 miles long by 53 miles wide, averages 282 feet deep, and has a maximum depth of 803 feet.

TIPS: From ice-out through April, flatline Smithwick Rogues off planer boards, around tributary mouths, in 3 to 7 feet of water, for brown trout averaging 7 pounds.

THE FISHING: A lake this size naturally spawns a lot of fish tales. Most are true. Constantly improving water quality, copious forage, lamprey control, and the annual stocking of millions of salmon and trout by the authorities conspire to make this place one of the world's top fisheries. And while a new exotic critter seems to crop up every year (spiny water fleas, zebra mussels, and round gobies are its most notorious illegal immigrants), threatening to trash the habitat, Lake O makes the best of things, incorporating the invaders into her menu, pumping out massive quantities of trophy gamefish in the process. Indeed, chinook salmon over 40 pounds; coho salmon, lake trout, and brown trout weighing 30-something pounds; steelhead and domestic rainbow trout over 20 pounds; walleyes exceeding 10 pounds; 5-pound smallmouth bass; and 20-pound catfish are caught so often, anglers are getting spoiled.

This lake has a reputation for spitting out record fish—and controversy. For instance, the current International Game Fish Association's

47

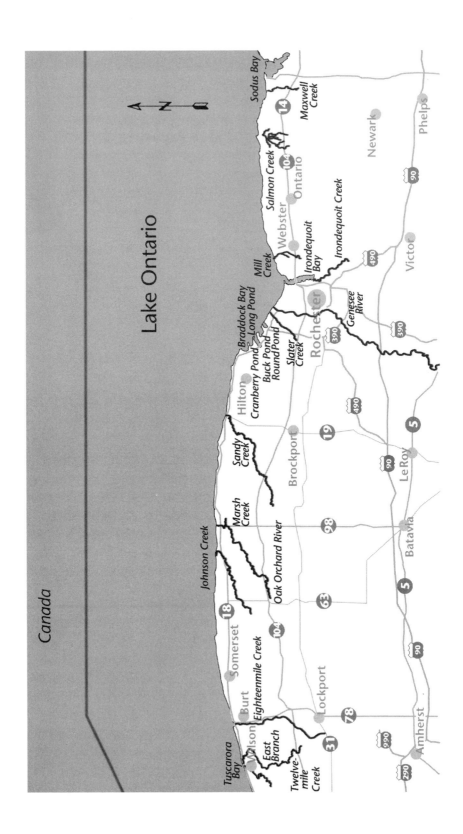

all-tackle record coho salmon (a species native to the Pacific Ocean, incidentally) is a 33-pound, 7-ounce beauty caught on August 13, 1998, in the Salmon River. Problem is, it may be a chinook/coho salmon hybrid, a species so new they're still trying to come up with an appropriate name for it ("kingho"?). Indeed, it's not even certain whether the breed is created naturally by the current washing chinook milt over coho eggs or by humans accidentally corrupting the ingredients in the hatchery (probably both). Experts claim the only definitive way to tell them apart is to examine the innards. A few colorful locals—apparently skeptical of scientists reading animal entrails—claim the species is a mutant form of coho, attributing it to the witch's brew of antibiotics, growth hormones, and pharmaceuticals lining the lake's floor like the bottom a mad biologist's aquarium. Staying abreast of the times, the IGFA has a chinook/coho hybrid listing and recognizes a 35-pound, 8-ouncer caught in the Salmon River on October 21, 2001, as the all-tackle world record.

Fact is, trophies of every species that swims in the state's fresh waters thrive in the tiniest Great Lake. Since time immemorial, one group of gamefish has been swimming through the imaginations of more of this big pond's anglers than any other: salmonids. In the old days, the indigenous species were landlocked Atlantic salmon and lake trout; in recent years, chinook and coho salmon, brown and rainbow (steelhead) trout have been added to the list. Classified as cold-water fish, each spends summer in the open lake, where the most effective way to catch them is by trolling. Since they're highly sensitive to water temperatures, many anglers go for them by running lures through the targeted species' comfort zone: brown trout, landlocked Atlantic salmon, and steelhead prefer to hang out in water around 60 degrees Fahrenheit, coho and chinook salmon like it around 55 degrees, and lake trout are partial to around 48 degrees. Another school argues you should target hungry fish because they're the ones most likely to bite, and they hang out in temperatures the forage prefers: Smelt like a cool 45 degrees; alewives like it around 65 degrees. Then there's those like cousin Staash, the most practical guy in the family, who argues: "Five feet here, five feet there, what's the difference? They all hang out in or around 'the zone' most of the time and as long as your bait's close, they'll see it, and go for it." He's talking about the thermocline, a narrow layer between 5 and 20 feet deep that develops each summer when lake temperatures stratify. Separating the lake's warm upper layer from its cold depths, the temperature within the thermocline drops quickly from the 60s to the 40s, the comfort zone.

Fly-fishing in a tributary's plume.

Spring is a different story. At ice-out, lake temperatures are below 40 degrees, a level uncomfortable to most fish. Searching for any warmth they can find, they abandon the cold open water for slightly warmer temperatures found inshore, especially around tributary mouths; in essence, they congregate in 10 percent of the lake. A couple of factors are at work here. Shallow bottoms are easily disturbed by waves, clouding up with particulates and small organisms swept out from under pebbles. Likewise, freshets are generally a couple of shades darker because of the mud and debris they carry. The sun's rays are drawn to the color and, since they don't have to penetrate too deeply, warm the shallows quickly. Equally important is the abundance of food. Runoff carries a cornucopia of insects, worms, and other delights. Forage is naturally drawn to the murkier, warmer, food-rich shallow water, and the big boys are right on their tails.

As spring progresses, the warmer inland water spreads out farther into the lake. Since warm and cold water don't like to mix, a vertically oriented transition called the thermal bar forms, separating the relatively warm, inshore waters from the cold, open lake. When summer heats the entire lake's surface, the bar flips and goes horizontal, becoming the thermocline.

Each year the state stocks roughly 1,761,600 chinooks, 245,000 coho, and 50,000 Atlantic salmon into Lake Ontario's tributaries. Pelagic by nature, the Pacific strains beat fins for the open lake as soon as they can, and head for the strongest current around: the mighty Niagara River, source of 80 percent of the lake's water. As summer rolls along and the fish get bigger, the largest start heading east, so that by August, the majority of mature chinooks and cohos—the biggest, ugliest, and meanest of the bunch—are in the eastern basin, staging off the Salmon, Oswego, and Black Rivers. This west-to-east movement is so foolproof, charter captains like Darryl Raate launch each season from the western ports of Olcott and Wilson, move operations to Rochester and Oswego, respectively, as summer progresses, and end up chasing muskies in the Thousand Islands from mid-September through December 15 or first ice—whichever comes first.

In spring, target Pacific salmon in relatively shallow water by trolling cutbait, spoons, and flies behind flashers and dodgers. As summer heats up and the fish spread out into the lake and go deep, troll the same combinations off downriggers, anywhere from 60 to 150 feet deep, over water up to 500 feet deep. As their spawning hour approaches, they head back to their natal streams. Milling around the mouths waiting for the irresistible urge to run upstream to spawn, they'll hit crankbaits and spoons flatlined around, and through, the stream's plume by day. At night, many conduct reconnaissance runs into the lower reaches of tributaries and can be taken on raw skein still-fished on bottom just off the mouths.

Unlike their West Coast cousins, the majority of Atlantic salmon gravitate to the central part of the lake, the Oak Orchard and Genesee River areas. The most warm-water-tolerant of their kind, they seek out the open lake's shallower waters and are often caught on lures targeting brown trout in areas where the thermocline comes close to bottom. Still, some make it out into the middle of the lake but suspend in the upper reaches of the comfort zone. Good numbers run the Salmon River in summer but leave the stream when the first kings appear in late August.

In the open lake, steelhead prefer to hang out higher in the water column than other salmonids. Before the thermocline develops, look for them along thermal bars and below scum lines. When temperatures stratify, they like the upper layers of the thermocline, even in temperatures above their comfort zone. In fact, when the lake is calm, they'll rise for terrestrial bugs blown out into the open water by earlier winds, and aquatic insects hatching on the surface. Lately, a new class of angler is responding to this unusual fishing opportunity by heading out in kayaks and belly boats and fly fishing for them by matching the hatch. Still, chromers are mostly targeted secondarily with small spoons run off cheaters, sliders, or divers by anglers trolling for salmon.

Numerous guides and charter captains consider brown trout their bread-and-butter fish, especially in spring. The most warm-water-tolerant of the trout, ice-out finds them cruising in shallow water within range of crankbaits like Smithwick Rogues and Bass Pro XPS Floating Minnows cast from shore, particularly around freshets and tributary mouths. They remain close to shore well into May, and bank anglers adjust their tackle to compensate for the warmer temperatures scattering them farther out into the lake by switching to heavier lures like Little Cleos, and casting from points, piers, or breakwalls—any structure that pokes into the water a little way. Still, spring finds the great majority 200 to 300 feet out, in 12 to 20 feet of water. This close proximity to shore makes them popular targets with anglers in small craft ranging from kayaks and canoes to McKenzie boats, even rowboats. Most flatline for them by row-trolling, a technique Captain Ryan "Tiny" Gilbert calls "silent death because the fish don't hear any motor. When the wind's blowing, I can reach speeds up to 2.5 mph rowing with it. On calm days, I can row up to 1.9 mph." As spring progresses, browns go deeper, often congregating where the thermal bar touches bottom. When flatlining these areas, avoid spooking the notoriously skittish browns with your motor by using planer boards or divers to keep your lures off to the side. Come summer, the thermocline scatters the bait all over the lake, forcing browns to give chase; a popular way to get them is to troll spoons like Michigan Stingers through the forage's comfort zone.

Back at the turn of the century, large lake trout were so common that many charter captains considered them a nuisance, even though lakers saved many fishing trips when the more popular species weren't biting. Unfortunately, they were almost always taken deep; when horsed to the surface, their air bladders expanded so they had to be burped (sliding the hand gently from the vent toward the mouth to ease excess air out of the bladder) before release. Since lakers are most fertile when they're 25 to 30 inches long, the state, in its desire to reintroduce this native son to its home waters, imposed a slot limit requiring all lakers in that range be released. Taking them for granted, most guys didn't know how to burp them or didn't care, and simply threw them over the side. The majority, already weakened by the fight to shake the hook, floundered in the warm water and died—so many, in fact, that it was common to go out on a calm August day and see cadavers floating around like rogue whitecaps. The laws were changed, and anglers are now allowed to keep one fish in the slot limit per day. The species is rebounding, and many experts believe it's only a matter of time before the days of multiple 20-pounders per trip are common again. Lakers like cold water (60 to 150 feet deep) over level bottoms and respond to spoons, plugs, trolling flies, and cutbait run deep (don't be afraid to let the cannonball bounce off bottom) behind flashers, dodgers, and multi-bladed trolling rigs (cowbells and Christmas trees).

While smallmouth bass numbers have been down lately, especially in the Mexico Bay area (some attribute the disappearing act to a massive fish kill, caused by VHS, in 2006), there are still enough around everywhere else to make targeting them worthwhile. Pound for pound, the smallmouth is the feistiest fighter in fresh water, a trait that endears it to anglers, making it the lake's most popular warm-water gamefish. Look for them early in the season around tributary mouths, in open water on hot summer days, around rip-rap and breakwalls after heavy summer blows, and close to shore again as their season ends. They like live minnows drifted over boulder fields in 5 to 15 feet of water early and late in the season; and crayfish fished over the same structure, in 15 to 25 feet of water as summer heats up. Another of the species' claims to fame is its willingness to take artificial lures ranging from spoons and hard crankbaits to soft plastics. They'll hit just about anything in the tackle

Pier Fishing on Lake Ontario.

box, from stickworms and bucktail jigs (fished plain or tipped with live bait) to Berkley Twitchtail Minnows worked on drop-shot rigs, jigheads tipped with soft plastics like curly-tail grubs, Carolina-rigged 4-inch finesse worms dragged slowly on bottom, bladebaits retrieved steadily or jigged vertically, prop baits and Zara Spooks fished walk-the-dog-style in the calm of the morning and at dusk, surface poppers on still days . . . you get the picture.

Third deepest of the Great Lakes, Lake O is shaped like a bowl and is relatively poor in largemouth habitat, so bucketmouths are rare in the open pond. Still, a few can be found in the weeds and rip-rap along the lake sides of breakwalls and in weedy bays, mostly found on the lake's northeastern corner.

From the walleye opener through mid-June, post-spawn fish in the 5- to 13-pound range mill around the plumes at the mouths of major rivers like the Niagara, Oswego, and Black; and return to these areas on the tails of bait looking for warmer water in late fall. Target them by casting bucktail jigs and weight-forward spinner rigs tipped with worms or curly-tail grubs around structure like breakwalls, and by flatlining minnowbaits like Bomber Long A's or night crawlers on spinner-rigged harnesses along current edges and through the plumes of tributaries. In June they filter back into the lake and stage in places like the Niagara Bar and off the inshore islands of the Golden Crescent. From August through September they congregate around offshore islands like Calf and the Galloos. These summer fish respond to bucktails tipped with worms or minnows and bladebaits vertically jigged over boulder fields and shoals 20 to 40 feet deep; and to Smithwick Rogues and Bombers flatlined behind a few colors of lead core. If spinning tackle loaded with monofilament is all you've got, use planer boards to get the lure away from the motor, and keel or snap-on sinkers to get it down. October finds them closer to shore again, on boulder fields and shoals 10 to 40 feet deep.

Monster channel catfish so big (15 to 25 pounds) they look like miniature Minotaurs thrive in the lake. Called "giant Lake Ontario pussy cats" by locals, they pack into deep holes at the mouths of rivers, especially during the autumn salmon runs, and take strips of salmon milt, skein, cutbait, or large minnows control-drifted on bottom, or dangled a couple of inches off the floor below slip bobbers, along eddies and current breaks. So many congregate in the channel between Little and Big Galloo Islands that the channel is called Catfish Bowl. Since the water is up to 80 feet deep, the cats suspend and many are caught incidentally on crankbaits targeting walleyes and bronzebacks.

Sheepshead grow huge out in the lake; 10-pounders are common, and 20-something-pounders are possible every time you go out. They like to feel bottom under their fins—or at least have it in view—and hang out in relatively shallow water, anywhere from 2 to 25 feet deep. They have a taste for fresh flesh like crayfish, worms, and minnows fished on bottom, but will also take artificial baits. Indeed, a drum's propensity for striking lures has led to more than one angler dreaming a world-record smallmouth or walleye was at the end of the line . . . until the whites of its sides came into view.

Yellow perch up to 14 inches and rock bass exceeding a pound can be found near shore in water up to 40 feet deep. They are especially drawn to boulder fields, piers, rip-rap, breakwalls, and any other insect- and crayfish-rich cover. They strike worms, crayfish, minnows, and small lures like Berkley's Atomic Teasers and Beetle Spins. In addition, googl-eyes take surface baits like flies and poppers.

DIRECTIONS: Woven from many roads, blazed by square green signs bearing a pair of soles stepping over waves, the Seaway Trail runs the length of the lake.

ADDITIONAL INFORMATION: At press time, black bass season in Jefferson County and the St. Lawrence River and its tributaries runs from the third Saturday in June through November 30; fishing for them during the closed season, even catch-and-release, is prohibited. Asked how anglers without GPS systems are supposed to figure out the boundary between Jefferson and Oswego County, Frank Flack, a fisheries biologist with DEC Region 6, answers: "Don't fish north of Sandy Pond's outlet for post- or pre-season bass." An invisible line separates the United States from Canada at mid-lake. If you're going to be fishing out there, especially in the main shipping channel, and aren't sure where the international border is, carry New York and Canadian fishing licenses—the Canadian authorities have no sense of humor when it comes to Americans fishing their territorial waters without licenses. "They've been known to confiscate everything you got with ya, exceptin' your wife and firstborn, if they catch ya," claims cousin Staash. Numerous annual fishing competitions like the LOC (Lake Ontario Counties) derbies (spring, summer, and fall) and the Lake Ontario Pro-Am Series Tournaments (Niagara, Orleans, Wayne, and Oswego Counties) are held each year; details are available at tourism offices.

CONTACT: New York State Department of Environmental Conservation Regions 6 (Jefferson and St. Lawrence Counties), 7 (Cayuga and Oswego Counties), 8 (Orleans, Monroe and Wayne Counties), and 9 (Chautauqua,

Erie, and Niagara Counties); Buffalo Niagara Convention & Visitors Bureau; Niagara County Tourism and Convention Corporation; Orleans County Tourism; Greater Rochester Visitors Association (Monroe County); Wayne County Office of Tourism; Cayuga County Tourism; Oswego County Promotion & Tourism; Thousand Islands International Tourism Council (Jefferson County); and Seaway Trail Inc.

11A. Niagara Bar

DESCRIPTION: Niagara Bar is the popular name given to the highly productive shelf at the mouth of the Niagara River. According to Bill Hilts Jr., Niagara USA's highly popular outdoor sports specialist: "You know you're off the bar if you're in water over 60 feet deep." Off the deep end the bottom drops to over 200 feet, creating good year-round habitat for lake trout and salmon.

THE FISHING: Fish consider the Niagara River Lake Ontario's greatest attraction. In addition to drawing fish from all over the west end of the lake with its penetrating plume, it keeps them at the bar with uniform temperatures and the ever-present food supply riding its current. The

Capt. Frank Campbell (left) and Niagara County Tourism's Bill Hilts Jr., admire a nice bronzeback Hilts took on the Niagara Bar in the shadow of Fort Niagara.

bar's 10- to 30-foot depths hold incredible numbers of smallmouth bass and walleyes. Best baits for the bronzebacks are minnows and their imitations in spring and fall; crayfish, tubes, and jigs in summer. Walleyes respond to minnow-imitating crankbaits, bucktail jigs, and worms bottom-bounced or trolled deep on spinner harnesses. Both species also like lipless crankbaits like Rat-L-Traps swimmed or yo-yoed through the water column, and vertically jigged bladebaits. Pacific salmon spend winter in the soothing, relatively warm temperatures. Ice-out sees armadas taking advantage of the new season's first meaningful fishing for the species; the action lasts well into June. Cohos and kings hit all the usual suspects: A-Tom-Mik flies, cutbait, and spoons run behind flashers and dodgers. In late summer, the biggest salmon on this end of the lake stage off the bar in preparation for their spawning runs up the Niagara River. Highly aggressive, they'll strike crankbaits flatlined in their paths. Brown and lake trout find the bar's holes and humps to their liking, too. Both take Michigan Stingers trolled near bottom relatively close to shore in spring and fall, out along the drop-offs and deep water off the bar's edges in summer. What's more, the lakers are famous for their taste for spoons jigged on bottom. Steelhead constantly move in and out of the river and find the bar comfortable just about everywhere and anytime. Target them by trolling spoons and crankbaits in the upper layers of the water column at speeds a little faster than you'd run for other salmonids.

DIRECTIONS: The bar reaches out into the lake for about 3.5 miles and stretches (east to west) from Fourmile Creek to Canada's Welland Shipping Canal.

ADDITIONAL INFORMATION: Fort Niagara State Park, a fee area located at the mouth of the Niagara River (NY 18F, a little north of Youngstown), boasts two paved double ramps, parking for 100 rigs, and toilets.

11B. Wilson and Olcott

DESCRIPTION: Located on NY 18, roughly 12 miles and 18 miles, respectively, from the mouth of the Niagara River, the waters off both hamlets are famous haunts of salmonids.

THE FISHING: These ports offer the best spring and early-summer salmon fishing on the lake. The waters are so fish-friendly, a lot of captains simply drop their lines over the side right out of the harbor and troll north until they catch what they're looking for, then spend the rest of the day fishing the same depth, east to west. August sees monster kings cruising near shore in water less than 100 feet deep. In late summer, the oldest salmon grow increasingly aggressive as they mature, and start staging off the mouths of natal streams, moving closer and closer to shore as they ripen. By mid-September, they're in close enough to target by flatlining large spoons and J-plugs. Spring browns carpet the inshore waters and respond to small spoons trolled through areas where the thermocline rubs bottom. Steelhead thrive in the offshore waters and respond to plugs and spoons run through the surface layers of water 200 to 400 feet deep.

Built to provide a spawning site for lake trout, the Niagara Pro-Am Artificial Reef, a 205-foot-long combination of red shale, concrete blocks, and 359 tons of cut limestone, draws great quantities of all kinds of forage—which, in turn, attracts predators. Yellow perch congregate here in spring and fall, smallmouth bass like it in summer, and lake trout spawn here in autumn. The site is located 4.5 miles east of Wilson and 1.5 miles west of Olcott, in 25 to 35 feet of water.

ADDITIONAL INFORMATION: Wilson Tuscarora State Park, a fee area located on the west side of Wilson, offers, a paved ramp and parking for 50 rigs, emergency storm shelter docks, picnic sites, and a 4-mile nature trail through 475 acres of mature woods, meadows, and marshland. Piers on the East Branch of Twelvemile (see site 13A) and Eighteenmile (see site 14B). Creeks provide superb casting platforms for bank anglers throwing spoons and minnowbaits for coho and chinook salmon, rainbow and brown trout in spring and fall. The Town of Newfane Marina, a fee area on West Main Street, Olcott, offers a three-lane paved launch and parking for 50 rigs.

11C. Point Breeze

DESCRIPTION: The water off the mouth of Lower Oak Orchard Creek (site 17) ranks as one of the best steelhead and landlocked Atlantic salmon spots on the lake.

THE FISHING: The state annually stocks about 20,000 landlocked Atlantic salmon yearlings into Orleans County waters. They grow quickly on the area's rich food supply. Since big Atlantics didn't get that way by being stupid, they know a good thing when they see it and stick around for their entire lives, offering anglers who troll crankbaits, spoons, and streamers good shots at trophies running 15 pounds or better. In fact, numerous entries in the Lake Ontario Counties spring derbies are caught each year off Point Breeze. Troll for them at a quick clip, and stack your spoons in 5- to 10-foot increments throughout the water column.

The authorities stock good numbers of steelhead around here, too. With ideal spawning grounds and winter habitat in Oak Orchard Creek, and loads of minnows and great water temperatures in the lake the rest of the time, they have no reason to leave. In fact, the Oak's plume actually draws steelies from other parts of the system. You see, when the creek's warmer waters meet the lake's colder ones, thermal bars, crowned in scum lines, are formed: Bait likes to hang out in the comfort zones afforded by the bars; terrestrial insects and other floating goodies accumulate on the scum line. Indeed, Mark Lewis, a local tournament angler who financed his way to a graduate degree by working in the area's fishing business (filleting, hiring on as first mate, cleaning boats . . .) during summer vacations, back in the 1980s, cashes a lot of checks by playing the local water conditions. His advice: "Never ignore fish you see high in the water column. I watch the graph and if there's fish there, I don't care if it's 68 degrees, I'll run my lures through it. I cleaned countless monster steelhead back in the day that had yellow jackets, beetles, all kinds of bugs in their stomachs."

Come summer, maturing Pacific salmon, drawn east from the Niagara River region by the incipient urge to spawn, start showing up in great numbers. "Normally, summer kings and steelhead will work the same bait pod," Lewis offers, "the steelies feeding from the top, the kings from the bottom." Both respond to spoons and trolling flies.

Browns like the area's gentle slope: The lake bottom drops about 100 feet for every mile you go out for the first 5 miles or so. Run spoons and crankbaits in spots where the thermocline scrapes bottom.

Point Breeze smallmouths grow fat on a summer diet of crayfish and gobies. Fall's dropping temperatures herd them into large schools in anywhere from 10 to 25 feet of water. Winter's approach spurs them into a feeding binge, and they'll hit just about any bite-sized morsel that acts alive. Search for them by dragging Carolina-rigged finesse worms on bottom. When you locate a feeding school, toss anything from minnows and bucktail jigs to diving crankbaits, bladebaits, hard-bodied plugs like Bagley Killr' B's, and Balsa B's.

Yellow perch spend summer in weeds, over boulder fields and around any other structure they can find, including the breakwall. They're especially plentiful at the water plant intake about 0.5 mile west of the "Oak's" mouth. Fish for them in anywhere from 15 to 25 feet of water with minnows, crayfish, and small plastics like Atomic Teasers and 2-inch Berkley Power Grubs.

DIRECTIONS: From New York State Thruway exit 48 in Batavia, head north on NY 98 for 24 miles to the end and turn left onto Ontario Street.

ADDITIONAL INFORMATION: Orleans County Marine Park's boat launch and parking for about 20 rigs is at the end of Ontario Street. When heading out of Oak Orchard Creek, or coming in, take the west opening in the breakwalls; the water on the east entrance can be a little tricky.

11D. Rochester Area

DESCRIPTION: Lake Ontario's Rochester shoreline is rich in bays, ponds, and fertile tributaries like the Genesee River and Irondequoit Creek. In addition, the lake's floor slides quickly to depths over 100 feet. This combination of rich nutrients and a wide range of temperatures makes the water around this major metropolitan area a veritable fish magnet.

THE FISHING: Coho, chinook, landlocked Atlantic salmon, steelhead, brown trout, and lake trout hang out in the area all year long. Early spring's warming waters attracts hordes of browns and steelhead. They cruise the inshore shallows, in anywhere from 3 to 15 feet of water, especially around the openings of bays and the mouths of streams. They'll hit flatlined spoons and minnow-imitating crankbaits. Late spring through summer, growing numbers of large kings start showing up offshore, joining the chromers and browns forced into deeper, cooler water by rising temperatures. The chinooks respond to spoons, flies, and cut-bait run behind flashers and dodgers, and trolled deep off downriggers. Steelies hit cheaters riding the bow of lines running off downriggers, and spoons flatlined off planer boards. Browns will hit all these combinations. Dying summer calls humongous schools of salmon to stage off the mouth of the Genesee River—indeed, in front of all the area's tributaries. Feeding voraciously in the open lake by day, and close to shore by night, they grow fat in preparation for the signal that'll stop them feeding and send them storming into the rapids of tributaries to spawn and die. While they wait to make their final run, they'll take spoons trolled behind downriggers anywhere from 30 to 90 feet down in the open water during daylight, J-plugs and minnow-imitating crankbaits flatlined in 10 to 30 feet of water at night.

DIRECTIONS: This fabulous fishery stretches for roughly 8 miles east (Ninemile Point) and 8 miles west (Lighthouse Point) of Rochester.

11E. Pultneyville

DESCRIPTION: Warmed by numerous tributaries, including the Genesee River and Salmon and Bear Creeks, and the discharge from the Ginna nuclear power plant, the inshore water west of the hamlet ranks among the lake's warmest in early spring. Favorable temperatures combined with steep drops, bait-holding shoals, humps, and boulder fields add icing to this angling paradise.

THE FISHING: In April brown trout hang out near shore, in 4 to 8 feet of water, from Hungerford Shoal (about 2 miles west of the harbor) to the Ginna power plant. In addition, March and April find lakers and steelhead drawn to the cobble floors off the mouths of the area's numerous small streams. Most are caught by flatlining Junior Thundersticks, Smithwick Rogues, and Michigan Stinger spoons. As spring turns to summer, steelhead and Pacific salmon are drawn to the wealth of points and depth variations running from the east side of the hamlet all the way to Sodus Bay. Known affectionately as Rainbow Alley, this stretch of the lake is famed for great quantities of shallow-running salmonids, less than 45 feet down over water about 100 feet deep. Mix things up like the locals do: Flatline XPS minnows off planer boards, run dodger/fly combos off divers, and drag flasher/cutbait combos or Northern King spoons off downriggers anywhere from 15 to 40 feet deep.

The area's relatively gently sloping cobble floors—especially off points—are ideal spawning grounds for smallies. What's more, Hungerford Shoal and nearby rock fields hold decent populations of smallmouths in the 12- to 20-inch range all summer long. A simple technique favored by locals is to cast a live minnow—crayfish in summer—wait for the sinker to hit bottom, count to 10, and set the hook. If you're partial to artificial baits, try swimming or jigging bladebaits, or dragging tubes and 3-inch Berkley Power Grubs on bottom. Rock bass and massive schools of perch thrive on the crayfish and round gobies living off the area's copious zebra mussels and insects. Go for them with minnows just off bottom anywhere from 5 to 15 feet deep in spring, and 20 to 40 feet deep in summer.

DIRECTIONS: The hamlet is located halfway between Oswego and Rochester. Take CR 101 (the Seaway Trail) for about 13 miles west of Sodus Point.

ADDITIONAL INFORMATION: While the marina in Pultneyville has a hard surface ramp, most anglers prefer to avoid paying the fee and put in for free at Sodus Bay, about 10 miles east—namely at the Harriman Park Boat Launch on NY 14 and Margaretta Road, just south of the hamlet (hard surface ramp and parking for 20 rigs), and Sodus Point Beach Park, at the end of Wickham Boulevard, next to the Coast Guard Station (hard-surface ramp and parking for about 100 rigs; this site is closed Memorial Day through Labor Day). Pultneyville Harbor's entrance is straddled by cribs that can ruin a motor. When coming in, boaters are advised to follow a straight path set by lining up the two shore markers (white rectangles on poles with a green stripe running down the middle). After the 9/11 terrorist attacks, the authorities slapped a security zone around all nuclear power plants. Buoys mark the restricted area. If you venture inside the wire, be prepared for something nasty to happen, like being challenged by the Coast Guard, boarded by grumpy Navy SEALs, buzzed by a drone, maybe even torpedoed.

11F. Oswego (Nine Mile One and James A. Fitzpatrick Nuclear Plant Discharges)

DESCRIPTION: Besides boasting the mouth of the Oswego River, Lake Ontario's second largest tributary, the city of Oswego is only about 6 miles west of two nuclear power plants that discharge hot water into the lake.

THE FISHING: From mid-October through May, warm water from the above sources attracts walleyes, trout, and salmon. For browns, troll crankbaits and spoons along the shoreline in 3 to 10 feet of water from ice-out through April, and move into waters from 30 to 70 feet deep as summer

Oswego County Tourism's Janet Clerkin struggling with a rod loaded with a king salmon, as Capt. Dick Stanton gives moral support.

intensifies. Hog walleyes spawn in the river and hang around the mouth for most of May. Many "oops walleyes" are caught on lures targeting browns just off the Oswego River's mouth in May. From July through September, the lake's greatest concentration of monster kings and cohos stage off the mouth of the river in preparation for their spawning runs upstream in October. They can be found anywhere from 60 to 100 feet deep over water up to 500 feet deep, and respond to the usual suspects: cutbait, spoons, and trolling flies trolled behind dodgers and flashers. Steelies get as excited preparing for the autumn runs as the salmon do, and stage with kings and cohos in late summer. Chromers are generally targeted by salmon anglers running spoons on cheaters or divers.

DIRECTIONS: This area stretches from a couple of miles west of the city of Oswego to the nuke plants; the huge concrete cooling tower of Nine Mile Two (the most recently built nuke plant) marks the spot.

ADDITIONAL INFORMATION: The city of Oswego's Wrights Landing, a fee area on the west side of the river (from NY 104, head north on West 1st Street, travel four blocks, hook a left onto Lake Street, and continue for a couple hundred yards), offers a six-lane paved ramp, parking for 150 rigs, toilets, and showers. After the 9/11 terrorist attacks, the authorities slapped a security zone around all nuclear power plants. Buoys mark the restricted area. If you venture inside the wire, you'll be in hot water, and face being buzzed by a drone -packing a Cruise missile or, even worse, boarded by angry Immigration and Naturalization authorities, and God only knows where that can lead.

11G. Mexico Bay

DESCRIPTION: Stretching from Nine Mile Point to the mouth of the Salmon River, a distance of roughly 9 miles, this bay is blessed with several tributaries and a gently sloping floor that can take over a mile to reach 30 feet deep.

THE FISHING: This bay's near-shore waters are a brown trout hot spot from ice-out through May. The fish respond to minnow-imitating crankbaits flatlined off planer boards in 3 to 10 feet of water. As summer heats up, they move out a little way and hit spoons and stickbaits trolled just off bottom, anywhere from 40 to 80 feet deep. Large lakers and chinooks hang out in the deep water, several miles out, all summer long and are taken mostly on cutbait/flasher combos trolled behind downriggers 75 to 125 feet down. In late summer, ripe kings sweep through the area on their way to the Salmon River and Little Salmon Rivers. In early August, they can be taken just about anywhere in the bay by running spoons or trolling flies 75 feet or deeper. Still, you can better your chances of scoring by concentrating your efforts on the waters off the mouths of the streams. As they ripen, the salmon move in closer, and by mid-September they can be taken by flatlining large lures like J-Plugs in water 30 feet deep or less. At night, they come right to the mouths of both streams and will take raw skein still-fished on bottom.

ADDITIONAL INFORMATION: Mexico Point Boat Launch, a fee area in the hamlet of Texas (take NY 3 south from Port Ontario for 4 miles, turn west onto NY 104B, continue for 1 mile to CR 40, turn north and travel about 0.5 mile) offers a double-lane concrete ramp, parking for 150 rigs, shore-fishing access, and restrooms. Campers at Selkirk Shores State Park (site 36A) are allowed to launch free. All others are charged a day-use fee from April through October. Free launching is allowed off season.

11H. Henderson Trench

DESCRIPTION: Cut by a glacier during the last ice age—maybe even before that—the trench measures roughly 4 miles long by 1 mile wide. Its steep walls quickly drop 80 feet before hitting a gentler slope and sliding another 40 feet to an average depth of 120 feet.

THE FISHING: Containing summer's coldest and deepest water in the Black River Bay area, this spot holds salmonids all year long. From August through mid-September, it turns into a lunker magnet, drawing and holding mature kings that feast like pigs while milling around waiting for the biological signal that causes them to stop feeding and ascend the Black River to spawn. They respond to all the usual suspects but are especially inclined to strike cut bait.

DIRECTIONS: Heading west out of Henderson Harbor, go through the cut (the narrow channel between the mainland and Hoveys/Association Islands); the trench is to the south, the channel between Stony Point and Stony Island.

ADDITIONAL INFORMATION: The Town of Henderson offers a paved, four-lane launch ramp, with parking for 85 rigs, on the south end of Henderson Harbor, off Military Road (CR 178).

11I. The Wall

DESCRIPTION: Submerged under 60 feet of water in the main shipping channel, the wall is a cliff-like structure that drops about 100 feet, and stretches northeast to southwest for about 1.5 miles.

THE FISHING: Strong current, deep water, and an abundance of bait keep lunker chinook salmon and lake trout here all summer long. For summer chinooks, troll black-and-silver spoons like Northern King 28s and Michigan Stingers, or cutbait tight to the wall in 90 to 125 feet of water. Lakers hang out 30 feet deeper and strike Spin N Glos and Wobble Trolls (peanuts) fished behind cowbells.

DIRECTIONS: Located in the main shipping channel, between Galloo and Canada's Main Duck Islands, the middle of the wall is about 5 miles west of the southern tip of Galloo Island.

ADDITIONAL INFORMATION: The state's Stony Creek boat launch, roughly 13 miles east of the wall, offers a concrete double ramp, parking for about 80 rigs, toilets, and picnic facilities. Get there from Henderson Harbor by taking Harbor Road (CR 123) south to the edge of town. Cross Military Road, take the next right onto Danley Road (CR 152), travel 1.9 miles to the stop sign, turn right onto Nutting Street Road, and continue for 0.2 mile.

11J. Golden Crescent

DESCRIPTION: Nestled into the northeastern corner of the lake, this area boasts the heaviest concentration of islands, shoals, and small bays on the American side of the lake.

THE FISHING: This is the most productive walleye territory in the book. After spawning in tributaries like Kents Creek and the Black River, walleyes remain near shore for as long as they can to prey on all the bait drawn there by warm temperatures. As summer approaches, they slowly move back to open water. Mid-May finds hogs off Point Peninsula; July generally sees them moving north to the steep drops on the south side of Dablon Point, and out deeper, off Fox and Grenadier Islands; August's and early autumn's blistering temperatures send them even farther out, to the waters off Stony, Calf, and the Galloo Islands. While they're still close to the mainland around Point Peninsula, they can be taken by working bucktail jigs and bladebaits over shoals and rock fields in 10 to 25 feet of water. As they move toward Fox and Grenadier Islands, you can still cast for them, but you'll find trolling shallow diving crankbaits like Smithwick Rogues 15 to 30 feet deep (use lead-core line, keel sinkers, or snap-on sinkers to get you down) more productive. In late summer, they congregate on Galloo Shoal (Gas Buoy Shoal), Calf Island Reef, and Calf Island Spit, and respond to shallow diving crankbaits trolled 15 to 30 feet down over drop-offs. Smallmouth bass ranging from 1½ to 5 pounds love this area, too, especially the steep drops-offs around

Galloo and Stony Islands, and respond to live and soft plastic minnows on drop-shot rigs and Carolina-rigged finesse worms in the deep water, as well as spinnerbaits in the shallows around the islands and on the shoals. The shallow channel between Fox Island and the mainland often sprouts massive weed beds, providing some of the best largemouth bass fishing on the open lake. For explosive confrontations with bigmouths, toss wacky-rigged stickworms and Texas-rigged rubber worms, or cast buzzbaits into weed openings and edges.

DIRECTIONS: The Golden Crescent stretches from Cape Vincent to Stony Point.

ADDITIONAL INFORMATION: A hard-surface ramp with parking for about 50 rigs and 20 cars is located at the corner of CR 57 and Flanders Road, on the lake side of the Isthmus.

12. TWELVEMILE CREEK AND EAST BRANCH

KEY SPECIES: Chinook salmon, steelhead, brown trout, bullhead, sunfish, and yellow perch.

DESCRIPTION: These skinny creeks are heavily influenced by runoff and all but dry up in summer and early fall. Indeed, "Where's the creek?" is a common complaint heard from guys scouting the streams for early salmon and steelhead.

TIPS: Fish these streams a couple of days after a downpour.

THE FISHING: Autumn rains, winter thaws, and snowmelt swell both creeks temporarily to ideal spawning size. From late September through mid-November, ripe chinooks up to 30 pounds, and a few cohos averaging 8 pounds stage spawning runs after heavy rains. Browns up to 10 pounds move in about the same time, but continue showing up, when water levels permit, through December. Steelhead up to 15 pounds start pouring in around mid-October to feast on all the fresh caviar. In addition, a few steelies trickle in during winter thaws, and, come spring, they swarm in to spawn. Under such iffy conditions, Pacific salmon are territorial and extremely aggressive, and strike streamers, spoons, and fresh skein with amazing savagery. The browns and rainbows respond with relish to egg sacs and anything that looks like salmon eggs.

Approaching their mouths, the creeks reach the same gradient as the lake and slow down to a crawl. Largely bordered by marsh, the lower reaches load up with panfish in spring and early summer. Bullheads can go 2 pounds, bluegills and pumpkinseeds reach the size of small frying pans, and yellow perch can stretch up to 14 inches. They hit worms fished on bottom. The sunfish and perch will also hit 1-inch curly-tail grubs, tiny jigs, and wet flies.

DIRECTIONS: Located on the west side of Wilson; Hulbert Road parallels Twelvemile Creek; Youngstown and Daniels Roads parallel the East Branch.

ADDITIONAL INFORMATION: The lower reaches of both creeks straddle Wilson-Tuscarora State Park, NY 18, west of Wilson. The facility offers boat ramps, shore-fishing access (including ramps for the handicapped on both branches), picnic areas, and playgrounds. A day-use fee is charged from May 1 to Labor Day.

CONTACT: New York State Department of Environmental Conservation Region 9 and Niagara County Tourism and Convention Corporation.

12A. Public Fishing Rights

DESCRIPTION: Two miles of public fishing rights on Twelvemile Creek stretching upstream of Wilson-Tuscarora State Park.

DIRECTIONS: Access from southwestern corner of Wilson-Tuscarora State Park.

12B. Public Fishing Rights

DESCRIPTION: Shoulder parking and about 1 mile of PFR on Twelvemile Creek upstream of the bridge.

DIRECTIONS: Head west out of Wilson on Youngstown Road for about 3 miles.

12C. Public Fishing Rights

DESCRIPTION: Shoulder parking and roughly 2 miles of PFR on the East Branch; 1 mile upstream of the bridge, and 2 miles downstream.

DIRECTIONS: Take Youngstown Road west out of Wilson for about 1.5 miles, turn left onto Daniels Road, and continue for a few hundred feet to the bridge.

12D. Public Fishing Rights

DESCRIPTION: Shoulder parking and about 1 mile of PFR on the East Branch upstream of the bridge.

DIRECTIONS: From site 12C, continue south on Daniels Road for about 1.5 miles.

12E. Public Fishing Rights

DESCRIPTION: Shoulder parking and a few hundred feet of PFR on the East Branch downstream of the bridge.

DIRECTIONS: From site 12D, continue south on Daniels Road for about 0.5 mile, turn left onto Brayley Road, and continue for 0.5 mile to the bridge.

13. TUSCARORA BAY

KEY SPECIES: Pacific salmon, brown trout, steelhead, largemouth bass, northern pike, and panfish.

DESCRIPTION: Also called Wilson Harbor, this relatively shallow, 100-acre bay is fed by the east branch of Twelvemile Creek (when it's running) and is separated from the lake by a narrow strip of land called the Island.

TIPS: Vertically jig spoons like Kastmasters and Swedish Pimples through the ice for steelhead and brown trout.

THE FISHING: One of only a handful of bays on the western end of the lake, this place gets visited by salmonids in winter. Many are caught serendipitously through the ice on wax worms and minnows targeting panfish and pike. The bay has good populations of warm-water species year-round. Largemouth bass ranging from 1½ to 5 pounds, and northern pike going from 22 to 30 inches, respond to minnows, spinnerbaits, and crankbaits worked around docks and weed edges. Lake-run perch averaging 10 inches and rock bass running over a pound invade the weeds and mudflats in April and May, and respond to small minnows. Loads of 5- to 7-inch sunfish and a few crappies up to 14 inches are also available. In warm weather, the sunfish like worms and small poppers, and the crappies hit minnows and Beetle Spins. Both take jigs tipped with insect larvae through the ice. Lake-run bullheads ranging from 7 inches to 2 pounds swarm into the west side, around the creek's mouth, in April and respond to worms fished on bottom.

DIRECTIONS: Located on the west side of the village of Wilson.

ADDITIONAL INFORMATION: Wilson-Tuscarora State Park, a fee area skirting the bay's west bank, offers a paved ramp, parking for 30 rigs, shore-fishing access, including a platform for handicapped anglers, and restrooms. A day-use fee is charged from May 1 to Labor Day.

CONTACT: New York State Department of Environmental Conservation Region 9 and Niagara County Tourism and Convention Corporation.

13A. Wilson East Pier

DESCRIPTION: This site offers parking for about 10 cars, toilet, and access to the Federal Pier, a popular fishing hot spot.

THE FISHING: The chute is the only way lake-run fish can get to the East Branch of Twelvemile Creek. Cast spoons, in-line spinners, and crankbaits in autumn for Pacific salmon, brown trout, and steelhead; and float-fish egg sacs and worms in spring for chromers. Make a couple of casts on the lake side, too, especially for spring browns. In April and May, massive schools of yellow perch and rock bass come through on their way to the spawning grounds in the bay. They'll hit minnows, worms, and small jigs. Post-spawn smallmouths load the channel for the first week or so of the season and hit minnows, worms, crankbaits, spoons, jigs—you name it. Sheepshead and catfish like the chute's gently flowing waters in summer, and bite best when boat traffic is low, early in the morning and around dusk. The catfish take shrimp, cutbait, and Berkley Catfish Bait Chunks; the drum like crayfish; both hit worms.

DIRECTIONS: At the west end of Ontario Street, in the hamlet of Wilson.

14. EIGHTEENMILE CREEK (NIAGARA COUNTY)

KEY SPECIES: Coho salmon, chinook salmon, brown trout, steelhead, northern pike, largemouth bass, yellow perch, sunfish, and brown bullhead.

DESCRIPTION: Named for its distance from the Niagara River, this gentle, angler-friendly stream offers about 2 miles of world-class seasonal salmonid fishing.

TIPS: October sees the greatest numbers of the Big Four: brown trout, steelhead, kings, and coho salmon.

THE FISHING: "This is the most popular tributary in the western basin of the lake if the state's creel census is any indication," claims Bill Hilts Jr., outdoor sports specialist for Niagara USA. Gallon for gallon, this skinny creek's incredible autumn runs of salmon and trout make it one of Lake Ontario's most productive tributaries. In addition, steelhead overwinter, and fresh runs of ripe chromers enter in the spring. Each species hits fresh skein, egg sacs, glo bugs, and streamers in the fast water and spoons, spinners, and plugs in slow stretches.

The flat water near the mouth is a popular warm-water fishery. Northern pike up to 36 inches are targeted by locals with live minnows and spinnerbaits. Bucketmouths averaging 2½ pounds thrive in the weeds and respond to bass bugs and poppers worked around lily pads, along and with Texas-rigged worms worked along weed edges and windfalls. Yellow perch averaging 9 inches, sunfish up to 8 inches, and brown bullheads from 1 to 2 pounds are available in quantity and hit worms. Crappies averaging 10 inches are available and respond to minnows for about the first month after ice-out, but afterward like more active baits like Berkley Atomic Teasers tipped with a red Berkley Honey Worm, or Beetle Spins.

DIRECTIONS: NY 78 parallels the stream from Burt to Olcott.

ADDITIONAL INFORMATION: The Town of Newfane Marina, West Main Street, Olcott, offers a three-lane paved launch and parking for 50 rigs.

CONTACT: New York State Department of Environmental Conservation Region 9 and Niagara County Tourism and Convention Corporation.

14A. Burt Dam Fishermen's Park

DESCRIPTION: This fee area offers parking for about 100 cars, toilets, and gentle trail down to the fast-water portion of the river stretching for about 0.25 mile up to the Burt Dam. A wall of environmentally friendly limestone blocks skirts the eastern bank from the trestle for a few hundred feet upstream, offering anglers a long, stable, relatively safe casting platform.

DIRECTIONS: On NY 78, 1 mile south of the village of Olcott.

ADDITIONAL INFORMATION: According to Hilts, roughly a million dollars was spent in this area recently to stabilize the banks and install habitat improvements.

14B. Olcott Piers

DESCRIPTION: Two piers straddle the mouth of Eighteenmile Creek.

THE FISHING: These structures offer hundreds of yards of easy casting for brown trout, steelhead, coho, and king salmon in autumn, coho, steelies, and browns in the spring, and everything from smallies to perch, sheepshead, and catfish in summer. The salmonids hit spoons, minnowbaits, and in-line spinners run at a moderate to fast clip; bronzebacks respond to crayfish suspended a couple of inches off bottom below a slip bobber; perch like minnows, worms, and small tubes fished deep; sheepshead take worms and crayfish on bottom; and the catfish like shrimp or large minnows fished on bottom.

DIRECTIONS: Located in the hamlet of Olcott: Get to the east pier by heading north on Lockport Road to its end and turning west onto Ontario Street; for the west pier, head north on Jackson Street to the parking lot at its end. If the lake's too rough to walk the beach to the pier, go to the road, turn left onto Beach Street, then left again past the third house onto the fenced-in path leading to the pier.

14C. Golden Hill State Park

DESCRIPTION: This fee area, famous for its striking, decommissioned lighthouse (offering three bedrooms, it's available for rent year-round), offers 50 campsites (some electric), hot showers, and a paved boat launch with parking for 50 rigs. The campground is open from mid-April through mid-October. A day-use fee is charged non-campers in season.

THE FISHING: The rip-rap protecting the entrance to the harbor is popular with anglers casting crankbaits and spoon-feeding spring browns and an occasional steelie. Steelhead run Golden Hill creek to spawn, water levels permitting, and respond to egg sacs, beads, and garden worms chuck-n-ducked or fished below floats. Bullheads swarm into the harbor to spawn after ice-out and hit worms still fished on bottom. Come summer, the weed beds at the entrance to the harbor hold yellow perch, sunfish, and smallmouth bass. The panfish strike worms and small jigs tipped with scented plastic baits like Honey Worms. Bronzebacks take buzzbaits worked over vegetation; Texas-rigged worms dropped into the openings or worked along the edges; and floating crankbaits like XPS Floating Minnows twitched on the surface in the morning before boat traffic gets too intense, and at dusk when traffic dies down.

DIRECTIONS: From Olcott, take NY 18 east for about 10 miles, turn north onto Carmen Road, then east 1 mile later onto Lower Lake Road.

15. JOHNSON CREEK

KEY SPECIES: Pacific salmon, brown trout, steelhead, black bass, northern pike, panfish, and catfish.

DESCRIPTION: Although this spring creek's water levels are influenced by vagaries in the weather, and it's been known to scrape bottom during drought years, it generally has enough flow to host lake-run salmonids up to the dam in Lyndonville, a distance of 8 miles as the crow flies.

TIPS: While the short stretch from NY 63 to the dam doesn't offer the stream's most striking scenery, it's one of its most productive spots.

THE FISHING: This creek gets stocked with roughly 6,700 steelhead each year. However, it's one of only a handful of tributaries on the west side of the lake, so it draws more than its fair share of lake-run fish with spawning on their minds. Ripe kings, cohos, browns, and steelies, many stretching to wall-hanging proportions, storm the place in their time. They'll hit sponge, egg sacs, and egg-pattern flies. The lower reaches, from the mouth for about a mile inland, are slow and deep, ideal warmwater habitat. Northerns run from 22 to 26 inches, bucketmouths up to 4 pounds, and smallies from 12 to 15 inches. They respond to minnows, spinnerbaits, and swimbaits. In autumn, yellow perch storm into the slow waters, joining resident populations of sunfish and crappies. Spring sees massive quantities of lake-run rock bass, bullheads, and white perch. Target the bullheads, sunnies, and silver bass with worms; the perch, rock bass, and crappies with minnows. Ron Bierstine, owner of Orleans Outdoor, a tackle shop specializing in fly fishing, says some monster channel cats call the lower creek home. They'll hit worms, cutbait, and shrimp.

DIRECTIONS: NY 18 parallels the stream for a couple of miles west of Kuckville, and Alps Road parallels it for a few miles east of Lyndonville.

ADDITIONAL INFORMATION: Lakeside Beach State Park offers 274 campsites with electricity, hot showers, a camp store, and access to the stream's mouth. The campground is open from the last week in April through October; free day use off season. The state offers several hundred feet of public fishing rights upstream of the Blood Road Bridge (off Alps Road) east of Lyndonville. In addition, there's a lot of informal access off NY 18.

CONTACT: New York State Department of Environmental Conservation Region 8 and Orleans County Tourism.

16. MARSH CREEK

KEY SPECIES: Chinook and coho salmon, brown trout, and steelhead.

DESCRIPTION: Watered by several feeders, this skinny creek feeds the Oak Orchard River at the Bridges—a triangle of steel created by Oak Orchard River Road and Roosevelt Highway (NY 18) crossing the Oak Orchard River, and Oak Orchard Road (NY 98) crossing Marsh Creek.

TIPS: Local fly-fishing expert Ron Bierstine says: "The best time to fish this stream is soon after a rain, when water clarity has returned and the level is dropping back to normal."

THE FISHING: This stream gets stocked with about 7,100 steelhead annually. However, its relationship to Oak Orchard River results in it getting good runs of each of the big four in autumn. What's more, winter offers some good opportunities for browns and steelies during thaws. Chromers run in spring. Nymphs and egg patterns are good in the fall, egg sacs are the best winter fare, and egg sacs, 3-inch trout worms, and cone-headed streamers work in spring.

DIRECTIONS: Marsh Creek Road and Kent Road parallel the stream.

ADDITIONAL INFORMATION: While the state owns numerous small patches of public fishing rights easements, posted signs are few. Many access the stream from bridges and along the shoulder at places like Bills and Sawyer Roads near the mouth all the way to the Ridge Road Bridge (NY 104).

CONTACT: New York State Department of Environmental Conservation Region 8 and Orleans County Tourism.

17. OAK ORCHARD RIVER (OAK ORCHARD CREEK)

KEY SPECIES: Coho salmon, chinook salmon, landlocked Atlantic salmon, steelhead, brown trout, northern pike, largemouth bass, smallmouth bass, and panfish.

DESCRIPTION: Spawned in Genesee County's Oak Orchard Swamp, the river snakes through Orleans County before feeding Lake Ontario at Point Breeze. The Waterport Dam, located about 5 miles from the mouth, blocks Lake Ontario's fish from migrating farther upstream. Averaging about 100 yards wide and 2.5 feet deep, the river's temperature and water volume are ideal from fall through spring for seasonal runs of salmonids.

TIPS: In spring, swing an Egg-Sucking Leech through the current on a sinking leader.

Salmon trying to jump the falls, Oak Orchard Creek.

THE FISHING: The lower stretch of Oak Orchard River is world-class trophy salmonid water. It's made this way by the state annually stocking roughly 140,000 chinook fingerlings and 21,000 steelhead yearlings. Chinook salmon reaching up to 40 pounds run the river from early September through mid-November. Cohos up to 20 pounds start showing up in October and run into December, providing "Christmas cohos," according to Ron Bierstine, owner of Orleans Outdoor, a local tackle shop specializing in fly fishing. "In recent years, the river has seen a modest resurgence of Atlantic salmon, usually in the early part of the run," adds Bierstine. The Pacific salmon strike streamers and salmon skein; the landlocked Atlantics prefer flies, and will hit a worm after a rain.

While the salmon enjoy a good following, most anglers are drawn to the "Oak" by brown trout. Its autumn runs are legendary, offering fish ranging from a paltry (relatively speaking) 3 pounds to over 20 pounds. Though the state's stocking list indicates that none is stocked directly into the stream, Lake O's residents cotton to the flow and converge on the place to spawn. Browns start trickling in around mid-September and stay as late as January. Steelhead up to 20 pounds run in their wakes, and continue entering the river all winter, taking advantage of the stream's slightly warmer temperatures and fattening up on the steady supply of red caviar washed out from under the rocks by ever-shifting currents. Come spring, snowmelt draws massive quantities of ripe chromers into the swollen rapids to spawn. These trout hit nymphs, streamers, egg sacs, and worms while in the rapids, as well as spoons and minnowbaits cast from the breakwalls.

Northern pike thrive in the still water of the lower river. A hard blow out of the northeast usually spurs them into a feeding frenzy, especially in the stretch between the Lake Ontario State Parkway and the break-wall. Smallmouth bass and a few largemouths are also present in the lower reaches and respond to minnows, crayfish, soft jerkbaits worked along weed edges, and finesse worms tossed into the weeds on Charlie Brewer's Spider Classic Slider Heads. Walleyes enter the river to spawn, and some stick around a couple of weeks into May, offering trophy opportunities to anglers trolling for them between the piers with crankbaits. Schools of lake perch pour into the lower river autumn through spring and respond to minnows, worms, and small lures. Sunfish, sheepshead, catfish, and white perch are popularly sought by anglers bottom-fishing off the piers with worms.

DIRECTIONS: Head north out of Batavia on NY 98 for about 24 miles.

CONTACT: New York State Department of Environmental Conservation Region 8 and Orleans County Tourism.

17A. Oak Orchard Fishing Access Site

DESCRIPTION: This DEC site has parking for about 40 cars.

THE FISHING: The power plant and adjoining waterfalls block salmon from advancing any farther upstream. The tailrace and plunge pool load up with the frustrated fish, milling around trying to figure out their next move.

DIRECTIONS: From the village of Albion, head north on NY 98 for about 4.5 miles, turn left onto Waterport-Carlton Road, travel for 2.1 miles, turn right onto Park Avenue, and continue for 0.3 mile.

17B. Park Avenue Extension Public Access

DESCRIPTION: This site offers shoulder parking for 10 cars on the west side of the unpaved street, and paid parking in the field on the other side of the road.

THE FISHING: The trail down to the stream ends where the choicest fly-fishing water begins.

DIRECTIONS: From site 17A above, head north on Park Avenue for about 0.4 mile, and continue straight when the road banks sharply to the right.

17C. Orleans County Marine Park

DESCRIPTION: Located in the Oak Orchard River Gorge, this safe harbor offers a paved ramp, parking for 50 rigs, fishing ramps and piers, 71 rental slips, and hot showers. Open April 15 through November 1.

THE FISHING: Chinook and coho salmon enter this slow, deep harbor as early as late August and mill around for a while before charging upstream. They can be taken on crankbaits and spoons, and by drifting egg sacs and skein. Brown trout also enter about this time and respond to the same baits, as well as worms. Trophy steelhead are available from mid-November through April and take all the above baits, as well as Rooster Tails and plugs like Hot Shots and Lazy Ikes.

DIRECTIONS: Follow the directions to site 17A, but instead of turning on Park Avenue, continue on NY 98 for about 2 miles to the park's main entrance on the west side of the road.

ADDITIONAL INFORMATION: Bank anglers have thousands of feet of slow-water access in the 0.5-mile-long park and on the pier and jetty at the river's mouth. A no-fee paved launch with parking for 10 rigs is located a couple hundred yards north, at the end of NY 98.

17D. St. Mary's Archers Sportsman's Club

DESCRIPTION: This private club owns hundreds of yards of riverfront and allows free public fishing but charges a parking fee; you can avoid it by parking on top of the hill.

THE FISHING: Salmon generally run right past this area on their way up to the dam. On the other hand, steelhead and browns find the area's gentle currents and pools terrific spots to rest and feed. They respond to streamers swung through the current, dead-drifted nymphs and egg imitations.

DIRECTIONS: From the NY 98/Carlton-Waterport Road junction, head west on Waterport-Carlton Road for about 4 miles to its end, turn right onto Waterport Road (NY 279), and cross Waterport Pond (Lake Alice). When you come to the T in the road shortly afterward bear right to stay on NY 279, travel for a few hundred feet, turn right onto Clarks Mills Road, and travel a few hundred yards to the club's entrance on the right.

ADDITIONAL INFORMATION: The club holds an annual three-day fly-fishing, catch-and-release trout derby the third week of October.

17E. Oak Orchard Marine State Park West

DESCRIPTION: This fee area has a four-bay paved launch, parking for about 25 rigs, a picnic area, and a comfort station.

DIRECTIONS: Head south on NY 98 from Point Breeze for 1.7 miles to NY 18, turn right, travel 0.7 mile to Archibald Road, turn right, and travel 1 mile to the park on the right.

17F. Lakeside Beach State Park

DESCRIPTION: This fee area offers 274 campsites with electricity, hot showers, and a camp store. The campground is open from the last week in April through October; free day use off season.

DIRECTIONS: Two miles west of Point Breeze, at the end of the Lake Ontario State Parkway.

18. SANDY CREEK (MONROE COUNTY)

KEY SPECIES: Coho salmon, chinook salmon, brown trout, steelhead, black bass, northern pike, crappies, yellow perch, and brown bullheads.

DESCRIPTION: This skinny creek's fishery is very runoff-dependent. While there's just about always something around worth catching, when the water's running high—after an autumn storm or winter thaw, for instance—salmonids storm the place en masse. Its lower reaches and mouth contain dynamite warm-water habitat.

TIPS: Swing streamers through the tails of runs.

THE FISHING: The state stocks roughly 90,000 fingerling chinooks and 20,000 steelhead averaging 5 inches each year. Seasonal returns are good. Early autumn sees runs of kings averaging 20 pounds, coho salmon ranging from 6 to 10 pounds, and brown trout up to 15 pounds. The salmon aren't into feeding, but the spawning urge makes them macho, and they'll strike lures, streamers, and clumps of raw skein. The browns don't shut down as utterly as the salmon, but their appetites are suppressed by the spawn they're carrying. Still, they'll hit small stuff like pieces of worm, egg sacs, and nymphs. Steelhead up to 20 pounds run from November through March and take egg sacs, beads, and small spinners in the rapids, and plugs like Hot Shots in smooth water. Largemouth bass ranging from 2 to 5 pounds and northerns up to 10 pounds lurk in the lower creek's weeds, reeds, and other cover, where they grab minnows, spinnerbaits, and wide-bodied plugs like Bass Pro XPS Square Bills. Smallmouth bass invade the place every spring to spawn and usually stick around for a couple of weeks after the season opens. Famished after making whoopie, they only range between 1 and 2½ pounds, but what they lack in size, they more than make up for in scrappiness, eagerly challenging lures crossing their path. Brown bullheads up to 14 inches and yellow perch in the 8- to 12-inch range swarm in from April through mid-May, gobbling up every worm they can find; the perch will take minnows and jigs, too.

DIRECTIONS: From Rochester, take Lake Ontario State Parkway west for about 15 miles to the Westphal Road exit and follow the signs to the fishing access site.

ADDITIONAL INFORMATION: The Westphal Road fishing access site offers shore fishing, a paved ramp, parking for about 50 rigs, and a portable toilet.

CONTACT: New York State Department of Environmental Conservation Region 8 and Greater Rochester Visitors Association.

18A. Public Fishing Rights

DESCRIPTION: About 0.25 mile of PFR upstream and a mile of PFR downstream of the bridge; shoulder parking.

THE FISHING: Lake-run trout and salmon find this area's deep runs and rapids to their liking. It's ideal water for float-fishing beads and 3-inch plastic worms, chuck-n-ducking egg sacs and night crawlers, or casting in-line spinners.

DIRECTIONS: From the Westphal Road fishing access site (site 18), head south on Westphal Road for about a mile, turn right onto North Hamlin Road, travel about 1.5 mile and turn left onto Lake Road West Fork, continue for about 1.5 mile, turn right onto Church Road (NY 360), and continue for a few hundred yards to the bridge.

18B. Public Fishing Rights

DESCRIPTION: About 0.25 mile of PFR upstream and downstream of the bridge.

DIRECTIONS: From site 18A, continue west on Church Street for about a mile, turn left onto Redman Road, travel 1.5 miles, turn right onto Roosevelt Highway, and travel a few hundred feet to the bridge.

18C. Hamlin Beach State Park

DESCRIPTION: This 1,100-acre fee area offers hundreds of campsites with electric hookups, hot showers, playgrounds, and a fishing pier. In addition, Yanty Creek on its east side draws seasonal runs of brown trout, steelhead, and salmon, and bullheads and panfish enter the marsh in the spring.

DIRECTIONS: Off Lake Ontario State Parkway, about 3 miles west of Westphal Road.

19. BRADDOCK BAY

KEY SPECIES: Northern pike, chain pickerel, largemouth bass, yellow perch, white perch, black crappies, sunfish, rock bass, brown bullheads, bowfin, and carp.

DESCRIPTION: Fed by West, Salmon, and Buttonwood Creeks, this 357-acre bay's shallow waters offer an incredible collection of warm habitats ranging from ancient pilings and massive weed beds to undercut cattail mats, rock fields, new and abandoned docks, bridge abutments—you name it.

TIPS: On calm summer days, work darters and prop baits over weeds and along mats of vegetation for largemouth bass.

THE FISHING: Bucketmouths running 2 to 4 pounds are the norm, but heavier hawgs are caught regularly. Drag Texas-rigged worms along weed edges, cattails, and other structure; cast Flukes or hard jerkbaits under docks, making sure to hit the uprights every now and then to sound the dinner bell; and pitch jig-n-pigs into slop. Spinnerbaits and crankbaits cast along any weed line and weed edge, especially in the creeks, will meet the teeth of northern pike ranging from ax handles to 28 inches long, but be prepared for brutes up to 36 inches, too. As plentiful as the northerns and almost as big, chain pickerel thrive in the bay and respond to worms worked just below the surface on spinner-rigged harnesses (don't worry about reeling too fast—they swim quicker than your fingers can turn the handle) and crankbaits. A highly productive nursery for everything from minnows and tadpoles to aquatic insects, Braddock Bay is a year-round home to good populations of yellow perch in the 8- to 12-inch range and crappies ranging from 9 to 12 inches. They like the deeper water found in Salmon Creek and have a taste for small minnows, jigs, and 2-inch Berkley Power Grubs. Bluegills and pumpkinseeds reach mind-boggling size—some over a pound—on all the insects, invertebrates, and stuff. Go for them with spikes, mousies, and wax worms through the ice; garden worms and spikes in early spring; and night crawlers, cork poppers, wet flies, and Berkley Honey Worms late spring through fall. Spawn-heavy rock bass up to 2 pounds swarm into Salmon Creek in May and take minnows, small jigs, and worms. Bullheads invade the place from ice-out into May and hit worms fished on bottom, particularly at night. Rafts of white perch, some weighing up to 2 pounds, storm in to spawn in the spring and strike worms and anything that resembles a minnow; their numbers are very cyclical, with some years seeing numerous lunkers, other years only runts, and some years hardly any at all of any size. Bowfin are plentiful and strike minnows, crayfish, and cutbait fished on bottom. Carp grow huge, up to 40 pounds, and hit bread balls, baked potato, and corn.

DIRECTIONS: Lake Ontario State Parkway runs along the south shore about 5 miles west of Rochester.

ADDITIONAL INFORMATION: The shallow mouth is littered with pilings and sandbars. If you come in from the lake, follow the channel marked by the beacons. This bay, Rose Marsh just west of Braddock Point, and the three Greece Ponds to the east are part of the 2,125-acre Braddock Bay Fish and Wildlife Management Area.

CONTACT: New York State Department of Environmental Conservation Region 8 and Greater Rochester Visitors Association.

19A. Town of Greece Braddock Bay Marina

DESCRIPTION: This fee area, a cooperative effort of government and private enterprise, offers complete marina services, a ship-and-shore store, a paved boat launch, parking for 50 rigs, picnic tables, and restrooms. The launch ramp is open from ice-out (April) to the end of November. A free canoe launch with parking for about 10 cars is just before the entrance gate, on the right. Bank fishing is permitted at the canoe launch but not on marina grounds.

THE FISHING: Right after ice-out, the marina loads up with yellow perch, crappies, rock bass, sunfish, bullheads, and white perch. The perch, sunfish, and bullheads will take worms fished on bottom; the crappies, perch, and rock bass will take minnows, small jigs, and tubes fished below floats.

DIRECTIONS: From Rochester, take Lake Ontario State Parkway west for about 7 miles, turn onto East Manitou Road, and travel a few hundred yards.

19B. Public Access

DESCRIPTION: The bottleneck of Salmon Creek just below the Lake Ontario State Parkway Bridge is a popular bank-fishing spot for perch and bullheads in early spring.

DIRECTIONS: From 19A, head west on the Lake Ontario State Parkway for about a mile, get off at the Manitou Beach Road exit; the lot will be on the right a few yards later. You'll have to walk along the highway for several hundred feet to get to the water.

19C. Cooper Pond

DESCRIPTION: Only about 3 acres, this partially man-made pond on Buttonwood Creek averages 3 feet deep and drops to a maximum depth of 10 feet.

THE FISHING: Largemouth bass range from 2 to 6 pounds and have a taste for Flukes ripped over emergent vegetation and Texas-rigged 7- to 10-inch plastic worms gently jiggled on bottom in deep spots. Northerns up to 10 pounds are present and respond to large minnows suspended below bobbers and to buzzbaits ripped over submerged weeds. Its crappies reach up to 16 inches, bluegill bigger than a large man's hand, and yellow perch up to 12 inches. Strawberry bass are partial to jigs tipped with minnows, Berkley Atomic Teasers tipped with Honey Worms, and curly-tail grubs rigged on spinner forms; the sunfish like worms and 1-inch, scented, curly-tail grubs; both love wax worms, spikes, and other maggots fished through the ice; and the yellow perch love all of the above.

DIRECTIONS: Head up weedy Buttonwood Creek, Braddock Bay's eastern tributary. The channel to the pond is on the east side, about 1,000 yards upstream of the Lake Ontario State Parkway Bridge.

ADDITIONAL INFORMATION: Don, from the Bait Shop in Spencerport, says some of his customers fish this site regularly but they seldom talk about it . . . This site is accessible by boat only.

20. CRANBERRY POND

KEY SPECIES: Largemouth bass, northern pike, walleye, yellow perch, black crappies, sunfish, and bowfin.

DESCRIPTION: Connected to Long Pond by a channel, this 226-acre pond is a superb warm-water fishery.

TIPS: Fly fish with bass bugs on windless days.

THE FISHING: Largemouth bass in the 2- to 3-pound range, and northern pike typically running 2 to 6 pounds occupy weed edges and readily take spinnerbaits and soft plastic jerkbaits. Come winter, the place is popular with ice anglers looking for northern pike, walleye, crappie, and perch dinners. Large minnows fished off bottom on tip-ups account for most of the northerns, including pikeasauruses over 10 pounds. Swedish Pimples and Rapala Jigging Raps tipped with minnows, shaken so gently they barely move, catch a lot of walleyes. Insect larvae and small minnows work for the resident perch running 6 to 10 inches and crappies ranging from 9 to 12 inches. After ice-out, lake-run walleye, perch, and bullheads swarm into the pond and respond to worms fished on bottom; the perch and walleye will take minnows, jigs, and minnowbaits, too. Bowfin are numerous and take crayfish, minnows, and worms.

DIRECTIONS: From Rochester, head west for about 5 miles on Lake Ontario State Parkway. Take East Manitou Road north for about 0.5 mile to its end, turn right onto Edgemere Drive, and travel a few hundred yards.

ADDITIONAL INFORMATION: A public access site with a beach launch for cartoppers and parking for 10 cars is located at the northwestern corner of the bay, at the corner of Edgemere Drive and Cranberry Road. In addition, informal access and parking is available at the shoulder of Edgemere Drive.

CONTACT: New York State Department of Environmental Conservation Region 8 and Greater Rochester Visitors Association.

21. LONG POND

KEY SPECIES: Northern pike, chain pickerel, largemouth bass, walleye, yellow perch, black crappies, rock bass, bullheads, sunfish, channel catfish, and carp.

DESCRIPTION: Heavily developed on three sides and surrounded by weed beds, this 442-acre pond averages 5 feet deep and has a 100-acre hole in the middle that drops to a depth of 9 feet.

TIPS: After ice-out, bottom-fish with worms for bullheads.

THE FISHING: This is a great warm-water fishery. Largemouths averaging 15 inches, with a lot of bigger ones to keep things interesting, rule the weeds. They eagerly take wacky-rigged stickworms dropped into weed openings, 4-inch Texas-rigged tubes worked in slop and emergent vegetation, and finesse worms on Charley Brewer Slider Heads shaken through thick weeds. Northern pike and chain pickerel between 22 and 26 inches are commonly taken in summer on buzzbaits and jerkbaits, but some 30-inch pickerel and northerns up to 40 inches are caught each year through the ice on large shiners. Some large walleye and huge numbers of yellow perch ranging from 11 to 13 inches come in from the lake in late autumn and respond to minnows and crankbaits. In winter, they join the pond's year-round population of 6- to 10-inch yellow perch, 9- to 14-inch crappies, and monster sunfish, offering some of the best ice-fishing action on the lake's south shore. Additional schools of perch and bullheads are drawn to the place to spawn from ice-out through April; and huge quantities of white perch, white bass, and rock bass come in from late April through May. They hit worms, minnows, and small lures. April sends crappies on feeding binges, and they'll nail small tubes, Beetle Spins, and minnows. In summer, fly fishers find heart-pounding action working weedless streamers through weeds for bass and pike, and casting poppers for panfish. A decent population of channel cats ranging from 14 to 30 inches calls the place home, too. They're most active in summer and hit worms, minnows, shrimp, even bread balls, fished on bottom. Carp reach monstrous proportions and take dough balls dipped in sweet syrups and peanut butter.

DIRECTIONS: Take Lake Ontario State Parkway west out of Rochester for about 3 miles, turn north onto Long Pond Road, continue for 0.75 mile, and turn left onto Edgemere Drive.

ADDITIONAL INFORMATION: Edgemere Drive offers informal parking and shore-fishing access. Car-toppers can launch at Cranberry Pond (site 20), follow the north shore, and take the narrow channel into Long Pond; you'll have to go under a bridge with a 3-foot clearance.

CONTACT: New York State Department of Environmental Conservation Region 8 and Greater Rochester Visitors Association.

21A. Public Access

DESCRIPTION: Parking for about 10 cars and a trail leading to the Lake Ontario State Parkway Bridge.

THE FISHING: In spring, massive schools of bullheads and yellow perch move in and out of the bottleneck at the parkway's bridge. This is a popular bank-fishing site for anglers bottom-fishing with worms, or suspending emerald shiners below bobbers.

DIRECTIONS: From its intersection with Edgemere Drive on the northwestern corner of the pond, take Lowden Point Road south for about

0.5 mile to the lot on the left. Hike the trail at the southeastern corner a few hundred yards to the bridge.

22. BUCK POND

KEY SPECIES: Largemouth bass, northern pike, bluegill, black crappies, and yellow perch.

DESCRIPTION: Averaging 6 feet deep, this 174-acre pond is surrounded by marsh. It smells like a fresh fish in deep summer, and average folks consider this place a backwater suitable only for waterfowl and mosquitoes—which is another way of saying it's a dynamite fishing hole.

TIPS: Work Zara Spooks in the water lilies.

THE FISHING: Bucketmouths reach 6-plus pounds and northerns more than 30 inches on the pond's cornucopia of ducklings, baby muskrats, minnows, and frogs. Both species respond best to large minnows. The biggest northerns are caught through the ice. The place is also a great ice-fishing spot for bluegills and crappies ranging from ½ to ¾ pound and perch ranging from 8 to 14 inches. They are normally targeted with teardrop jigs baited with grubs or minnows.

DIRECTIONS: Head west out of Rochester on Beach Avenue. When it dips south, continue straight on Edgemere Drive for about 1.5 miles.

ADDITIONAL INFORMATION: Buck Pond's public access site, located on Edgemere Drive at the northeastern corner of the pond, has parking for 10 cars.

CONTACT: New York State Department of Environmental Conservation Region 8 and Greater Rochester Visitors Association.

23. ROUND POND

KEY SPECIES: Largemouth bass, white perch, sunfish, brown bullheads, and carp.

DESCRIPTION: This 38-acre pond is the shallowest and smallest of the four Greece—not grease—Ponds on the western outskirts of Rochester. Averaging 3 feet deep, full of weeds, and skirted on the west bank by cattails and marsh, this pond's muddy wakes and vocabulary of splashes and sucking sounds (made by monster carp) are enough to give normal people nightmares.

TIPS: Cast small plugs and spinners for white perch in the spring.

THE FISHING: Largemouth bass running from 1½ to 4 pounds live under the slop and respond to plastic worms and snakes ripped across the surface. Carp thrive in the place and respond to bread balls and pieces of boiled potato. Sunfish the size of small frying pans are available and are especially cooperative in spring, when they can't resist garden worms fished on bottom or spikes hooked onto ice jigs and dangled from bobbers. There's a good run of 10- to 14-inch bullheads in the spring; they'll hit worms fished on bottom.

DIRECTIONS: A couple hundred feet west of the corner of Dewey Avenue and Edgemere Drive, just west of Rochester's city limits.

ADDITIONAL INFORMATION: While the place is surrounded by roads, posted signs are all over the place; the best way to get in is by entering from the lake.

CONTACT: New York State Department of Environmental Conservation Region 8 and Greater Rochester Visitors Association.

24. SLATER CREEK

KEY SPECIES: Steelhead.

DESCRIPTION: This short stream bubbles out of a residential area on the west side of Rochester.

TIPS: Float-fish an egg sac wrapped in white mesh when the water's murky; blue and orange when it's clear.

THE FISHING: This used to be a primo steelie haunt in winter and early spring when the power company was discharging warm water regularly in the early part of the century. That's over with and the only water the creek gets now is what nature dishes out. Currently, the volume is very skinny under the best conditions—so bony, in fact, that only the panfish seem to find it tolerable. However, high water from heavy rains and snowmelt can swell the creek to levels spawn-minded steelies find attractive, and they'll storm in out of curiosity if nothing else. The public access site's convenient location on Beach Street draws attention to the place, and it's fished a lot by self-respecting locals who can't resist taking a few casts whenever they're crossing the stream.

DIRECTIONS: Beach Avenue, on Rochester's west side.

ADDITIONAL INFORMATION: The public fishing access site on Beach Avenue, just downstream of the power plant, has parking for about 25 cars.

CONTACT: New York State Department of Environmental Conservation Region 8 and Greater Rochester Visitors Association.

25. GENESEE RIVER

KEY SPECIES: Coho salmon, chinook salmon, brown trout, steelhead, black bass, northern pike, walleye, channel catfish, freshwater drum, yellow perch, and silver bass.

DESCRIPTION: This shallow, roily stream flows right through Rochester, the third largest city in New York. It offers about 0.75 mile of fast water below the lower falls, followed by a 5.5-mile stretch of flat water all the way to the lake.

TIPS: In autumn and spring, cast spoons and spinners into the chute from Ontario Beach Park's Charlotte Pier (west bank) and Summerville Pier for salmonids.

THE FISHING: Each year the state stocks about 140,000 chinook fingerlings and 22,000 steelhead. From mid-September through mid-November, kings averaging 20 pounds and cohos running 5 to 12 pounds stage their spawning runs, along with a smattering of brown trout averaging 6 pounds, and steelhead up to 20 pounds. Chromers and browns continue moving in and out of the river straight through April. Troll for them with spoons and plugs, especially between the O'Rorke Bridge (Pattonwood Drive) and the mouth. Bank anglers will do almost as well casting spoons, in-line spinners, plugs, egg sacs, and beads. Another option is the fast water below the lower falls where egg sacs, skein, streamers, yarn flies, and in-line spinners produce fish. From opening day through June, the piers at the mouth are popular hot spots for walleye reaching up to 10 pounds. They respond to crankbaits like Bass Pro XPS Minnows, jigs, and worms on harnesses (spinner-rigged and plain) dragged slowly on bottom. Lake-run smallmouths averaging 2 pounds join the resident population, providing some of the best bronzeback action imaginable until mid-July. They hit crayfish and worms still-fished on bottom, free-lined minnows, scented plastic finesse worms and 3-inch leeches on drop-shot rigs, 3-inch tubes and curly-tail grubs dragged along the river floor, crankbaits—you name it. Hawg largemouths and northerns of pikeasaurus proportions rule the weed beds. They respond to spinnerbaits and jerkbaits worked over weed edges, under docks, around culverts, and parallel to break lines. Sheepshead and channel catfish running from 1 to 15 pounds are popularly targeted in deep summer by bank anglers bottom-fishing with crayfish and shrimp, respectively. Lake-run yellow perch up to 14 inches and rock bass over a pound swarm the place in spring, and take minnows, curly-tail grubs, and small spoons. While their numbers fluctuate wildly from year to year, rafts of lake-run white perch and white bass invade the stream in late May, sometimes reaching such great numbers they look like piranhas feeding on the surface. Generally running 6 to 8 inches—some years they stretch over a foot long—they move in and out of the harbor all summer and take worms, minnows, and small lures like Bill Lewis's Tiny Traps.

DIRECTIONS: Lake Avenue parallels the stream in Rochester.

ADDITIONAL INFORMATION: Monroe County's Ontario Beach Park occupies the last few hundred yards of the river's west bank, offering shore-fishing access, toilets, a paved ramp with parking for about 100 rigs, and unlimited parking for shore anglers.

CONTACT: New York State Department of Environmental Conservation Region 8 and Greater Rochester Visitors Association.

25A. Genesee River Fishing Access Site

DESCRIPTION: This site offers parking for about 50 cars, shore-fishing access, and a Johnny-on-the-spot.

THE FISHING: Located on the east bank of the harbor just south of the river's mouth, this site offers relatively deep water and is favored by summer-time anglers bottom-fishing for everything from smallmouth bass to catfish.

DIRECTIONS: From its intersection with Lake Avenue, head east on Pattonwood Drive to its end, about 0.5 mile, then turn left onto St. Paul Boulevard and travel about 0.5 mile to the access site at the end.

25B. Summerville Pier Access

DESCRIPTION: Jutting out of the east side of the mouth of the Genesee River, this pier reaches several hundred yards into the lake.

THE FISHING: This spot is a popular platform for casting skein, egg sacs, and lures for autumn-running salmon and trout; and for spoon-feeding browns and float-fishing for steelies in spring.

DIRECTIONS: From the northeastern corner of site 25A's parking lot, walk the road past the gate to the Coast Guard station, and take the narrow trail out to the pier.

25C. Seth Green Lower Falls Public Fishing Area

DESCRIPTION: Parking and fishing access in the rapids below the lower falls.

DIRECTIONS: On Seth Green Drive, about 100 yards west of its junction with St. Paul Street.

25D. Maplewood Park Access

DESCRIPTION: Parking and a footpath on the west side of the river to the lower falls.

DIRECTIONS: Backtrack to St. Paul Street from site 25C, head south for about 0.25 mile to Driving Park Avenue, turn right, cross the bridge, then turn right again onto Maplewood Avenue.

26. IRONDEQUOIT CREEK

KEY SPECIES: Steelhead, brown trout, chinook salmon, and coho salmon.

DESCRIPTION: Boasting a watershed stretching for over 300 miles, Irondequoit Creek winds through Monroe County, including the southeastern outskirts of Rochester, like a confused snake, ultimately coming to rest in Irondequoit Bay. Its numerous tributaries keep it sufficiently watered and at the right temperatures to draw some of autumn's earliest runs of salmon and browns, and steelhead from October through early spring. Roughly half of it flows through municipal parks, offering anglers miles of access.

TIPS: Work Crystal Buggers and Egg-Sucking Leeches through the heads and tails of pools.

THE FISHING: This stream boasts Monroe County's longest stretch of stream habitat for lake-run salmonids. The state stocks the place annually with about 10,000 browns, including 2,000 two-year-olds between 13 and 14 inches long, and 27,500 steelhead. In addition, Monroe County kicks in over 15,000 trout annually that it raises in a hatchery it operates at Powder Mills Park. The chromers beat fins for the lake as soon as the water gets uncomfortably warm, usually by June. And while most of the browns follow, a lot of them settle in and stay year-round. Those lucky enough to survive their tours in the lake always return. The browns come back in autumn to spawn; rainbows invade the place from October through April, to feast on salmon and trout caviar in fall and winter, and to spawn in the spring. Both hit egg sacs, worms, in-line spinners, and the litany of glo bugs and streamers that fly tiers have developed to entice them. Although Pacific and Atlantic salmon aren't stocked, naturally spawned fish and stragglers from plantings elsewhere wander over in large enough numbers to draw followings of anglers. A few landlocked Atlantic salmon trickle in June through September and respond to streamers anytime and worms after a rain; Pacific salmon run in autumn and strike skein, streamers, and crankbaits.

DIRECTIONS: Interstates 490 and 590 parallel the stream.

ADDITIONAL INFORMATION: Flowing through one of the state's largest metropolitan areas, Irondequoit Creek is punctuated with numerous municipal parks offering fishing access. They include: Ellison County Park (Blossom Road) and Linear Park (Penfield Road, NY 441) in the town of Penfield; Spring Lake Park (Whitney Road) and Perinton Park (Baird Road) in the town of Perinton; Deblase Park (Thornell Road) and Powder Mill Park (Park Road) in the town of Pittsford.

CONTACT: New York State Department of Environmental Conservation Region 8 and Visit Rochester.

26A. Channing H. Philbrick Park

DESCRIPTION: Nestled in a scenic valley, this 19-acre park's trail system skirts one of the longest stretches of rapids on Irondequoit Creek, offering cleared access to some of the stream's finest pocket water. Bank improvements include huge blocks of cut limestone that make great holding areas and hiding spots for salmonids, and super fishing platforms for anglers and critters ranging from blue herons to mink, while preventing further erosion of the park's spectacular bluff, a high-rise for cliff swallows.

THE FISHING: Mark Moskal, owner of Summit to Stream Adventures, says this stretch of stream is one of his favorite go-to spots. Its highly oxygenated waters draw lake-run salmonids like a magnet; they find the pools and runs ideal for courting, and the pebbles carpeting its riffs perfect for spawning. They eagerly respond to flies, especially egg imitations and egg-sucking streamers. What's more, this is one of the spots the state stocks with browns, making it a productive summer fishery, too.

DIRECTIONS: On Linear Road, two blocks west of the NY 441/Five Mile Line Road intersection in the town of Penfield.

ADDITIONAL INFORMATION: This park's upper (10 cars) and lower (25 cars) parking areas, playground, toilets, and picnic tables, all steeped in some of the most picturesque scenery imaginable, make it the perfect site for family outings.

27. IRONDEQUOIT BAY

KEY SPECIES: Brown trout, steelhead, coho salmon, chinook salmon, northern pike, chain pickerel, walleye, black bass, and panfish.

DESCRIPTION: Located on the east side of Rochester, this 1,800-acre bay is fed by Irondequoit Creek. Bluffs, scarred by the elements, loom over its shoreline, spawning such place-names as Inspiration Point and Point Lookout. A deep trench runs down the center. In summer anaerobic degradation of organic material on the floor drastically lowers oxygen levels below 18 feet.

TIPS: Work the central basin's drop-offs with 3-inch scented plastic minnows on drop-shot rigs, or crayfish, 12 to 18 feet down, for summer smallmouths.

THE FISHING: This is the Rochester area's likeliest bay to save the day when winds whip Lake Ontario into a frightful latticework of whitecaps and swells. In early spring, football-sized brown trout averaging 6 pounds, a smattering of steelhead ranging from 4 to 10 pounds, coho salmon from 3 to 5 pounds, and kings up to 15 pounds move in to pig out on the alewives basking in the bay's warmer waters; spring sees ripe chromers pass through on their way to spawn in Irondequoit Creek. They hit small spoons and minnow-imitating crankbaits flatlined off planer boards. The bay's best-kept secret is its black bass fishery. Bucketmouths up to 6 pounds rule the weed beds and can be lured out with Texas-rigged worms worked along the edges and in holes. Good numbers of 2- to 4-pound bronzebacks are present. Vertically jig for them with bladebaits or drag soft plastics on bottom, around abutments, docks, and other structure in 15 feet of water. Walleyes in the 3- to 5-pound range are common, with 8-pounders possible. In spring fish for them at night by casting or flatlining crankbaits like XPS Minnows and Smithwick Rogues; in July they go deeper and respond to bladebaits snap-jigged in 10 to 18 feet of water, or worms bottom-bounced on spinner harnesses or slow death hooks. Northern pike, many over 10 pounds, and pickerel up to 30 inches prowl the weed edges in 5 to 15 feet of water, eagerly awaiting the opportunity to pounce on bite-sized morsels ranging from minnows and fat-bodied crankbaits to Mepps Aglias and noisy lipless lures like Rat-L-Traps. The two piers at the mouth are local hot spots for folks casting spoons, stickbaits, and egg sacs into the chute for autumn-running salmon and trout; and spring steelies and browns. Lake-run yellow perch, bullheads, and rock bass storm in from ice-out through May; and good populations of resident perch, sunfish, and crappies thrive in the bay year-round. All but the crappies like worms; and all but the sunfish and bullheads slam minnows and small lures.

DIRECTIONS: NY 590 parallels the west bank; Bay Road parallels the east shore.

ADDITIONAL INFORMATION: Irondequoit Bay State Marine Park, a fee area at the intersection of NY 590 and Lake Road, has a paved ramp, parking for 30 rigs, shore- and pier-fishing access, and toilets.

CONTACT: New York State Department of Environmental Conservation Region 8 and Greater Rochester Visitors Association.

27A. Irondequoit Bay County Park West

DESCRIPTION: This park offers a beach launch for car-top craft and parking for five cars.

DIRECTIONS: Off South Glen Road in Rochester.

27B. Hand Launch

DESCRIPTION: This public launch is suitable for car-toppers.

DIRECTIONS: Off Empire Boulevard (NY 404), on the bay's south end.

27C. Webster Park

DESCRIPTION: This 550-acre Monroe County park offers 40 campsites with electric hookups, hot showers, picnic facilities, pier fishing, and access to Mill Creek (site 28). The campground is open mid-May through October 15.

DIRECTIONS: Take Lake Road east out of Rochester for about 4 miles to Park Road and turn right.

CONTACT: Monroe County Parks.

28. MILL CREEK (MONROE COUNTY)

KEY SPECIES: Pacific salmon, brown trout, and steelhead.

DESCRIPTION: This creek runs through Webster Park. Problem is, it's about as skinny as they come and it doesn't take long to get fished out . . . under normal water levels.

TIPS: After a good rain, chuck-n-duck single plastic eggs for autumn salmonids.

THE FISHING: When its flow is stained and swollen with runoff, fish run it in droves. All the usual suspects work, including worms.

DIRECTIONS: Four miles east of Rochester on Lake Road.

ADDITIONAL INFORMATION: The beach parking lot at the mouth of Mill Creek has room for 30 cars and is open year-round.

CONTACT: New York State Department of Environmental Conservation Region 8 and Monroe County Parks.

29. SALMON CREEK (PULTNEYVILLE)

KEY SPECIES: Brown trout, steelhead, and Pacific salmon.

DESCRIPTION: This stream is about as lanky as skinny creeks come; a lot of traveling anglers judge it by its size and keep on driving. Indeed, the only indication motorists get that this spit of water even exists is the SALMON CREEK sign at the foot of the bridge. Its name gives silent testimony to the massive runs it used to host up until the middle of the 19th century, when Lake O contained the world's greatest population of landlocked Atlantic salmon.

TIPS: Fish this stream after autumn rain or snowmelt raises and colors it a skosh.

THE FISHING: While some customers patronize the Pultneyville Deli Company because they can eat their sandwiches while admiring the stream from the Lake Road bridge, few can even imagine such a narrow "crick" holds large minnows, let alone mature salmon or trout. But all that changes quickly after seeing a large, submerged form splashing downstream, towing an excited angler stumbling behind it. You see, a salmonid sees the place differently: as an ideal spawning site, in fact, or food station loaded with eggs left by those who came before it. Early autumn's first hard rain generally lifts water levels enough to draw respectable numbers of kings, browns, and chromers. Steelies continue moving in and out—water levels permitting—all winter long, and stack up in amazing quantities when spring runoff invites them in to spawn. Such a confined area makes spawn-minded kings grumpy, and they strike just about anything that crosses their paths. Browns, on the other hand, are instinctively interested in their own spawn's survival and gently crush any competing eggs they encounter. Their hit is so light and quick, you have to strike back at the first sign. Steelies hit a little more aggressively, and, like the browns, will take single eggs, sacs, and glo bugs.

DIRECTIONS: Salmon Creek runs through the heart of the hamlet of Pultneyville.

ADDITIONAL INFORMATION: There is no official public access. However, at press time (and for the 10 years I've been fishing the spot) there weren't any posted signs for a couple hundred yards upstream of the Lake Road (CR 101) bridge. Shoulder parking for three cars and a trail down to the water are on Jay Street, a few feet north of the Williamson Water Utilities Waste Water Lift Station building; shoulder parking for about four cars is at the southeastern corner of the Lake Road bridge.

CONTACT: New York State Department of Environmental Conservation Region 8 and Wayne County Tourism.

30. MAXWELL CREEK (SALMON CREEK)

KEY SPECIES: King salmon, steelhead, brown trout, northern pike, largemouth bass, and panfish.

DESCRIPTION: Named Salmon Creek on many maps, this stream is called Maxwell Creek by locals to avoid confusing it with Salmon Creek in neighboring Pultneyville. Wayne County Tourism's Chris Kenyon says, "Shallow and narrow, extremely runoff-sensitive, hard autumn rains and snowmelt swell its rapids into Wayne County's best fast water for trophy salmonids." Its bay is a dynamite bank-fishing spot for panfish, especially in spring.

TIPS: Fish the upper half of the estuary channel with a $\frac{1}{16}$- to $\frac{1}{32}$-ounce marabou or bucktail jig suspended about 2 feet below a float for late-winter steelhead.

Mark Moskal, Summit to Stream Adventures, with a steelie caught on a glo bug in Maxwell Creek.

THE FISHING: This stream gets stocked with about 23,000 five-inch steelhead annually. They return from fall through spring, ranging from 4 to 12 pounds, punctuated with a few 15-pounders to keep things interesting. Depending on water levels, mature kings can start running in early September. Normally, however, they don't appear in meaningful numbers until October and continue streaming in through mid-November. Spawn-heavy browns accompany the first kings, but continue running well into December. The salmon strike gobs of skein and streamers, while the trout like egg sacs, glo bugs, and small lures, particularly in-line spinners.

Maxwell Bay boasts lake-run bullheads and yellow perch after ice-out, and loads of sunfish throughout spring. The sunnies and bullheads are partial to worms; the perch like them, too, but also cotton to more active baits like 2-inch scented curly-tail grubs or Johnson Beetle Spins. Northern pike up to 30 inches long and largemouth bass averaging 2 pounds call the place home, too. They respond violently to floating minnowbaits like Bass Pro Lazer Eyes twitched on the surface around windfalls and along emergent vegetation early in the morning and at dusk.

DIRECTIONS: Head west out of the hamlet of Sodus Point on Lake Road (CR 101) for about 2 miles.

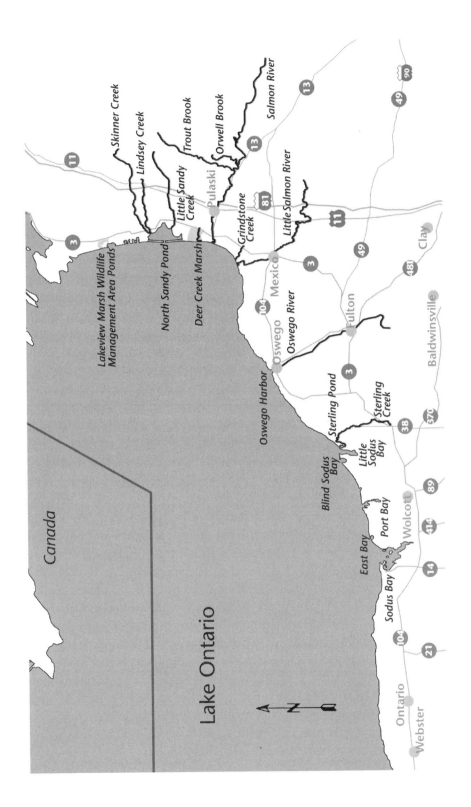

ADDITIONAL INFORMATION: Maxwell Bay fishing access site, located at the northeastern corner of the Lake Road bridge, offers parking for about 25 cars and a trail leading to the estuary; additional parking for 10 cars and a trail to a couple hundred yards of the fast water upstream of Lake Road is at the southwestern corner of the bridge. Beechwood State Park, a former Girl Scout camp, skirts the west side of Maxwell Creek from CR 101 all the way to the lake. Sprawling over 150 acres, including 3,500 feet of Lake Ontario Beach, its aging lean-tos, complete with built-in sleeping platforms, sit on a low rise less than 100 feet above the creek.

CONTACT: New York State Department of Environmental Conservation Region 8 and Wayne County Tourism.

31. SODUS BAY

KEY SPECIES: Northern pike, largemouth bass, coho salmon, chinook salmon, brown trout, steelhead, sheepshead, rock bass, yellow perch, white perch, bullhead, crappies, bowfin, and gar pike.

DESCRIPTION: Covering about 3,700 acres, this bay's shoreline is heavily developed. It has three islands (from east to west: Leroy, Eagle, and Newark); a vast, shallow south end (the mouth of Sodus Creek); numerous creek mouths; and a generally shallow, weedy shoreline. Averaging 25 feet, its maximum depth is 40 feet. Two piers, one with a metal lighthouse, straddle its mouth.

TIPS: For the first couple weeks of the season, troll minnowbaits like Smithwick Rogues and Bomber A's in the chute, from sundown to about 10 p.m., for monster walleyes.

THE FISHING: Late in the last century, northern pike averaging 8 pounds, with many going twice that size, were so plentiful, misguided anglers considered them a nuisance. So many were mishandled that their numbers nose-dived. Fortunately, they were missed and a lot of their former persecutors started treating them with a little respect, leading to a rebound in their numbers. While they're not averaging 8 pounds yet, they're at a solid 5, and 10-pounders are common. From opening day through mid-June, they're particularly plentiful around the islands and can't seem to resist large minnows and minnowbaits. The chute is popular with guys targeting pike on Rat-L-Traps or by jerking suspending minnowbaits. The rest of the year they can be anywhere and respond to spinnerbaits and buzzbaits worked over submerged vegetation, and fat-bodied crankbaits run along the edges of weeds and drop-offs.

Largemouth bass in the 2- to 4-pound range are plentiful around the islands and in the southern basin, and 6-plus-pounders are available. A few ways to attract their attention include casting Texas-rigged worms around cribs and under docks, making sure to hit the uprights with your sinker every now and then to wake the fish up; tossing wacky-rigged stickworms into openings in weed beds; and jerking Flukes along weed edges and breaklines. Bronzebacks aren't as plentiful as they used to be, but enough are still around to warrant a dedicated following. They like jigs and tubes bounced or dragged on bottom around drop-offs.

Early in the fall, cohos between 4 and 7 pounds and chinooks from 15 to 25 pounds move into the bay and mill around for a while looking for places to spawn. Invariably, they're joined by brown trout up to 15 pounds and steelhead averaging 7 pounds. Highly aggressive, these fish respond to spoons and stickbaits trolled in the deep water off the chute and west of Newark and Eagle Islands.

The walleye bite comes and goes. At the turn of the century, the bay was one of the best-kept walleye secrets on Lake Ontario's south shore. Then the population decreased drastically. Currently, a few monster walleye are caught every year, mostly by flatlining minnowbaits in and around the chute. Some report decent results by bottom-bouncing worms, rigged on slow death hooks or spinner harnesses, along weed edges and drop-offs.

Crappies are plentiful around the islands, particularly the east sides, in fall and winter, and in the southern basin early spring through summer. Go for them with small tubes, jigs, and minnows fished below tiny floats in spring and fall, and through the ice with jigs tipped with grubs. Local angler Corky Cansdale claims: "The first heavy rain after ice-out sends runs of resident and Lake Ontario bullheads, some up to 16 inches long—natives call them yellow bellies—into the southern shallows." The Ridge Road Bridge (CR 143) is popular with anglers bottom-fishing for them with worms; be prepared for shoulder-to-shoulder conditions. Monster sheepshead, large rock bass, and some white and yellow perch always hang out in the chute, especially around the entrance, but you have to get there early, before boat traffic shuts them down. They'll hit worms, crayfish, jigs, and minnowbaits. Spurred by cold northerly winds, schools of yellow perch storm into the bay from late autumn through May. They hit minnows and insect larvae.

This place is a hot spot for gar and bowfin. Both hang out in the small bays. Bowfin like live minnows suspended below bobbers or fished on bottom, and jigs tipped with scented soft plastics like Berkley Honey Worms. Gar will hit these baits, too, but their mouths are so bony that hookups are all but impossible. Get around this minor problem by using a rope lure: Hook one end of a 3- to 6-inch section of nylon rope to a jighead, and splay its back end so the threads catch in the fish's teeth or wrap around its mouth.

DIRECTIONS: NY 14 parallels the bay.

ADDITIONAL INFORMATION: While there aren't any campgrounds on the bay, several motels and commercial campgrounds are in the area.

CONTACT: New York State Department of Environmental Conservation Region 8 and Wayne County Tourism.

31A. Harriman Park Boat Launch

DESCRIPTION: This town park has a paved two-lane ramp and parking for about 50 rigs. It is marked with a square brown sign with yellow lettering saying HELP PROTECT WATER QUALITY on top and NYS DEPARTMENT OF ENVIRONMENTAL CONSERVATION on the bottom.

THE FISHING: The area in front of the boat ramp is popular with ice fishermen using tip-ups loaded with minnows for northerns. In summer, largemouths and northerns hang out along the drop-off south of the launch and respond to swimbaits, bucktail jigs tipped with minnows, and Flukes jerked violently through the water column. The mouth of First Creek attracts bullheads, sunfish, and crappies in March and April. The bullheads and sunfish are partial to worms, and the crappies take minnows.

DIRECTIONS: Located at the NY 14/Margaretta Road intersection, less than 1 mile south of the hamlet of Sodus Point. The parking lot is across the street.

31B. Sodus Point Park

DESCRIPTION: This large park offers a paved two-lane boat launch (next to the Coast Guard station) and parking for about 100 cars. Fishing from the concrete pier is permitted year-round, but bank fishing in other areas of the park is prohibited in summer.

DIRECTIONS: Take Greig Street to 1st Street in the hamlet of Sodus Point.

32. EAST BAY

KEY SPECIES: Largemouth bass, northern pike, black crappies, sunfish, yellow perch, and brown bullheads.

DESCRIPTION: Covering only 100 acres, this shallow bay's floor is carpeted with weeds. Its entrance is kept open in summer by the local property owners association. Come autumn, when the lake level is at its lowest, the opening is filled in to maintain water levels in the Lakeshore Marshes State Wildlife Management Area.

TIPS: Early in the season, head up the bay's arms and tributaries and work soft plastic jerkbaits in holes, around fallen timber, and along undercut banks for post-spawn northern pike.

THE FISHING: This bay, famed for largemouths ranging from 3 to 5 pounds, is a favorite alternative spot during local bass tournaments staged in nearby Sodus Bay. Hawgs respond to all the usual suspects but are especially partial to jig-n-pigs worked in shallow weeds and slop, spinnerbaits ripped over weed beds, and fat-bodied, shallow-running crankbaits worked along breaks. Northerns ranging from 4 to 8 pounds are most common, but 15-pounders aren't unheard of. They're usually targeted by drifting large minnows, or anchoring and fishing them below bobbers. Pikeasaurus also respond well to 7-inch worms tipped on painted jigheads or bucktail jigs and yo-yoed around structure; and buzzbaits and spinnerbaits worked over weeds. Black crappies are most active from late March through the second week of May, eagerly hitting minnows, Beetle Spins, and Berkley Atomic Teasers tipped with scented plastics like Berkley Honey Worms and Power Wigglers. Bullheads swarm into the bay in the spring and respond to worms fished on bottom, especially at night. Yellow perch ranging from 8 to 13 inches sweep in each fall and respond to minnows and 2-inch curly-tail grubs. Bluegills and pumpkinseeds up to a pound are plentiful and respond to worms and fly-rod-sized poppers during warm weather, as well as spikes and mousies through the ice.

DIRECTIONS: From the light in the heart of Wolcott (at the bare-breasted statue of Venus), head west on Main Street (Ridge Road) for 1 mile, turn right onto Lummisville Road, travel 4 miles, turn right onto East Bay Road, and continue for 3.7 miles to its end.

ADDITIONAL INFORMATION: East Bay Road ends in a single-lane paved ramp, with parking for about three rigs on its north shoulder. Chimney Bluffs State Park, the most striking example of bluff sculptures on the lake (chimneys, saddles, and spires cut out of the hill by the elements), is on the west side of East Lake Road, at the sharp turn just before road's end. There is no public camping on the bay, but commercial campgrounds are in the area.

CONTACT: New York State Department of Environmental Conservation Region 8 and Wayne County Office of Tourism/History.

32A. Public Access

DESCRIPTION: A gravel car-top launch on Mudge Creek, the bay's largest tributary, and parking for five rigs.

DIRECTIONS: From the bare-breasted statue of Venus in the heart of Wolcott, take Main Street (Ridge Road) west for about 3 miles to North Huron Road (CR 156). Head north for 2.8 miles, turn west onto Slaght Road, and continue for 1.2 miles.

32B. Public Access

DESCRIPTION: This site offers access to the east side of the barrier beach, parking for six cars on North Huron Road, and space for two cars on the barrier bar below. The 0.3-mile unpaved road down to the beach is steep and subject to being washed out at times.

THE FISHING: This site is popular with bank anglers targeting panfish.

DIRECTIONS: Follow the directions to site 32A, but instead of turning left onto Slaght Road, continue straight on North Huron Road for another 2.3 miles.

33. PORT BAY

KEY SPECIES: Largemouth bass, smallmouth bass, northern pike, walleye, brown trout, black crappies, yellow perch, sunfish, and brown bullheads.

DESCRIPTION: Spread over 520 acres, this bay's sides are relatively steep, quickly dropping to an average depth of 20 feet; its maximum depth is 30 feet. Fed by two creeks, its west side and south end contain Port Bay's most expansive weed beds. With the exception of the barrier beach spanning the north end and the marsh on the southeastern corner, the shoreline is heavily developed with private residences.

TIPS: From opening day through May, fish for walleye by working a jig tipped with a piece of night crawler along the west bank of the Narrows (the bay's eastern arm), from Tompkins Point south to where the bottom starts rising—about halfway to the south end's fishing access site.

THE FISHING: Port Bay is famed for bucketmouths in the 3- to 6-pound range. Fish for them by working suspending jerkbaits and vertically jigging bladebaits over deep weed beds; ripping soft jerkbaits around submerged structure; and casting Rat-L-Traps or walking Zara Spooks around timber and lily pads. Chris Kenyon, recreational promotional coordinator for Wayne County Tourism, suggests casting spinnerbaits into docks and other structure in the Narrows. Smallmouths typically go 1½ pounds, but many over 3 pounds are available. They'll take a minnow or crayfish drifted along deep weed edges and over humps. Northern pike range from 22 to 36 inches and take buzzbaits ripped along weed lines, spinnerbaits worked parallel to weed edges, and white bucktail jigs worked around dock uprights and along drop-offs. The state has been stocking walleye for a couple of decades, and a resident population has taken root. They're normally targeted in the deep water off Graves, Loon, and Tompkins Points, and off the barrier beach by locals throwing jigs tipped with worms during daylight; or casting or trolling minnowbaits parallel to shore, in 3 to 10 feet of water, from dusk till just after dawn. Small jigheads tipped with curly-tail grubs and tubes, and worked in weed openings, along weed edges, and over breaks, are dynamite for catching perch ranging from 8 to 10 inches. Corky Cansdale, a local who's been fishing the bay for over 50 years, claims, "Perch numbers are down a bit lately but the bay is loaded with slab-sized crappies, 13 inches, even better . . . if you can find 'em." Regardless of the season, crappies respond best to minnows, jigs, small tubes, and curly-tail grubs. In spring, look for them in shallow water, especially around timber and brush; come summer they generally move deeper, along drops-offs in 10 to 20 feet of water; and in the fall they can be found just about anywhere. The entire southern basin is hot in the spring for bullheads, which love worms fished on bottom at night or on rainy days. Weedy areas are loaded with bluegills and pumpkinseeds up to ¾ pound. Work $\frac{1}{32}$-ounce Hula Poppers over holes in vegetation and along weed edges. "We used to catch loads of white perch up to 2 pounds, but their numbers nosedived after zebra mussels appeared. They seem to have adjusted to the aliens, though, and they're on the rebound. They're not always around like they used to be but every now and then you'll run into a school," says Corky. Particularly fond of worms, they'll still take just about any lure under the sun.

From late April through May, brown trout invade the bay and can be taken by casting Challenger Minnows or Smithwick Rogues from the wall at the mouth, or by trolling Michigan Stingers in the open waters of the bay.

DIRECTIONS: East and West Port Bay Roads parallel the place north of the village of Wolcott.

CONTACT: New York State Department of Environmental Conservation Region 8 and Wayne County Office of Tourism/History.

33A. Public Access

DESCRIPTION: This site has a paved ramp, parking for 50 rigs, a handicapped fishing ramp, and a portable toilet.

DIRECTIONS: From the heart of Wolcott, take Lake Avenue to the end (about 0.5 mile), turn right onto West Port Bay Road, travel about 3.5 miles, and turn right onto the dirt road.

33B. West Barrier Public Access

DESCRIPTION: Located at the bay's mouth, this site has two paved ramps, parking for 25 rigs, and hundreds of yards of shore-fishing access on the bay, its mouth, and Lake Ontario.

DIRECTIONS: Head north on West Port Bay Road out of Wolcott for about 6 miles to its end and turn right.

34. BLIND SODUS BAY

KEY SPECIES: Largemouth bass, smallmouth bass, northern pike, walleye, and panfish.

DESCRIPTION: This 240-acre bay averages 14 feet deep and has a maximum depth of 24 feet. Its shoreline is roughly half private residences, half bottomland forest. Lake storms seal this bay's outlet regularly, but the locals always clear it again.

TIPS: Work jigs along the inside of the barrier beach.

THE FISHING: Generally shallow and weedy, this bay supports an extraordinary warm-water fishery. Largemouth bass up to 5 pounds are common, with hawgs to 8 pounds possible. Work jig-n-pigs and spinnerbaits tipped with trailers against weed edges and submerged timber. Smallmouths move in from the lake to spawn and quite a few stick around afterward, many tipping the scales at over 4 pounds. They respond to shaken worms worked on drop-shot rigs in deep water; and they take soft jerkbaits ripped around weed edges in the shallows. Northern pike generally go 22 to 26 inches, but 15-pounders are also present. Big or small, they can't seem to keep their mouths shut when a Rat-L-Trap or spinnerbait swims by. Walleye can be found year-round in the deep water off the barrier beach. Fish the deep weed edges with bucktail jigs tipped with worms or minnows, or work plain jigheads tipped with scented curly-tail grubs or tubes. Pumpkinseeds and bluegills ranging from ½ to ¾ pound are plentiful. Some crappies up to 1 pound; perch from 8 to 12 inches are also available. The perch and sunnies take worms; crappies and perch like minnows; and they all hit tiny tube jigs like Berkley Atomic Teasers tipped with Berkley Honey Worms or Power Wigglers. Come ice time, the pond is a favorite of locals who target its panfish with minnows and insect larvae like spikes.

After ice-out, browns are drawn to the channel and are taken just inside the bay on Little Cleos and Smithwick Rogues.

DIRECTIONS: Take NY 104A west out of Fair Haven for about 1 mile. Turn north onto Blind Sodus Bay Road and continue for a couple of miles.

ADDITIONAL INFORMATION: There is no public access. Most anglers get there by launching in Little Sodus Bay, going out into the lake, turning left, and motoring into the entrance several hundred yards later. Another option is launching from Lee's Shady Shores Campground (www.shadyshorescampground.com), tucked into the northeastern corner of the bay, right at the outlet; you'll have to pay a fee. Get there from Fair Haven by traveling west on NY 104A to the edge of town, turning north onto West Bay Road, and traveling 2.7 miles.

CONTACT: New York State Department of Environmental Conservation Region 8 and Wayne County Tourism.

35. LITTLE SODUS BAY

KEY SPECIES: Black bass, northern pike, walleye, yellow perch, sunfish, black crappies, white bass, and bullheads.

DESCRIPTION: Sprawling over 750 acres, averaging 25 feet deep, and having a maximum depth of 36 feet, this bay's shoreline is almost totally developed with summer cottages and year-round homes.

TIPS: Work Berkley Power Jerk Shads over weeds clinging to drop-offs.

THE FISHING: Smallmouth bass pour into the bay to spawn, and many stick around into midsummer, some all year. Typically ranging from 1 to 3 pounds, they eagerly take crayfish and minnows worked along

Light House at Little Sodus Bay.

drop-offs and weed lines. Largemouth bass from 2 to 5 pounds thrive in the weeds and under docks, especially in the shallow southern basin. They respond to jig-n-pigs, Texas-rigged worms, 4-inch worms tipping bucktail jigs, and YUM Dingers. Northern pike averaging 7 pounds can be found on drop-offs and respond to large minnows, spinnerbaits, and crankbaits. Walleyes typically go from 3 to 7 pounds and are taken in daylight by trolling minnowbaits like Thundersticks in 20 to 30 feet of water. They move close to shore at night and are targeted by guys casting crankbaits like Challenger Minnows and Rat-L-Traps from the north shore, particularly around the Fair Haven State Park boat launch, off the southern edge of the eastern pier, and around the outlet just before the chute and in the chute. Come ice time, they respond to Swedish Pimples tipped with minnows or their heads, and jigged or shaken gently just off bottom in about 20 feet. Black crappies up to 1 pound are plentiful and are easiest to catch in the spring when they congregate in marinas and around culverts, and hit minnows and small tubes like Berkley Atomic Teasers. Bluegills up to ¾ pound—some even better—are mostly targeted through the ice on tiny jigs tipped with grubs, fished in 5 to 10 feet of water. Perch averaging 12 inches crowd into the bay in winter and are taken through the ice, with minnows and jigs, in the deep water due west of the park boat launch. Brown bullheads generally occupy the shallow north and south ends and respond to worms fished on bottom. White bass like to suspend in schools over deeper water and strike small lures and jigheads tipped with worms or buckeyes.

A few chinooks and browns enter the bay in autumn and are targeted by guys casting spoons and crankbaits into the chute. Additionally, browns and steelhead return after ice-out to indulge in the warmer shallow waters while feasting on alewives that are also seeking warmer temperatures; most of the chromers are gone by mid-April, but the browns stick around longer, often into mid-May.

DIRECTIONS: Located in the village of Fair Haven.

ADDITIONAL INFORMATION: West Barrier Bar Park, located at the end of West Bay Road, offers toilets, a single-lane hard-surface ramp, and loads of shore-fishing access, including the outlet's western breakwater. Fair Haven State Park (a fee is charged during summer) offers fishing access to the mile-long eastern breakwater at the bay's outlet, and several hundred yards of bank access on the northeastern corner of the bay (see site 35C).

CONTACT: New York State Department of Environmental Conservation Region 7 and Cayuga County Tourism.

35A. Municipal Boat Launch

DESCRIPTION: This site offers a single-lane, hard-surface ramp, parking for about a dozen rigs, and toilets.

DIRECTIONS: From NY 104A, turn north onto Bell Avenue and hook the first left onto Cottage Street.

35B. Village of Fair Haven Public Boat Launch

DESCRIPTION: This site offers a single-lane hard-surface ramp and shoulder parking for about eight rigs.

DIRECTIONS: From NY 104A, head north on West Bay Road for a little over 0.5 mile, turn right onto King Road, and travel about 0.2 mile to the end.

35C. Fair Haven Beach State Park

DESCRIPTION: This 865-acre fee area offers 191 campsites (44 electric), 32 cabins, hot showers, paved ramps on Little Sodus Bay with parking for 50 rigs, and rowboat rentals. The park's breakwall and three old Lake Ontario piers offer great casting platforms for brown trout and steelhead up to 15 pounds, autumn and spring.

DIRECTIONS: On the east side of the village of Fair Haven.

36. STERLING CREEK

KEY SPECIES: Chinook salmon, brown trout, and steelhead.

DESCRIPTION: This tributary feeds Sterling Pond in Fair Haven Beach State Park.

TIPS: Use egg sacs from ice-out until the end of snowmelt time, usually around mid-April.

THE FISHING: This skinny creek gets stocked with over 70,000 kings annually. They return each fall averaging 25 pounds and respond aggressively to streamers and raw roe. Lake-run brown trout also run in autumn and take the same baits. Roughly 4,600 steelhead are stocked each year. Growing to between 6 to 15 pounds, some return in the fall, in the wakes of the salmon, but the greatest number runs from ice-out until mid-April. They respond to egg sacs, glo bugs, bead-head nymphs, and worms.

DIRECTIONS: Head west out of Oswego for about 3.5 miles on NY 104, turn west onto NY 104A (Sterling Valley Road), and travel for about 6.5 miles to the hamlet of Sterling.

ADDITIONAL INFORMATION: Limited parking is available at the playground adjacent to the village barn on Williams Road (west side of the NY

104A bridge) and at the village offices a couple hundred yards west of the bridge. Additional informal access, on a slow, marshy stretch, is available at the bridge on Old State Road. Sutter Creek Campground on Sterling Valley Road offers access to a mile of stream for a fee.

CONTACT: New York State Department of Environmental Conservation Region 7 and Cayuga County Tourism.

37. STERLING POND

KEY SPECIES: Northern pike, largemouth bass, sunfish, and brown bullheads.

DESCRIPTION: This 83-acre pond averages 4 feet deep and drops to a maximum depth of 10 feet.

TIPS: Monster bluegills and pumpkinseeds up to a pound invade the place from late May through mid-July.

THE FISHING: Fed by Sterling Creek, most of this natural pond's floor is carpeted in thick weeds, making it a remarkable, though challenging, warm-water fishery. Its deepest water is in the bay southeast of the chute. Northern pike running from 22 to 30 inches prowl the edges of this deep, open area. The best time to get them is in the spring by suspending large minnows below bobbers and casting to the edge of the weeds and the old creek channel. Although largemouth bass can reach 6 pounds, they typically run from 1½ to 4 pounds and respond to jig-n-pigs worked in slop, Flukes run parallel to weed edges, and surface poppers and darters worked through vegetation. A decent resident population of bluegills and pumpkinseeds is available year-round; however, the easiest time to get massive quantities of big sunnies is during the early-summer spawn. They'll hit anything from wet flies and poppers to garden worms, red worms, and spikes. In spring brown bullheads up to 14 inches swarm into the pond and eagerly hit worms fished on bottom. Brown trout, steelhead, and king salmon have to pass through the pond to get to spawning sites in Sterling Creek. They respond to spoons, crankbaits, egg sacs, nymphs, and streamers cast into the north end of the pond, including the chute, from mid-September through December and from ice-out through early April.

DIRECTIONS: Located in Fair Haven State Park, on the east side of the village of Fair Haven.

ADDITIONAL INFORMATION: Fair Haven Beach State Park, an 865-acre fee area, offers a paved ramp on Sterling Pond with parking for 25 rigs, boat rentals (canoe, paddleboat, and rowboats), several piers jutting into Lake Ontario (great casting platforms for spring brown trout and steelhead), 183 campsites (46 electric), 32 cabins, three cottages, a swimming beach, playing fields, and hiking trails. Free day use is allowed off season, roughly from Labor Day to Memorial Day.

CONTACT: New York State Department of Environmental Conservation Region 7 and Cayuga County Tourism.

38. OSWEGO RIVER/OSWEGO HARBOR

KEY SPECIES: Chinook salmon, brown trout, steelhead, lake trout, walleyes, black bass, northern pike, catfish, sheepshead, gar, black crappies, and panfish.

DESCRIPTION: Lake Ontario's second largest tributary, this river drains the Oneida Lake and Finger Lakes watersheds. Dropping roughly 125 feet in its 23.7-mile existence, its last dam is right in downtown Oswego, the oldest port city on the Great Lakes. Its mouth is kept from roaming by jetties.

TIPS: Float-fish a Berkley PowerBait 3-inch Trout Worm in the rapids, a couple of inches off bottom, for steelhead and brown trout.

THE FISHING: In autumn, the river's last stretch of fast water below Varick Dam boasts world-class trophy fishing for chinook salmon, steelhead, and brown trout, punctuated with smaller numbers of lake trout and

Typical Oswego River walleye, caught off west linear park in the city of Oswego.

walleyes. Locals joke that when the salmon are running, they're so thick they raise the water level by a foot.

The state stocks roughly 100,000 fingerling kings annually into the downtown area. Some three and a half years later, small groups of early bloomers begin returning by late August. Their numbers remain insignificant until the main event begins in late September. Starting off slowly, a few rippling in every day for a week or so, the pace accelerates steadily, growing into major waves the first week of October and tsunamis soon after that. Everything is stood on its head. So many huge fish in such a confined area would be a sight anytime, anyplace. But during the spawning run, they're excited beyond belief: porposing, tailwalking, beaching themselves, fighting, bumping anglers, you name it. And the anglers ain't any better. About the only discernible difference between the two is that the fish celebrate quietly, seldom louder than a splash, whereas man whoops and hollers up and down the river. The salmon action peters out by mid-November.

Kings range from precocious two-year-olds (jacks and jennies) averaging 6 pounds, to fully mature 40-pounders. Upon entering the river, their hypothalami shut down, curbing all instincts except the one to spawn. Schooling up in the powerhouse's deep tailrace, they wait for high water to grant them easy passage through the shallow rapids leading to the dam. In drought years, they'll hold out until the need to procreate overwhelms their survival instinct, and storm into the old riverbed in water barely deep enough to cover their backs. And though they're not actively feeding, they're used to being the biggest kids on the block and will attack streamers and lures that get in their way, especially if they're on redds. In addition, they hit raw skein, egg sacs, sponge, glo bugs, and anything else imitating a competitor's spawn. Most anglers target them from the West Linear Park's fenced, concrete wall, a fishing spot notorious for offering the most comfortable and convenient combat fishing found anywhere. A small group of purists with a taste for adventure and fair play wades for them in the rapids between the powerhouse and dam (personal flotation devices are mandatory while fishing this area).

Roughly 80,000 brown trout are stocked into Lake Ontario's Oswego County territorial waters each year, half of them into the mouth of the river. Hanging out in the lake, putting on a couple of pounds, maturing, they stage spawning runs upriver about the same time the kings do. The run is staggered, and groups continue trickling in through December. Many stay through January to bask in the relatively warm currents. In autumn, they take crankbaits, egg sacs, and minnows worked in the rapids. From early winter through January, most browns stay in the relatively slack water below the lock on the east bank, responding to egg sacs still-fished on bottom, and in-line spinners and Berkley 3-inch Twitchtail Minnows worked slowly just off the floor. Still, the rapids contain good numbers at this time, too, and they'll hit egg sacs, ceramic beads, and 3-inch trout worms float-fished in the seams and pockets punctuating the white water. Snowmelt draws them back in late winter and they remain until April, hanging out in the deeper water downstream of NY 104 (Bridge Street), striking small spinners, Little Cleo spoons, and crankbaits like Smithwick Rogues.

The state stocks about 23,000 steelhead each year. After spending a short time in the river learning the ropes of their new habitat, they beat fins for the lake to start their new lives. Chromers ranging from 3 to 15 pounds begin trickling back into the stream in the wakes of the kings to feed on their caviar. By mid-October their numbers grow to the point where you can specifically target them, and enough move in and out all winter long to attract a dedicated following. Most anglers go for them with egg sacs, wax worms, Berkley PowerBait 3-inch floating Trout Worms, and ceramic beads chuck-n-ducked or float-fished a couple of inches off bottom on centerpin equipment. Come March, steelies charge

Brown trout taken in downtown Oswego.

the river to spawn. However, runoff from the Oswego's vast watershed generally swells the rapids to just below flood stage, making it tough to fish. Still, persistent anglers target these aggressive fish with in-line spinners and small plugs like Junior Thundersticks and Lazy Ikes; many are taken incidentally by guys targeting browns in the slack water behind "motel row."

Larry Muroski, owner of Larry's Oswego Salmon Shop, reports: "Lakers are coming back. Last year [autumn 2012], several 10-pounders were caught off the wall behind the shop on egg sacs and stuff aimed at steelhead and browns."

Huge lake walleye up to 15 pounds migrate into the rapids to spawn in March and April. After doing the deed, many hang out in the fast water stretching from the pedestrian bridge to the harbor, feasting on perch and alewives well into June and beyond. After eating their fill, most return to the cooler depths of the lake. Lately, however, anglers have been taking them all summer long by casting crankbaits into the rapids and by still-fishing night crawlers on bottom, plain or on worm harnesses.

Resident bronzebacks thrive here, especially in the deeper reaches of the fast water, from the powerhouse tailrace all the way to the end of

Fishing at the Oswego River's Varick Dam.

the west bank's linear park, and in the shipping channel west of Wrights Landing. In deep water they respond to crayfish and minnows, and 4-inch finesse worms worked on drop-shot rigs; in shallow water they like spinnerbaits and wacky-rigged YUM Dingers tossed into openings in vegetation and along weed edges, and Berkley's PowerBait Jerk Shads ripped along breaklines and weed edges.

Lake-run smallmouth bass in the 1- to 3-pound range spawn in the harbor, often remaining there for the first couple of weeks of the season. Afterward they move out into the lake but return to the breakwalls during the calm following a few days of heavy winds. They take crayfish and minnows drifted parallel to structure, along with jigs and crankbaits cast toward shore and worked into deep water.

Resident bucketmouths ranging from 2 to 5 pounds and northern pike up to 36 inches occupy the weedy areas in and around Wrights Landing. Both take large minnows, spinnerbaits, buzzbaits, and suspending crankbaits like Bomber Long A's jerked over deep vegetation.

Sheepshead from 1 to 10 pounds can be found virtually anywhere. These powerful fighters are particularly fond of crayfish but will also hit worms and lures, particularly jigs and crankbaits.

Channel catfish weighing 2 to 10 pounds are plentiful in the harbor, and 15-something-pounders are available in the deep waters of the river's mouth. They take shrimp, cutbait, and large minnows fished on bottom.

The weed beds in Wrights Landing and adjoining areas are thick with bluegills and pumpkinseeds up to a pound, black crappies averaging 10 inches, and yellow perch from 6 to 10 inches year-round. Massive quantities of lake-run rock bass the size of salad plates and bullheads up to 2 pounds migrate into this area in the spring to spawn. The sunfish, perch, rock bass, and bullheads like worms. While you can't beat a worm for bullheads and sunnies, a lot of anglers avoid using them because of all the round gobies they attract. Indeed, some took to fishing worms below bobbers hoping to discourage hits from the bottom-feeding exotics, but then the gobies learned to look up and hit suspended baits. Realizing gobies feed by smell and ignore scentless baits, panfish enthusiasts met the challenge by switching to artificial lures like Beetle Spins, poppers, tiny jigs, and wet flies.

Gar pike up to 3 feet long invade the rapids in late spring and early summer. Difficult to hook because of their long, bony mouths, they've been challenging creative anglers for years. Recently, rope lures (3- to 6-inch-long sections of nylon rope or shoestring, unraveled on one end to allow the strands to wrap around the critter's teeth, and knotted on the other for hook placement) exposed the beasts to a whole new following. Most guys sight-fish for them in the rapids in spring.

ADDITIONAL INFORMATION: The Oswego River is big water whose levels are regulated by nature. If you decide to wade out to the wall, the ledge across from the powerhouse, or Leto Island, the power company requires you wear a personal flotation device. While out there, keep an eye on water levels. If the flow at your feet or coming over the dam seems to be rising, head for shore immediately. West Linear Park, a family-friendly river walk complete with railings, has several parking lots with space for hundreds of cars, and offers shore-fishing access to about 70 percent of the west bank. East Linear Park offers free parking and shore access to about 50 percent of the east shore. The city has numerous motels, some right on the water. The author conducts several kids' fishing classes on the river each summer.

CONTACT: New York State Department of Environmental Conservation Region 7 and Oswego County Tourism.

Emergency platforms in the city of Oswego offer anglers safety in the event of flash flooding on the Oswego River.

38A. Leto Island

DESCRIPTION: This lock island is jointly owned by the state and private interests.

STATE LAND: At press time, the access bridge crossing the lock is closed for repairs. Curiously, no provision has been made for pedestrian traffic to get over there. The only way to get to the island is by wading across the river, a dangerous proposition at times (see "Additional information," below). When and if the bridge is repaired and reopened, things should revert to normal and fishing should once again be allowed on public land: the natural riverbank downstream of the culvert running under the lock. Even if the bridge isn't repaired, local anglers hope the authorities will allow them to walk over on the lock—but that, according to lock keepers, seems unlikely. Free parking for about 10 cars is available in the public lot off the right side of Lock Road, just before the bridge.

PRIVATE LAND: The southwest half of the island, stretching roughly from the culvert beneath the southern end of lock 07 to a point below Varick Dam, has been owned by private interests for years. Before renovations began on the bridge, they offered parking, camping, and fishing for a fee, and even opened a restaurant in the old mill. It's uncertain whether these services will continue in the future, however, because the barrier at the old bridge has locked the island down—and no one seems to know if the bridge will ever be repaired or a pedestrian bridge built in its footprint.

THE FISHING: The rapids in the old riverbed hold chinook salmon, brown trout, and steelhead in the fall, steelhead all winter long, some walleye in May, and smallmouths through summer. In spring, panfish load up in the "Dug Out," the area around the culvert below the lock.

DIRECTIONS: Off East 1st St. (NY 481).

ADDITIONAL INFORMATION: The Oswego River's water levels are regulated by nature and unpredictable—high water generated by a storm in the Finger Lakes, 100 miles away, takes hours to reach the river's mouth. If you decide to wade out to Leto Island, keep an eye on the water coming over the dam. Normally, the river is only wadeable when a broken flow is coming over. If you're out there and notice water coming over the top uniformly, head for shore immediately. The power company, owner of half the riverbed, requires all individuals, regardless of what you're doing, wear personal flotation devices while in the area stretching from the north end of the powerhouse to the dam.

38B. Wrights Landing

DESCRIPTION: Protected by the harbor's breakwalls, this city-run fee area offers a six-lane, paved ramp, 166 seasonal slips, 57 transient slips, a 1-ton boat hoist, a fish-cleaning station, showers, parking for about 150 rigs and 50 automobiles. Open April through October; 315-342-8186.

THE FISHING: In autumn, the shipping channel on the north end of the marina and the turning basin to the west often load up with ripe salmon. Frustrated over their inability to climb the dam, they'll strike at spoons and streamers cast in front of them. Steelhead can be found in the channel from autumn through late spring and take in-line spinners and plugs like Hot Shots and Flatfish. For much of May, monster walleyes are taken in the channel by trolling crankbaits like Thundersticks and worms on spinner harnesses. In summer, the south shore grows the only meaningful weed beds in the area, becoming a bucketmouth and pikeasaurus hot spot for anglers throwing everything from soft plastics to hard jerkbaits and crankbaits.

ADDITIONAL INFORMATION: Bank fishing, with free parking, is permitted in designated areas of the marina.

DIRECTIONS: Head north on West 1st Street to Lake Street.

38C. West Breakwall

DESCRIPTION: This jetty is a combination of decaying concrete pier and limestone blocks. Beginning right below the steam plant's obsolete discharge tunnels, the wall runs along the north side of the shipping channel, then banks north and runs for about another 0.5 mile to the lighthouse.

THE FISHING: This is a local hot spot for shore anglers targeting salmon in autumn with spoons, crankbaits, and streamers. In early spring, steelhead mill around the turning basin and respond to egg sacs, small spoons, and Rooster Tails. In May, walleyes follow in the wakes of the chromers and strike crankbaits like Red-Fins.

DIRECTIONS: Take West Bridge Street (NY 104) to Washington Boulevard. Turn right a couple of blocks later onto 6th Avenue and follow it to the end.

ADDITIONAL INFORMATION: The landing at the end of 6th Avenue has parking for about 10 cars.

38D. Driftboat Launch

DESCRIPTION: This site has a paved ramp and street parking for 10 rigs.

DIRECTIONS: From its intersection with Bridge Street (NY 104), head north on East 1st Street and turn left at the next light. Bear left a few yards later onto East Canal View Drive and continue to the ramp at the base of the lock.

39. LITTLE SALMON RIVER

KEY SPECIES: Chinook salmon, steelhead, brown trout, largemouth bass, smallmouth bass, northern pike, bullheads, and sunfish.

DESCRIPTION: Formed by two major branches and numerous tiny feeders coming together east of Parish, this stream flows northwest for 30-something miles and feeds Mexico Bay in the hamlet of Texas.

TIPS: From ice-out through mid-May, cast crankbaits like Smithwick Rogues or spoons such as Bass Pro Flashy Times from the breakwalls at the mouth for large brown trout and an occasional steelhead.

THE FISHING: Back in the 19th century, this stream was one of Lake Ontario's most important spawning grounds for landlocked Atlantic salmon. Currently kings, brown trout, and steelhead enjoy followings in autumn, and steelhead continue drawing trophy seekers winter through early spring. These salmonids take the usual suspects: egg sacs, in-line spinners, streamers, and worms. Unfortunately, free public access is nonexistent in the fast-water areas and most guys are content with float-fishing egg sacs, tiny jigs, and 3-inch Berkley Floating Trout Worms in the channel between the jetties, or casting crankbaits like Bomber A's and spoons like Little Cleos into the lake from the jetties.

A dynamite warm-water fishery thrives in the estuary stretching from the NY 104A bridge to the mouth. Monster pikeasaurus prowl the weed edges, drop-offs, and river channel. Local subsistence anglers target them with minnows fished below bobbers. The marshy areas and marinas offer superb bass habitat. Bucketmouths ranging from 1 to 5 pounds hang out under docks, around windfalls, and near emergent weed edges, and respond to buzzbaits, poppers, and YUM Dingers. A small resident population of smallmouth bass thrives in the river—indeed, many believe this group is playing a leading role in restoring smallmouths to Mexico Bay after VHS all but wiped them out in 2006. They'll take jig-n-pigs and 4-inch Texas-rigged worms pitched into weed edges and 3-inch scented plastic minnows fished on drop-shot rigs, especially around clumps of weeds, fallen timber, and drop-offs. Large sunfish are plentiful in these insect-rich shallows and take worms, grubs, and flies. Lake bullheads swarm into the estuary in early spring to spawn and take worms still-fished on bottom.

DIRECTIONS: CR 16 runs parallel to the river from the village of Mexico to Texas; CR 40 parallels the east bank; and Mexico Point Drive parallels the west bank from NY 104B to the mouth.

ADDITIONAL INFORMATION: Free public access is limited to the two parks at the mouth, Mexico Point State Park on the west bank, and the Selkirk State Park Boat Launch on the east side. In addition, Yogi Bear's Jellystone Park Camp-Resort (800-248-7096) sits on about 0.25 mile of primo white water parallel to CR 16 and allows its guests to fish.

CONTACT: New York State Department of Environmental Conservation Region 7 and Oswego County Tourism.

40. GRINDSTONE CREEK

KEY SPECIES: Steelhead, chinook salmon, and brook trout.

DESCRIPTION: A skinny creek by anyone's standard, this stream hosts lake-run salmonids up to the dam in the hamlet of Fernwood, provided there ain't any beaver dams along the way.

TIPS: After an autumn rain, chuck-n-duck egg sacs into the run just above the mouth in Selkirk Shores State Park.

THE FISHING: The state stocks 5,000 fingerling steelhead annually. They return fall through spring and hit egg sacs, egg-pattern flies, and worms. After heavy autumn rains, chinooks storm in. However, they're tough to land in the forest lining remote sections; most guys simply fish for them off the concrete wall at the mouth in Selkirk Shores State Park with egg sacs, single plastic eggs, or sponge. The state stocked the place with brookies for years. While it's doubtful there are any survivors of these plantings, native-born squaretails outgrow the tributaries and end up in Grindstone, offering some challenging summer fishing. They'll take flies and worms.

DIRECTIONS: CR 28 parallels the stream.

CONTACT: New York State Department of Environmental Conservation Region 7 and Oswego County Promotion & Tourism.

40A. Selkirk Shores State Park

DESCRIPTION: This fee area offers parking for about 200 cars at the mouth, the creek's most productive stretch for salmon.

THE FISHING: Anglers have three dynamite fishing options within a stone's throw of the parking lot. A concrete retaining wall preventing the creek's mouth from wandering offers anglers a safe platform for casting into a long, deep run just above the stream's last set of rapids. The cobblestone

Pier fishing at Selkirk Shores State Park.

beach offers easy access to the plume at the mouth, a popular wading spot for fly fishers swinging streamers; pinheads floating egg sacs and 3-inch Berkley trout worms; and surf anglers bottom-fishing with egg sacs and worms. A pier jutting into the lake about 100 yards north of the mouth is great for spoon-feeding and cranking minnowbaits and swimbaits for salmonids in spring and autumn.

DIRECTIONS: From the NY 13/NY 3 intersection in Port Ontario, head south on NY 3 for about 1.5 miles.

ADDITIONAL INFORMATION: This 980-acre forested park offers two paved boat launches—one at Pine Grove on its north side, the other at the mouth of the Little Salmon River (see site 39)—148 campsites (88 electric), 24 rustic cabins, picnic facilities, hot showers, a swimming beach, playing fields, and hiking trails. Noncampers are charged a day-use fee from Memorial Day through Labor Day.

40B. Public Access

DESCRIPTION: Parking for five cars and 0.5 mile of public fishing rights.

DIRECTIONS: From the entrance to site 40A, head south on NY 3 for a couple hundred yards, turn left onto CR 28, and continue for a little over 1 mile.

40C. Public Access

DESCRIPTION: Parking for five cars and about a mile of public fishing rights upstream to site 40D and beyond.

DIRECTIONS: From site 40B, travel 0.5 mile farther east on CR 28.

40D. Public Access

DESCRIPTION: Parking for five cars and 1 mile of public fishing rights downstream to site 40C.

DIRECTIONS: From site 40C, continue east on CR 28 for about a mile, turn right onto CR 41, travel about 0.35 mile, turn right onto Manwaring Road, travel 0.35 mile, turn right onto Krebs Road, and continue for 0.1 mile.

40E. Public Access

DESCRIPTION: Parking for five cars and public fishing rights for 0.2 mile upstream and 0.5 mile downstream.

DIRECTIONS: From site 40D, head south on Krebs Road for 0.1 mile, turn left onto Manwaring Road, travel 0.35 mile, turn right onto CR 41, travel 0.6 mile, turn left onto CR 41A, and continue for 0.7 mile.

ADDITIONAL INFORMATION: The walk to the creek is about 630 paces, through light forest for the first couple hundred feet, field and meadow the rest of the way. You'll end up at the rusty, steel frame of an ancient bridge. Downstream, the creek runs through forest, and meadow upstream. At press time, there was a beaver dam upstream of the bridge.

41. SALMON RIVER

KEY SPECIES: Coho, chinook, and landlocked Atlantic salmon, brown trout, steelhead, northern pike, black bass, walleye, channel catfish, fallfish, suckers, and panfish.

DESCRIPTION: The most famous salmonid stream in the lower 48, the Salmon River snakes from the dam at the Lighthouse Hill Reservoir to its mouth at Port Ontario, a distance of 17 miles (13 as the crow flies). Draining roughly 280 square miles of mostly forest on the western edge of the Tug Hill Plateau—an area known for lake effect snow—it's New York's largest cold-water tributary to Lake Ontario. Fast and shallow, its base flow is regulated according to the needs of the seasons. In summer, when the fewest gamefish are in, Brookfield Renewable Power's Lighthouse Hill Dam (Lower Reservoir), a little way upstream of Altmar, maintains the

Dave Rath, former Oswego County Legislator, beams brightly as Capt. Nick Lee, Good Time Sport Fishing Charters, handles their first brown of the day; caught off the sticks (beacons at the mouth of the Salmon River).

flow so it averages 185 cubic feet per second; from September through December it's almost doubled to 335 cfs; and from January 1 to May 30 it's reduced to 285 cfs. Heavy runoff can force the power company to release 900 cfs and more, and snowmelt and rainstorms can send the water surging to 1,500 cfs or more (for current levels, go to www.h2o-line.com/365123.asp or call 800-452-1742 and enter code 365123). The state owns 12 miles of public fishing rights easements; its website offers a map showing locations, and another map showing pool locations and popular access sites.

TIPS: This is one of the most slippery rivers you'll ever wade. Wear traction devices or be prepared to swim.

THE FISHING: Two International Game Fish Association world records hail from here: coho salmon, 33 pounds, 4 ounces (a species native to the Pacific Ocean, no less), and chinook-coho salmon, 35 lb. 8 oz. In addition, the river boasts the Great Lakes record chinook, 47 pounds, 13 ounces, and the New York State record shorthead redhorse sucker, 11 pounds, 11 ounces.

Winter scene on the Salmon River.

Superior water quality, a wealth of spawning habitats, and massive human intervention make this stream a world-class salmonid fishery. Annually, the state stocks the place with roughly 160,000 steelhead, 80,000 cohos, 350,000 kings, 30,000 Atlantic salmon, and 2,500 brown trout. Autumn returns of Pacific salmon are unequaled in the lower 48 states; cohos over 30 pounds and 40-something-pound chinooks are caught every year. Massive quantities of brown trout weighing up to 15 pounds stage their spawning runs along with the salmon. Steelhead ranging from 3 to over 20 pounds follow in mid-October to feast on all the eggs. Many spend the winter, taking advantage of the cornucopia of aquatic insects, terrestrial goodies like worms carried in by runoff during thaws, and the continuous supply of caviar swept out of the pebbles by endlessly shifting currents. Ice-out through April sees additional chromers swarm in to spawn, and May through August sends good numbers of Skamania—a summer strain of steelhead—upriver. Landlocked Atlantic salmon ranging from 3 to 10 pounds enter the river in summer, too, and, unlike Pacific salmon that die shortly after spawning, they return to the lake for a few more years to feed and spawn again . . . some even a third time.

The only salmon indigenous to the tiniest Great Lake, Atlantics are the most warm-water-tolerant of the species and enter the river from May through August. They can be found anywhere, especially the tails of pools, until about mid-June. After that, summer heats the wide, shallow waters of the lower river to uncomfortable levels, forcing the fish to seek cooler temperatures around the mouths of tributaries like Spring Brook in Pulaski and Trout Brook (site 42) downstream of Pineville. What's more, a combination of numerous springs, the mouths of Orwell (site 43) and Beaverdam Brooks, and the dam's discharge keep water temperatures upstream of the Trestle Pool (site 41M) comfortable enough to hold Atlantics all summer long. Still, the majority of the fish congregate in the stretch from the dam's tailrace to the bridge in Altmar, the fly-fishing-only section. However, deep summer sees fresh runs during high-water events—after a downpour, for instance, and during scheduled recreational releases the power company provides for kayakers, tubers, and canoeists one weekend per month in May, June, August, and September, and two weekends in July (contact Oswego County Tourism for dates). During normal summer water levels, these fish respond to streamers swung through the current, nymphs cast upstream and

Fly-fishing lesson on the Salmon River.

worked back at dead drifts, and spinners and plugs cast upstream and retrieved fast enough to give the lures their proper action. Best of all, they'll slurp dry flies during a hatch. They'll strike the same baits in high water, and are especially fond of fat, juicy night crawlers after a rain.

Kings start showing up in the lower river in late summer. Captain Rick Miick, one of several local guides who offer night fishing for these early arrivals off "the sticks" (the lights at the end of the breakwaters at the mouth of the river), claims: "Itchy kings stage nightly reconnaissance runs upriver as early as the first week in August, reaching as far as the black hole before turning back in the morning." By the end of the month, precocious chinooks start trickling upstream to stay. The second week of September usually sees enough kings—and a smattering of cohos— spread throughout the system to make the evening news, drawing the legions of anglers that create the shoulder-to-shoulder fishing conditions locals call "combat fishing." The run builds in stages, drawing more and more fish until a magical time in mid-October when everything slams into reverse and the numbers start petering out, growing smaller and smaller until they simply stop coming in late November, and all that remain are mottled zombies milling around just below the surface in pools, waiting to join their dead kin already carpeting the floor.

The only thing that's guaranteed is that the salmon will come— even during drought years, when the water barely covers their backs. Fortunately, New York is a wet state and October often sees a good rain or two, and a rise in water levels of a few inches to a foot can spur holdouts in the lake to make their move. Another meteorological event known to spur runs is a spell of unseasonably cold days or nights.

The biggest kids on the block, Pacific salmon are used to having their way. What's more, their urge to reproduce is overwhelming, causing them to react carelessly in their bid to reach the spawning beds. Add their territorial, highly aggressive natures to the mix and you get fish that'll hit just about anything that crosses their paths. Bear in mind, they didn't reach maturity by being stupid, and if they're spooked by crazed anglers chasing after them, they'll clam up, and you might just as well go fishing to another spot. And while it's still possible to see a few crazies charging into the water after them flaying their rods like battle axes, most anglers are sportsmen and frown on them—letting 'em know it, too—and simply brandishing a cell phone is generally enough to get bandits to behave. As a result, the fish swim through the gauntlet about as calmly as can be expected by something on the verge of having sex, and they'll hit streamers, spoons, crankbaits, and in-line spinners swung through runs, worked in the tails of pools and through rapids; and blue and orange sponge, egg sacs, and raw skein chuck-n-ducked in pockets and the heads of pools.

Numerous browns, the most warm-water-tolerant trout, find the stream a comfortable year-round habitat. Stockies that decide to stay in the river can reach 24 inches. Called river browns by natives, they're differentiated from lake-run fish by their narrow, cylindrical shapes (lake-run fish are fat, shaped like footballs). Still, the most popularly sought browns are the spawn-minded lake fish that run along with the salmon in October and continue coming well into December, and sometimes beyond. They'll hit ceramic beads, Berkley 3-inch trout worms and egg sacs float-fished with centerpin equipment; worms, egg sacs, and glo bugs weighted down with split-shot sets and chuck-n-ducked in pockets.

If, as is often claimed, salmon provide an annual shot of adrenaline to the village of Pulaski's anemic economy, steelhead are the crutch that allows it to limp along for the rest of the year. You see, although they only reach about half the size of their Pacific cousins (rainbow trout are indigenous to the West Coast, too), chromers are every bit as challenging when hooked. They're a much classier fish, though, behaving in ways that appeal to the angler's elegant side. For instance, unlike kings, they seldom show off by leaping and porpoising needlessly, and in the moments when they do break the surface, it's for practical purposes like gently taking a floating insect, climbing a shallow rapid, nudging a mate into a better spawning position, or exploding out of the water in a violent attempt to shake a hook. Dressed in green backs fading into sides of proof silver (it makes them look like surface glare to an untrained eye) when freshly out of the lake, they slowly adapt to the limited confines of the river by losing the flash and assuming the colors of the rainbow, allowing them to more easily blend in with the river bottom. Finally, they have a taste for the better things in life like fine food and comfort, and accept great risk by climbing raging rapids in winter searching for water a couple of degrees warmer, and red caviar.

Two strains move into the Salmon River at different times of the year: Skamania (summer run; at press time hatchery fish have their left ventral—pelvic—fin clipped) and Washington (winter run). Skamania averaging 8 pounds trickle into the river as early as May, with peak numbers appearing from June through August. Runoff from heavy rains and increased power company water discharges for white-water weekends spur runs. In top shape during summer, they make it all the way to the dam in a few hours. The nicest thing about Skamania is that they're in when summer temperatures and water levels are perfect for wading and the sky and surrounding forest teem with wildlife, particularly deer, ospreys, kingfishers, and bald eagles. Go for these steelies with dry flies, Spey flies, large streamers, and nymphs in the fly-fishing zone; flies, worms, egg sacs, minnows, and in-line spinners everywhere else.

Washington-strain fish start running in the wakes of the salmon. They're so brazen, they've been known to station themselves a few feet below spawning kings five times their size, gobbling up rogue eggs caught by the current as they leave the female. During combat fishing time these chromers respond best to egg sacs, single plastic eggs, glo bugs, and other egg imitations fished at close range (cast too far and you'll cross someone) in the heat.

With all the eggs around, many spend the winter in the river and are joined by fresh fish during thaws. As a rule, steelies hang out in deeper, central parts of pools and runs during cold weather. Wading anglers do relatively well by swinging streamers and Spey flies on sinking leaders across the current, chuck-n-ducking nymphs and egg sacs, and center-pinning egg sacs, ceramic beads, and 3-inch floating trout worms.

Come January and February, wading in the river becomes much tougher, even downright dangerous. Not only do you have to climb high snowbanks left by plows just to get to the water, the area's heavy snow-fall makes hoofing through the woods arduous. What's more, when you reach the stream, you'll have to negotiate a high snowbank at the best of times, a shelf reaching several yards into the water in the worst cases, making walking out too risky for everyone but an angler with suicidal tendencies. And even if you manage to reach liquid water, your feet'll get cold awfully quick and ice buildup in your rod's eyes can turn the fishing trip into an exercise in frustration.

The safest, most productive way to fish at these times is from a drift-boat—something known as Cadillac fishing. Captain Ryan "Tiny" Gilbert explains: "You easily drift from one hole to another while searching for fish, stay on top of them when you locate active ones, and all the while the heater in the bow keeps your feet and hands warm." While all the baits and techniques listed above are effective, Cadillac fishing also allows for plugging (hotshotting), a dynamite technique in which rods loaded with minnowbaits or plugs like Lazy Ikes are set into holders while you si-lently drift through the rapids and gently drop your oars to slow the boat a skosh, just enough so the current can bring the lure to life.

Spring sees great quantities of chromers spawning. Afterward, they're extremely hungry and slowly head back to the lake. Called dropbacks, if they stop at all it's to feed in pockets and the tails of pools. They'll hit egg sacs (white, orange, and blue are good colors in clear water; chartreuse and orange when the water's cloudy), garden worms, night crawlers, minnowbaits, Spey flies, in-line spinners, you name it. The water is usually high at this time of the year, and the fish know how to use it to their advantage in their bid to get off the hook, making landing them even more challenging than it normally is.

Smallmouth bass find the length of the river to their liking, and you can count on at least one 3-pounder and numerous smaller ones in each hole. They'll hit the litany of baits their kind is known to strike but are especially exciting to catch by fly fishing streamers and crayfish patterns in pools and runs. They're even more plentiful and bigger down in the estuary, where they're suckers for minnows and Carolina-rigged 4-inch finesse worms worked in the channel early in the season; crayfish drifted over rocky bottoms, and buzzbaits and spinnerbaits ripped over weeds in summer; plastic leeches on drop-shot rigs or 3-inch curly-tail grubs dragged on bottom, in deep holes, in autumn.

Largemouth bass ranging from 2 to 6 pounds are available in the marshy area of the estuary. They hit minnows, crayfish, fat-bodied

Salmon River Coho.

crankbaits, Texas-rigged 7-inch worms, and top-water lures ranging from Hula Poppers and Zara Spooks to plastic snakes.

Northern pike up to 15 pounds share range with the bucketmouths but are especially fond of cruising drop-offs along the river channel and breaklines. They'll take spinnerbaits, jerkbaits, in-line spinners, lipless crankbaits, minnows, and bucktail jigs tipped with stickworms.

Resident channel catfish averaging 6 pounds hang out in the river from the mouth up to the first bend and take cutbait, shrimp, chicken livers, and commercial preparations like Berkley Catfish Bait Chunks. During the salmon run, some of the biggest catfish in the lake, up to 25 pounds, enter the river's mouth to feast on salmon cadavers and body parts. They respond to salmon bellies fished on bottom at night (check the special "Great Lakes and Tributary Regulations" in the New York State fishing guide for restrictions on night fishing in the river).

In recent years, several huge post-spawn walleye have been taken near and in the mouth on flatlined minnowbaits intended for browns, prompting some to predict that the species is reestablishing itself in the river naturally.

Fallfish, bright silvery fish often called chubs, can generally be counted on to bite when nothing else will. A small species, they typically run 6 to 10 inches, and a 16-incher is considered huge. Hard hitters and stubborn fighters, they'll strike streamers, wet and dry flies, small lures, and worms. While not exactly a gamefish, they enjoy a dedicated following of anglers who are trying to elevate their status. They're the largest minnows native to the northeastern United States, and most anglers who tangle with one are normally pleased with its spirited performance, treat it with the respect it deserves, and release it.

Schools of every sucker in the drink run the river's rapids in spring to spawn. The biggest are the shorthead redhorses. They'll take garden worms fished on bottom in pools.

Lake-run bullheads up to 16 inches long and yellow perch averaging 11 inches invade the river downstream of the NY 3 bridge in April and May. Resident crappies averaging 11 inches enter the shallows about the same time to spawn, especially around abandoned cribs and boat docks along the south shore. Bullheads, many over a foot long, occupy the estuary's mudflats, and sunfish and rock bass up to 10 inches long rule its weed beds, all summer. Crappies and perch love minnows. The bullheads hit worms and cutbait fished on bottom. The pumpkinseeds, bluegills, rock bass, and perch like worms, tiny jigs, and flies.

DIRECTIONS: NY 13 parallels the south bank from Port Ontario to Altmar, and CR 22 follows it to the dam on the lower reservoir.

ADDITIONAL INFORMATION: This stream has more bait shops, guide services, campgrounds, and motels than some Third World countries, mostly on NY 13 and US 11, particularly in the village of Pulaski. The state-of-the-art Salmon River Hatchery is located on CR 22 in Altmar, and is open daily for self-guided tours. The river upstream of the bridge in Altmar is a fishy affirmative-action set-aside for fly fishing (fly fishermen can use the entire river; bait fishermen, including children with worms, can't fish here) and catch-and-release. The Douglaston Salmon Run, a private, pay-to-fish preserve, covers the 2.5 miles of stream stretching from the west side of Pulaski to just upstream of the NY 3 bridge in Port Ontario. Camping is available at Selkirk Shores State Park, NY 3, about 2 miles south of Port Ontario.

CONTACT: New York State Department of Environmental Conservation Region 7 and Oswego County Promotion and Tourism.

41A. Pine Grove Public Boat Launch

DESCRIPTION: This fee area is part of Selkirk Shores State Park and is located within sight of the Salmon River's mouth. It has a paved ramp and parking for 50 rigs. Open from April 1 through the end of October.

THE FISHING: The bend just downstream loads up with perch after ice-out, and northerns swarm in after spawning to feast on them. Bullheads literally invade the estuary in front of the launch in April, and several trails striking off Pine Grove Road lead to landings that have been hosting nighttime bullhead fishing parties since the 19th century. Crappies become extremely active in March, too, especially around the south bank's abandoned sailboat harbor downstream of the NY 3 bridge, and in the channels slicing between the islands. Bullheads are partial to worms fished on bottom, crappies like minnows suspended a couple of feet below bobbers, perch take minnows and worms, and northerns strike anything that resembles perch or alewives, from red and white Dardevles (try jigging one so it alternately darts and flutters) and silver Little Cleos to white, yellow, or red-and-white jigs. Hawg largemouths, and huge rock bass, many well over a pound, rule the weed beds and the channels between the numerous islands, and respond to wacky-rigged stickworms dropped into holes, weed edges, and around other structure.

DIRECTIONS: Head west out of Pulaski on NY 13 for 4 miles. Turn south onto NY 3, then right 0.5 mile later onto Pine Grove Road and travel several hundred yards to the launch entrance on the right.

41B. Port Ontario Public Fishing Access with Handicapped Platform

DESCRIPTION: This site has an elevated handicapped platform and parking for nine cars.

THE FISHING: Located at the northwestern corner of the NY 3 bridge, this site overlooks a bottleneck in the estuary's relatively shallow north channel, allowing the disabled a casting platform right below the bridge. It's most productive during the early part of the salmon run.

DIRECTIONS: Take NY 13 north out of Pulaski for 4 miles, turn right onto NY 3, and cross the bridge; the access site is on the left.

41C. Black Hole

DESCRIPTION: The biggest, deepest pool on the river, it brushes against the village wastewater treatment plant. The village barn atop the hill on the north bank provides parking for about 100 cars—a parking fee is charged during salmon season—and access to a couple hundred yards of riverbank. The south bank is part of the Douglaston Salmon Run, a private fishing preserve.

THE FISHING: This spot always has fish. Rick Miick claims early Pacific salmon make nightly reconnaissance runs to this point in early August. Most return by morning but some stick around, offering the season's first shot at a trophy. At the beginning of the run, in early September, the place turns into a study in worlds colliding: salmon, staged shoulder-to-shoulder, roll on the surface or explode into the air like missiles; anglers, also shoulder-to-shoulder, clumsily pursue them, slipping and sliding, many dropping into the water like depth charges. As the run progresses, steelhead and browns mix with the salmon. Also in spawning mode, the browns shoot upstream, while the steelies, whose only interest is feeding on caviar, stage at the tail of the pool watching for salmon eggs. When the water temperatures drop drastically in late November, the steelies keep coming. Only now, they hang out in the deeper water downstream of the bend, mostly tight to the shelf below the cliff on the south shore. In fact, a rule of thumb for guys casting spinners, plugs, and egg sacs in winter is to cast close to the bank in the stretch running from about halfway down the bend to a few yards downstream of where the cliff reaches ground level. In spring, the trout hang in the bony water at the pool's head and tail. Some of the largest fallfish in the entire Great Lakes call this hole home, but don't hit much until sometime in April and continue feeding voraciously until the salmon run shuts them down. They'll take any bite-sized morsel that's alive—or appears to be—but they're notorious for hitting flies so violently you'll swear you're into a record Skamania. Smallmouth bass, some up to 4 pounds, start showing up around the same time the fallfish do and leave the river the same time, too; they'll hit minnows, crayfish, streamers, and plugs. Landlocked Atlantic salmon begin arriving pretty heavy sometime in May and stick around until June, when warm temperatures send them scurrying for cooler water upriver. A surprising number of fish averaging 8 pounds are taken in spring on worms, but they'll also hit jigs and lures.

DIRECTIONS: On Riverview Drive (off Bridge Street), in Pulaski.

41D. The Staircase

DESCRIPTION: One of the most spectacularly scenic spots on the river, it offers a series of pools and drops along a sheer cliff on the south bank, urban woods etched in archaeological ruins on the north shore.

THE FISHING: Downstream of the Long Bridge, the stream expands to one of its widest, boniest sections. From here to the black hole, a distance of less than 0.5 mile, it tumbles into several pools, sprouts a few islands, and ends by hitting a cliff on the north bank, just upstream of the Black Hole, that isn't negotiable by wading. Its pockets, pools, and runs are good resting and feeding stops for migrating salmonids, but it doesn't hold them for any length of time.

DIRECTIONS: From the NY 13/US 11 intersection, continue west on NY 13 for two blocks, turn right onto Jefferson Street, cross the long bridge, turn left onto James Street, and bear left at the end onto Forest Drive. There is limited street parking on Jefferson and James Streets, and access is at the handicapped parking area (three cars) on Forest Drive.

41E. Floodwall Walkway Access

DESCRIPTION: Completed in 2013, along one of the river's highest rapids in the heart of Pulaski, this site opens a path to a spot formally out of reach because of a cliff; parking for 50 cars.

THE FISHING: Class III rapids tumble into the head of the Village Pool just upstream of the US 11 bridge. This site grants anglers a toehold at the head, providing, according to Captain Rick Miick, "a remedy to the frustration anglers used to suffer while fishing this tempting village hot spot."

DIRECTIONS: On Maple Avenue, just around the corner from US 11.

41F. Dunbar Field Clamshed Pool

DESCRIPTION: Located in the heart of Pulaski, this site offers a driftboat launch and parking for about 100 cars.

THE FISHING: A big island splits the river in two. The deep runs along the undercut banks on its south side hold salmon and trout in autumn, ironheads all winter long. The Short Bridge (aka Village Pool) and Long Bridge Pools, a couple of the biggest and deepest holes on the river, are located a few hundred yards downstream. The Ball Park Run, an exciting stretch of white water, and the 81 Hole and Trooper Hole, quiet runs punctuating several hundred yards of rapids and pockets, are a short walk upstream.

DIRECTIONS: From the NY 13 railroad crossing in Pulaski, turn north onto Lewis Street and proceed for a couple hundred yards to the parking areas along the river.

41G. Haldane Community Center

DESCRIPTION: Parking for 50 cars.

THE FISHING: Located across the river from the Clamshed Pool, this site offers access to the north channel of the island mentioned in 41F. Wider and shallower than its sister channel, it boasts a pool at the mouth of Spring Brook that holds some nice bronzebacks in summer. During periods of high water, the community center offers the safest, most convenient access to the north banks of the I-81 Pool and the Trooper Hole.

DIRECTIONS: From the northernmost NY 11 light in Pulaski, head east on Maple Avenue for a few hundred yards to the curve and bear right on Maple Avenue Extension.

41H. Rucando Run, Lower Paper Hole, and Paper Hole (Railroad Bridge Hole) Access

DESCRIPTION: Parking for about 10 cars and access to river trails straddling the Conrail trestle crossing the stream.

THE FISHING: Large and deep, the Paper Hole (upstream of the railroad bridge) is notorious for holding kings and cohos in the fall, and lake-run trout from autumn through spring. Its sister hole (downstream of the bridge) is just a little smaller and boasts the same fish at the same times; it ends in the Rucando Run, a fabulous stretch of white water famed for its fish-friendly pockets and seams.

DIRECTIONS: From I-81 exit 36, head south on NY 13 for about a mile to CR 2A, turn left, and travel about a mile to the railroad crossing; park in the informal lot on the left, just across the railroad tracks.

41I. Long Hole, Side Hole, and Compactor Pool Access

DESCRIPTION: Two driftboat ramps (one paved, one hard-surface), parking for about 25 cars, and a portable toilet.

THE FISHING: The Long and Side Holes are stretches of relatively deep water in the bony section of the river downstream of the CR 2A bridge. The pool right below the north end of the bridge might not have a name but it usually has fish. Starting roughly at the head of the island upstream of the bridge and stretching to the bend in the river, the Compactor Pool is dynamite salmonid habitat. Deep and slow, situated above the bony water, it offers fish a respite from the dangers of the shallow rapids they just negotiated. Each of these spots offers good opportunities for autumn salmon, and steelhead in late winter and spring.

DIRECTIONS: Take NY 13 south out of Pulaski for about a mile, turn north onto CR 2A, and cross the bridge; the parking lot is on the right.

41J. Sportsman's Pool North Access

DESCRIPTION: This site has parking for about 50 cars and a very long footpath to the river's longest pool.

THE FISHING: The Sportsman's Pool is long, wide, deep, and always holds fish. Starting at a bend in the river, the current skirts this side of the pool. The long walk down from the parking area discourages most anglers, and the north bank is seldom crowded.

DIRECTIONS: From site 41H, head north on CR 2A for about 0.1 mile, turn right onto Centerville Road, and travel for 2.3 miles.

41K. Sportsman's Pool South Access

DESCRIPTION: This site has parking for 50 cars, a toilet, and a path to the pool.

THE FISHING: The walk down from the parking area is a little shorter than the north access site's, and crowds form quickly. Still, about the only time it sees real combat-fishing pressure is at the height of the salmon season. The rest of the time there's usually enough elbow room to chuck-n-duck, Spey cast, and centerpin.

DIRECTIONS: Take NY 13 south out of Pulaski for about 3 miles.

41L. Pineville Pool Access

DESCRIPTION: This site has parking for about 100 cars and a driftboat launch.

THE FISHING: Pineville Pool always holds fish. Autumn salmon mill around its head, trying to decide which channel to take around the island. From autumn through spring, the head is popular with chuck-n-duckers working egg sacs on bottom, and centerpinners float-fishing the usual suspects for steelies. From the bridge downstream for several hundred feet, the water runs deep and slow and is popular with Spey casters, particularly in deep winter. The unnamed run stretching from the bend downstream for 100 yards or so, and the Ace Hole, a few hundred feet farther down, are favorites of late-autumn steelheaders practicing all the arts man has devised to catch these beauties.

DIRECTIONS: Take NY 13 south out of Pulaski for about 4 miles to Pineville, turn left onto CR 48, cross the bridge, turn right onto Sheepskin Road, and continue for 100 yards.

41M. Trestle Pool North Access

DESCRIPTION: Nestled off to the side of the concrete remnants of an old railroad trestle, this site has a hard-surface gravel railroad bed (tracks have been removed) leading to it and parking for about 50 cars.

THE FISHING: After banking sharply about 100 yards downstream of the mouth of Orwell Brook, the river bottlenecks, rages for a few hundred feet, slides into the former trestle's center support, widens and deepens, and forms a pool carpeted in huge boulders. Atlantic salmon and Skamania find the habitat to their liking on all but the hottest days of summer. Autumn-running Pacific salmon and trout find that its cover and deeper waters offer a measure of safety from the gauntlet downstream and pack in so thick sometimes, you have to work to avoid foul-hooking them. Steelhead and a few browns spend the winter, but the 0.5-mile-long abandoned railroad leading to the river is usually snowed in.

DIRECTIONS: Take Sheepskin Road (see site 41L) out of Pineville for about 0.5 mile, turn right at the abandoned railroad bed, and continue for about 0.5 mile.

41N. Trestle Pool South Access

DESCRIPTION: This site has parking for about 25 cars.

THE FISHING: The same as site 41M. However, the distance from the highway is much shorter than the north access, so it gets plowed and draws all the winter anglers. You'll have to walk a few hundred yards to get to the river.

DIRECTIONS: About a mile south of Pineville on NY 13.

41O. Ellis Cove Access

DESCRIPTION: This site has parking for about 30 cars.

THE FISHING: Situated right at the corner where the river makes a sharp turn, this site offers easy access to a deep run skirting the road, a couple of nice runs lined with steep banks due south of the parking area, and the Muskrat Hole a little farther downstream. The north shore has some low spots that get extremely muddy. The easiest way to avoid getting bogged down, maybe even losing your traction devices, is to follow the footpath along the river; even here, you're gonna run into some awfully low areas where you'll sink up to a foot in mud.

DIRECTIONS: Head north out of Altmar on CR 52 for about a mile.

41P. Altmar North Parking Area

DESCRIPTION: Parking for about 25 cars.

THE FISHING: Less than 100 feet downstream of the Altmar Bridge, the river drops into a small but productive pool. About 100 feet later, the stream widens into the Barrels, a stretch of bony water punctuated with productive runs and pockets; when water levels are 500 cfs or better, the Barrel is popular with Spey casters swinging flies. Several hundred yards later, the river drops into the School House Pool, the upper and lower Wire Holes, and a couple of less significant pools and runs.

DIRECTIONS: At the northwestern corner of the CR 52 bridge, downtown Altmar.

41Q. Altmar Driftboat Launch and Lower Fly-Fishing Only Section

DESCRIPTION: This site, officially restricted to vehicles with driftboat trailers, is the river's uppermost driftboat launch, and has parking for about 20 rigs.

THE FISHING: Open autumn through spring, this site is the threshold to the lower fly-fishing, catch-and-release section. Its pools and runs are favored by Spey casters swinging streamers.

DIRECTIONS: At the southeast corner of the CR 52 bridge in Altmar.

ADDITIONAL INFORMATION: Check the special regulations for the Salmon River in the state fishing regulations guide for this section's seasons (the season varies for the upper and lower sections), times, and tackle restrictions (there's a lot of 'em).

Professional fishing guide and master Spey-caster, Pat Miura, showing his magic on the Salmon River in Altmar.

41R. Upper Fly-Fishing Section Access

DESCRIPTION: This site has a trail leading to the last leg of the special fly-fishing, catch-and-release-only set-aside in the Salmon River Gorge, and offers parking for about 20 cars.

THE FISHING: At press time, this section is closed in winter to protect bald eagles. When it's open in summer, it's the river's most productive spot for landlocked Atlantic salmon and Skamania. While most are taken by Spey casters swinging flies, Fran Verdoliva, the state's program co-ordinator for the Salmon River, claims they'll hit dry flies matching the hatch—and he's got the photos to prove it.

DIRECTIONS: About a mile east of Altmar on CR 22.

ADDITIONAL INFORMATION: Check the special regulations for the Salmon River in the state fishing regulations guide for this section's season, fishing times, and tackle restrictions.

42. TROUT BROOK

KEY SPECIES: Pacific salmon, brown trout, steelhead and brook trout.

DESCRIPTION: Springing out of deep woods in the Tug Hill Plateau, this stream stays cool its entire 10-something-mile length by snaking under the shadow of a mixed canopy of brush and forest before feeding the Salmon River about a mile downstream of Pineville. The state considers it the most productive nursery for wild steelhead in the watershed, outside of the Salmon River itself.

TIPS: The undercut banks and runs near the mouth hold Skamania from May through July.

THE FISHING: This medium-sized brook doesn't get stocked. However, it hosts great quantities of lake-run Pacific salmon and brown trout after moderate to heavy autumn rains pump it full of murky runoff; and it draws runs of spawn-heavy steelhead when snowmelt swells it to twice its normal size in the spring. In early summer, it's generally a couple of degrees cooler than the Salmon River, a factor that keeps Atlantic salmon and Skamania in the pool at its mouth, and draws some into its lower pools and runs, particularly during a hatch and after summer rains. The salmon will hit sponge and raw skein; steelies and browns like worms, egg sacs, and in-line spinners. Native brook trout ranging from 4 to 16 inches inhabit the stream's upper reaches. They'll take worms, minnows, and flies.

DIRECTIONS: Spawned in the town of Boylston, in northern Oswego County, this brook flows south and is paralleled by Van Auken Road in the town of Boylston, Wart Road and CR 48 in the town of Richland, and CR 48 in the town of Albion.

ADDITIONAL INFORMATION: Brook trout fall under the regular statewide angling regulations. The state owns 5.3 miles of public fishing rights easements on this stream and has a map of the locations on its website. The most popular and productive stretch runs for about 0.5 mile, from the state fishing access site at the CR 48 bridge (1.4 miles north of Pineville) to its mouth. A parking lot for about 10 cars is located on the east side of CR 48, just past its intersection with Centerville Road.

CONTACT: New York State Department of Environmental Conservation Region 7 and Oswego County Tourism.

42A. Public Access

DESCRIPTION: Shoulder parking at the bridge, and 1.5 miles of PFR upstream and 0.5 mile of PFR downstream.

THE FISHING: Located upstream of its junction with John O'Hara Brook, this stretch of Trout Brook is very bony, barely deep enough to cover a big fish's back. It's very runoff-sensitive, however, and all it takes to raise its levels to a salmon's comfort zone is a moderate rain. Still, a few careless salmonids always try climbing it even when the water level is at its stingiest. In summer and early autumn, heavy brush covers the brook in many spots; the best way to fish it is to gently wiggle through the cover, drop your offering into the middle of the stream, and let the current carry it naturally downstream.

DIRECTIONS: From its intersection with NY 13 in Pineville, head north on CR 48 for about 3.7 miles, turn right onto Wart Road, and travel a little under a mile.

42B. Public Access

DESCRIPTION: Shoulder parking at the bridge and 2 miles of PFR upstream, and 0.25 mile of PFR downstream to its union with an unnamed tributary.

THE FISHING: This section gets some salmonids during high-water events, but is primarily a local brook trout hot spot.

DIRECTIONS: From its intersection with CR 48 in the hamlet of Richland, head east on CR 2 for about a mile, turn left onto Jerry Look Road, and continue north for about 3 miles (in this span the road changes names to Lester Road, John Platt Road, and Van Auken Road) to the bridge at Van Auken Road.

43. ORWELL BROOK

KEY SPECIES: Pacific salmon, brown trout, steelhead, and brook trout.

DESCRIPTION: Pouring out of the Tug Hill Plateau, this spring brook flows south for about 8 miles as the crow flies, through heavy brush, pastures, and mature forests before feeding the Salmon River on the northwestern edge of the village of Altmar. Staying pretty tiny for the first 4 miles or so, it picks up a few tributaries, and runs the second half of its length as a midsized stream.

TIPS: From opening day through mid-May, fish the upper reaches with garden worms for some monster brookies.

THE FISHING: Human intervention is minimal on this stream; its fishery is maintained exclusively through natural reproduction. Its upper section is dynamite native brook trout territory and is easiest to fish early in the season, before the brush lining the banks in many spots covers the water in low naves of summer growth. The entire stream, but especially the lower half, is the year-round home for brown trout ranging from 8 to 20 inches. In autumn, Pacific salmon runs are heavy enough for an operation to make money charging anglers a fee to fish a long stretch of private property along Hog Back Road, about a mile upstream of the mouth. Some browns and ironheads enter the stream on the tails of the salmon, winter steelies run upstream in the spring to spawn, and Skamania run the place in summer. Brookies and resident browns hit worms, salted minnows, nymphs, and dry flies. One guy—speaking under condition of anonymity—says he gets monster brookies by slowly working mice patterns tied of deer hair, on the surface, along undercut banks, and around branches poking into the stream from the bank. The salmon respond to raw skein and large streamers; lake-run trout hit egg sacs, nymphs, and floating Berkley trout worms chuck-n-ducked into undercut banks and submerged timber or float-fished in pools and runs.

DIRECTIONS: CR 52 parallels the stream.

ADDITIONAL INFORMATION: Brook trout fall under the regular statewide angling regulations. The state owns 2.9 miles of public fishing rights easements and has a map of the locations on its website.

CONTACT: New York State Department of Environmental Conservation Region 7 and Oswego County Tourism.

43A. Public Access

DESCRIPTION: This site offers public fishing rights reaching 33 feet into the mouth of Orwell Brook.

THE FISHING: A few yards before its union with the Salmon River, Orwell Brook flattens out into a relatively deep, quiet stretch of water that often holds salmon and lake-run trout trying to decide whether to continue upstream or fall back into the river. Easily covered in half an hour or less, this is probably the most popular spot on the stream, so get there early.

DIRECTIONS: The mouth is located a few hundred yards upstream of the Salmon River's Trestle Hole North (site 41M).

43B. Public Access

DESCRIPTION: Two miles of PFR and parking for three cars.

THE FISHING: Perkin Brook feeds the stream at the PFR's halfway point. Above this juncture, Orwell Creek is narrow and shallow, dynamite squaretail territory; downstream, it's also good for brookies, especially in April and May, but the main attractions are the minor runs of Pacific salmon and brown trout it draws in autumn; and steelhead from late October through March. What's more, Pacific salmon and lake-run trout will migrate above the junction pool during high water. Go for them in the big pool below the Tubbs Road culvert, located a couple hundred yards east of the parking site.

DIRECTIONS: Take Bridge Street north out of Altmar for about 2 miles, bear right onto CR 52, and travel another 2 miles or so to the FISHING ACCESS sign.

ADDITIONAL INFORMATION: Perkin Brook offers good brook trout fishing all season long; it sees a few (very few) Pacific salmon, brown trout, and steelhead during high water. The state owns PFR on both sides from its mouth to about 500 yards upstream.

44. DEER CREEK MARSH

KEY SPECIES: Largemouth bass, northern pike, sunfish, yellow perch, black crappies, bullheads, and carp.

DESCRIPTION: On the last leg of its journey to Lake Ontario, Deer Creek slows to a crawl and meanders through the Deer Creek Marsh Wildlife Management Area. It moves so slowly in summer, the ground absorbs most of it; by the time it reaches the lake's edge, it's reduced to a trickle you can jump over.

TIPS: Flip soft plastic worms into the openings and edges of vegetation.

THE FISHING: Largemouth bass in the 1- to 3-pound range are plentiful, and monsters tipping the scale at over 5 pounds are available. They hide under the mats of vegetation lining the creek channel and cruise the steep drops at the foot of the dunes. Gently plop a small popper on a lily pad. If you're lucky, a hawg'll come out immediately to investigate what's hopping on its roof. Let the lure sit for a moment, then jump it into the water and brace yourself for a strike so violent and sloppy, it might just get you wet. If they're not hitting on the surface, try working the weeds with a 4-inch worm on a Charlie Brewer Slider Head. Look for clumps of weeds that are taller than surrounding ones and toss it right into the thick of things. Shake the bait gently a few times. If you run across a branch popping out of the water, that can be even better. Switch to a crankbait or Zara Spook, casting it so it hits the object and bounces into the water. If there's a bass—or pike, for that matter—in the vicinity, it'll be like sounding the dinner bell.

Northern pike tend to be small, stretching the tape anywhere from short hammer handles to 3-pounders. They prowl the edges of vegetation, violently striking any mouth-sized critter, from mice and ducklings to snakes and frogs. Lures imitating these life-forms are very productive. However, pike are partial to minnows and readily slam soft or hard jerkbaits worked in open water or parallel to shore, weed edges, and cover.

Sunfish up to 6 inches, yellow perch running from 5 to 10 inches, and brown bullheads averaging 12 inches thrive in the warm waters at creek's end. They all hit worms, but the perch and sunnies also hit flies. Black crappies up to 10 inches are available, too, and, along with the sunfish, love to take poppers off the surface, or Berkley Atomic Teasers tipped with Power Wigglers, worked a couple of feet below a tiny float.

Carp grow huge, up to 40 pounds. They can be found anywhere there's enough water to cover their backs but are especially abundant in the shallow flat running from the mouth of the creek upstream to the dunes. They'll take corn, bite-sized squares of baked potato, and bread balls. Die-hard carp enthusiasts mix a mash of grains flavored with bismuth or commercially made "carp juices and syrups" and heavily chum an area. They fish it by flattening a gob of the mash into a patty, dropping a hook baited with a kernel of corn or two into the center, packing the mixture around the hook-bait to the shape and size of a hard ball, and lobbing it out. It's allowed to sit on bottom where it slowly breaks up, spreading around the hook-bait like an edible place mat. When the carp catch wind of the chum, they arrive in massive numbers; you can catch hundreds of pounds in a couple hours.

DIRECTIONS: Head north out of Port Ontario for 2 miles on NY 3.

ADDITIONAL INFORMATION: The access site on NY 3 has a beach launch for car-top craft and parking for about 10 cars.

CONTACT: New York State Department of Environmental Conservation Region 7.

44A. Kelly Drive Access

DESCRIPTION: This dirt road ends in a cul-de-sac with parking for about six cars, and trails down to a remote spot on Deer Creek.

THE FISHING: In spring, bullheads up to 16 inches and various types of minnows swarm into this portion of Deer Creek to spawn. They hit worms fished on bottom. Largemouth bass and northern pike spawn here, too, and stick around to pig out on all the bait. They'll hit minnows, spinnerbaits, and crankbaits.

DIRECTIONS: From the intersection of NY 3/CR 5 in Port Ontario, head north for 1.7 miles to the unmarked road on the left, drive several hundred feet to the cul-de-sac, and follow the trails for about 100 yards to the creek.

44B. Barrier Beach Access

DESCRIPTION: This site offers parking for about 20 cars, and a trail through the center of a scenic dune to the barrier pond and the mouth of the creek.

THE FISHING: While the walk from the parking lot to the barrier pond takes about 10 minutes, it's worth the hike. The barrier pond behind the dune is one of the creek's most productive fishing spots for warm-water species. By August, most of the stream goes underground about 20 yards ahead of its mouth, leaving a shallow rivulet connecting it to the lake; during drought years, the mouth dries up completely, an isthmus is formed, and the pond becomes landlocked. While its autumn flow is generally too narrow and low for average kings to run, the mouth is only a few hundred yards from the Salmon River's mouth, and this proximity draws loads of chinooks to investigate. If a heavy autumn rain raises the creek a couple of notches, it'll dig a channel through the isthmus just deep and wide enough for kings and browns to storm in to spawn. Snowmelt usually sees water levels high enough to draw ripe steelhead into the creek to spawn.

Susan Rybaak hiking along the dune trail in Deer Creek Marsh WMA.

DIRECTIONS: Turn north onto NY 3 from its intersection with NY 13 in Port Ontario, travel 3 miles to Rainbow Shores Road, turn left, continue for 1.8 miles to the end, turn left, go 0.6 mile to the fork in the road, bear left, and drive another 0.3 mile to the parking area.

ADDITIONAL INFORMATION: Deer Creek Wildlife Management Area ends on the beach at the southern tip of the Eastern Lake Ontario Dune and Wetland Area, a spectacular, 17-mile-long series of barrier dunes, ponds, and wetlands boasting the highest sand dunes between Michigan and Cape Cod. Carpeted in poison ivy and beach grass, dune habitat is delicate and folks are encouraged to stay off. The easiest way to get to the mouth—and avoid the poison ivy lining the dune trail—is to walk the lake's beach. You'll pass a dune walkover that offers a decent fishing platform overlooking the pond.

45. LITTLE SANDY CREEK

KEY SPECIES: Steelhead, brown trout, chinook salmon, coho salmon, and panfish.

DESCRIPTION: Pouring out of the Little John Wildlife Management Area, on the western face of the Tug Hill Plateau, this creek averages about 15 feet wide and drains into the southeastern corner of North Sandy Pond. Spring-fed, running at a gentle gradient for its last few miles, it doesn't depend on rain to maintain water levels and carries a deep enough flow year-round to support resident suckers, fallfish, and young-of-the-year salmonids born in its fish-friendly currents. Its steady water levels allow salmonids to stick around in its pools, runs, and undercut banks even after runoff from heavy rains subsides.

TIPS: The best time to fish is when the creek is murky and too high to wade across.

THE FISHING: Pacific salmon run the creek after autumn rains raise its level a foot or so—it doesn't take much—remaining until they're all caught out, or spawn and die. A few browns and steelhead move in from late October through December. Snowmelt sees good quantities of steelhead enter to spawn. Target the salmon with raw skein; the browns and steelhead with egg sacs, streamers, and glo bugs. Bullheads, crappies, and sunfish run the creek's flat water to the first set of rapids below the NY 3 bridge. The bullheads and sunnies take worms; the crappies, minnows and scented tubes.

DIRECTIONS: CR 15 parallels the stream.

ADDITIONAL INFORMATION: One of the prettiest trout streams you'll find anywhere, this creek has such good habitat that the state set it aside as the crown jewel in a highly optimistic Atlantic salmon recovery program late in the last century. Things didn't work out because a thiamine deficiency, caused by the Atlantics feeding on alewives, rendered them sterile. The program was shelved after a few years. Currently, fishing is prohibited in the lower stream stretching from the channel junction 850 feet below the NY 3 bridge, upstream to the public fishing rights section when walleye season is closed.

CONTACT: New York State Department of Environmental Conservation Region 7 and Oswego County Promotion & Tourism.

45A. Norton Road Public Access

DESCRIPTION: This state site offers parking for 15 cars and about 2.5 miles of public fishing rights upstream of the bridge and a little over 0.5 mile of PFR downstream of it.

DIRECTIONS: Take North Street (CR 62) out of Pulaski for about 3.5 miles. At the stop sign, continue on CR 15 for 0.5 mile and turn left onto Norton Road.

45B. Public Fishing Rights

DESCRIPTION: Shoulder parking and about 0.2 mile of PFR upstream of the bridge and a few hundred feet downstream.

DIRECTIONS: At the US 11 bridge in the village of Sandy Creek.

46. LINDSEY CREEK

KEY SPECIES: Chinook salmon, coho salmon, and steelhead.

DESCRIPTION: Spawned in the deep woods of Winona State Forest, this narrow gem weaves through the Oswego and Jefferson County line for about 14 miles before feeding North Sandy Pond.

TIPS: Use a strike indicator while chuck-n-ducking glo bugs.

THE FISHING: Chinook salmon up to 20 pounds and a few coho salmon averaging 8 pounds run this skinny creek in autumn, during high water. They'll hit sponge, raw skein, and streamers. Steelhead enter in search of salmon eggs in late October and during winter thaws; they stage spawning runs from ice-out through mid-March, and will take egg sacs and glo bugs.

DIRECTIONS: Oswego County's Scott Road parallels most of the stream.

ADDITIONAL INFORMATION: Like all the creeks sired by springs jetting out of the side of the Tug Hill Plateau, this one stays cool enough to hold salmon and trout in its pools and runs just about anytime. The trick is to get there when runoff raises water levels enough to allow salmonids passage through the ripples.

CONTACT: New York State Department of Environmental Conservation Region 6.

46A. Public Fishing Rights

DESCRIPTION: Parking for five cars and roughly 6 miles of PFR downstream of the bridge.

DIRECTIONS: From I-81 exit 39 in Mannsville, turn west onto CR 90 (Lilac Park Drive), travel about 500 yards, and turn left onto CR 89. At its end in Cobblestone Corners, about 1.5 miles later, turn left, then a quick right onto CR 87, and continue about a mile to the parking lot on the northwestern corner of the second bridge.

ADDITIONAL INFORMATION: Jacobs Brook (the first bridge you cross on CR 87) draws some salmonids during high-water events; so many, in fact, the state bought 0.5 mile of PFR downstream of the bridge.

46B. Public Fishing Rights

DESCRIPTION: About 0.5 mile of PFR downstream of Weaver Road and parking at the shoulder.

DIRECTIONS: From site 46A, head south (right) onto CR 87 (turns into CR 22A in Oswego County, about 0.5 mile later), travel 0.8 mile, turn right onto Scott Road, continue for 2.5 miles and turn right onto Weaver Road, cross the bridge 0.2 mile later, and turn left onto Henderson Road; the PFR starts a couple hundred feet later (see "Additional information").

ADDITIONAL INFORMATION: The vast majority of the PFR easement is on the south bank. At press time posted signs lined the short stretch of PFR skirting Henderson Road on the north side of the creek. To avoid conflicts with whoever took the PFR signs down and put up the posted signs, or until the state resolves the issue by putting up new signs, most anglers park at the shoulder of the bridge on Weaver Road and head downstream on private property (it wasn't posted at press time) to the PFR.

47. SKINNER CREEK

KEY SPECIES: Chinook salmon and steelhead.

DESCRIPTION: Spit out of the west face of the Tug Hill Plateau like a kid squirting water through his teeth, this spring creek winds through a patchwork of scenic pasture, forest, and marsh before feeding North

Sandy Pond. The majority of lake-run fish only reach upstream as far as the culvert under the south lane of I-81.

TIPS: Salmon run best after an autumn rain.

THE FISHING: In early autumn, chinook salmon up to 20 pounds run the creek, water levels permitting. However, even during dry years reluctant stragglers, propelled by their unwinding biological clocks, stage small runs. They hit single plastic eggs, fresh skein, and skein-imitating materials. Steelhead enter the stream during high water, autumn through spring, and hit egg sacs, wax worms, and garden worms.

DIRECTIONS: The sections of stream with public fishing rights easements are paralleled by (east to west) CR 89, Dingman Road, and CR 121.

CONTACT: New York State Department of Environmental Conservation Region 6.

47A. Public Fishing Rights

DESCRIPTION: Parking for about 20 cars and about a mile of PFR upstream to US 11.

DIRECTIONS: From I-81 North exit 39 in Mannsville, head east on CR 90 for 100 yards, hook a right onto Brown Road, and travel 0.3 mile to the parking area at the curve.

ADDITIONAL INFORMATION: The shallow culvert under the south lane of I-81 blocks all but the toughest salmon and trout from getting any farther, so lake-run fish that make it up here are at the top of their class. You'll have to walk about 400 paces down a steep hill and through woods to get to the creek. In addition to the alpha fish mentioned above, this stretch gets stocked with about 300 nine-inch browns annually and has native brook trout.

47B. Public Fishing Rights

DESCRIPTION: Parking for five cars and access to 0.5 mile of PFR upstream and 1.5 miles of PFR downstream to CR 87.

DIRECTIONS: From I-81 North exit 39 in Mannsville, turn west onto CR 90, travel about 500 yards, turn left onto CR 89, and travel for about 1 mile.

ADDITIONAL INFORMATION: Getting down to the creek from the public access site is treacherous. Avoid it by taking the pipeline clearing about 100 feet west, off CR 89.

47C. Public Fishing Rights

DESCRIPTION: Parking for five cars and access to PFR upstream to site 47B and downstream for about 0.5 mile.

DIRECTIONS: From site 47B, continue west on CR 89 for about 1 mile to its end. Turn left onto Ellis Road then right almost immediately onto CR 87, continue for a few hundred feet, cross the creek, and park in the small lot.

47D. Public Fishing Rights

DESCRIPTION: Parking for 10 cars and PFR on the entire north bank, and most of the south bank, for a little over a mile upstream to Hobbs Road; and PFR downstream on both banks for about 0.25 mile, and an additional 0.5 mile on the north bank.

DIRECTIONS: From its intersection with NY 3, head east on CR 121 for 0.8 mile. At the curve, continue straight on the dirt road for about 100 yards, hook a right onto Weaver Road, and continue for about 0.2 mile to the parking area on the left, actually a widening of the shoulder.

ADDITIONAL INFORMATION: The parking area overlooks Big Deerlick Creek, a tributary of Skinner Creek. It gets runs of Pacific salmon and steelhead during high water, and the state owns PFR easements from the parking area to its mouth. An additional 0.25 mile of PFR is available on Deerlick Creek south of Dingman Road (head north on Weaver Road for 0.5 mile, turn right onto Dingman Road, and travel about 0.2 mile).

48. NORTH SANDY POND

KEY SPECIES: Largemouth bass, smallmouth bass, walleyes, northern pike, black crappies, and panfish.

DESCRIPTION: The biggest pond in the Eastern Lake Ontario Dune and Wetland Area, it covers 2,400 acres, averages 8 feet deep, and has a maximum depth of 13 feet. A popular summer destination, most of its shore is heavily developed with camps, year-round homes, and private marinas.

TIPS: Work jerkbaits along drop-offs and breaklines for bucketmouths.

THE FISHING: Largemouth bass ranging from 1½ to 5 pounds rule the pond's copious weed beds and reeds. They respond to all the usual suspects: Texas-rigged 4-inch tubes cast along the edges of emergent and submerged vegetation and jiggled lightly; YUM Dingers tossed around weed clusters atop sand flats; and Zara Spooks walked around lily pads, weed edges, breaklines, you name it.

While not as plentiful as largemouths, smallies in the 1- to 4-pound range find some of the pond's habitats to their liking. Local bass pro and guide Pat Miura claims that "a few usually hang out at the outlet and around the big island." They're known for being partial to 3-inch tubes, wacky-rigged YUM Dingers, and 4-inch finesse worms on drop-shot rigs.

Sandy Pond is one of the best places on Lake Ontario to nail large northern pike. Most range from 3 to 8 pounds, but there's a smattering of 10- to 15-pound fish to make things really interesting. They'll hit just about anything moving that remotely resembles a minnow, but are especially known for viciously slamming large in-line spinners, crankbaits like Smithwick Rogues swimmed or jerked over deep weed beds, and large minnows drifted along weed edges. Come winter, they're popular with icers using large minnows on tip-ups.

After dropping off for a couple of years, walleye numbers are on the rebound. Running anywhere from 2 to 8 pounds, they're targeted by locals who mainly drift worms on harnesses (plain and spinner-rigged), flatline crankbaits like Storm Thundersticks, or jig bladebaits.

Crappies up to 12 inches are the rage shortly after ice-out when they gather in the canals on the north and east shores. Move around silently, keeping an eye out for surface activity; when you find it, fish the area with small minnows or small tube jigs like Berkley Atomic Teasers. Sunfish averaging 6 inches and yellow perch running from 6 to 10 inches hang around vegetation and breaklines, and take tiny jigs tipped with scented plastics like Berkley Wigglers and Honey Worms. In addition, yellow perch are popular game in the winter when they're targeted on tiny ice jigs tipped with spikes and mousies. Bullheads enter the mouth of Little Sandy Creek after ice-out and take worms fished on bottom, especially at night.

DIRECTIONS: Take NY 3 north from Port Ontario for about 4 miles to the flashing yellow light, turn left onto CR 15, and continue for about 1.5 miles.

ADDITIONAL INFORMATION: Simply called Sandy Pond by locals, the place lives up to its name with a huge, shallow sandbar on its northwest side. Pat Miura claims, "I've won a lot of tournaments because guys got hung up on the sandbar." The best way to avoid it is to stay east of the large island. Several commercial operations with launch ramps ring the place. This pond marks the northernmost limit of the state's off-season, catch-and-release bass fishing; in other words, fishing for bass during the closed season is prohibited in the Jefferson and St. Lawrence County waters covered in this book.

CONTACT: New York State Department of Environmental Conservation Region 7 and Oswego County Tourism.

48A. Town of Sandy Creek Hazel M. Bardwell Launch

DESCRIPTION: Single-lane hard-surface launch.

THE FISHING: This site is a favorite of ice fishermen because the pond's deepest water is just north of it. Warm-weather anglers like launching here because they can avoid the huge sandbar on the north end.

DIRECTIONS: Head west on CR 15 from its intersection with NY 3 for about 1.4 miles, turn right onto Wigwam Drive, and continue to the end; the launch is on the right, tucked in between the restaurant (on the left) and a private residence.

ADDITIONAL INFORMATION: This no-fee public launch doesn't have a parking lot, but limited shoulder parking is available on the west side of Wigwam Drive, and the restaurant normally allows parking in its lot for a fee.

48B. Sandy Island Beach State Park

DESCRIPTION: Located on the channel connecting North and South Sandy Ponds, this park offers a launch for car-toppers at its lower parking lot.

DIRECTIONS: From site 48A, continue on CR 15 to the end of the road, cross the channel on the narrow bridge, and park in the lower lot just beyond the ticket booth.

ADDITIONAL INFORMATION: Famed for its splendid sand dunes and beach, this site has picnic areas, a guarded swimming beach, and a bathhouse. A fee is charged during summer.

48C. South Sandy Pond

DESCRIPTION: Spilling over 300 acres, this pond's average depth is 14 feet, and its maximum depth is 25 feet. Bowl-shaped, its shallow shoreline steadily drops to a deep center, making it ideal habitat for the same warm-water species found in North Sandy Pond.

DIRECTIONS: At press time there was no public access. The only way to get in is through the shallow channel connecting the ponds on the south-western corner of North Sandy Pond.

49. LAKEVIEW MARSH WILDLIFE MANAGEMENT AREA PONDS: LAKEVIEW, FLOODWOOD, GOOSE, NORTH COLWELL, AND SOUTH COLWELL PONDS

KEY SPECIES: Northern pike, largemouth bass, black crappies, yellow perch, bullheads, sunfish, bowfin, and catfish.

DESCRIPTION: This 3,461-acre wildlife management area is the largest un-developed parcel within the Eastern Lake Ontario Dune and Wetland Area, a 16-something-mile stretch of barrier beach with the tallest sand dunes between Lake Michigan and Cape Cod. Its five ponds are connected by channels navigable by canoe during years of normal rainfall.

TIPS: Ice fish for crappies around dusk and dawn with tiny jigs tipped with grubs.

THE FISHING: Northern pike are plentiful, but they're seldom longer than 24 inches. On the other hand, largemouth bass over 6 pounds are caught every year. Both of these predators react with extreme prejudice to soft and hard jerkbaits worked sloppily and quickly over openings in weeds and along weed edges. In addition, they prowl the edges of sand dunes, where they'll hit spinnerbaits and fat-bodied crankbaits. In years of average snow and rainfall, when Lake Ontario rises into reeds and over cattail mats, hawg bucketmouths move into the pockets in the vegetation and attack jig-n-pigs and Texas-rigged tubes pitched a couple of feet inside and shaken back to the edge; and weedless soft jerkbaits flipped deep into the cover and ripped back at high speed. Drifting free-lined worms or scented plastics like Berkley Power Wigglers below floats is a productive way to take sunfish averaging 5 inches. Crappies range from too small to over a pound. Fish for them on bottom in brush and around submerged timber with jigheads tipped with 2-inch scented curly-tail grubs or tubes; by casting Beetle Spins along weed edges and submerged driftwood; and by slowly pulling 3-inch scented plastic worms below floats along undercut banks, around the mouths of tributaries, and along the edges of channels. From mid-April through May, bullheads in the 8- to 14-inch range invade the ponds, and will gobble up every worm they can find. Bowfin range from 14 to 20 inches and hit minnows, cutbait, and scented plastics fished on bottom. Monster channel catfish up to 20 pounds thrive in the holes at the outlets, particularly at the mouth of Floodwood and Goose Ponds, a couple of miles south of Southwick Beach State Park. They'll hit cutbait, salmon skein, hunks of raw salmon milt, and large minnows still-fished on bottom or control drifted a couple of inches off the floor.

DIRECTIONS: NY 3 hugs the wildlife management area from Montario Point Road to Southwick Beach State Park.

ADDITIONAL INFORMATION: The sand dunes protecting these ponds and their wetlands from exposure to Lake Ontario's harsh conditions are very fragile; foot traffic is discouraged to prevent trampling of beach grass and other vegetation anchoring the sand. If the vegetation is removed, the wind catches the sand, eroding a hole in the dune and filling in the pond behind it.

CONTACT: New York State Department of Environmental Conservation Region 6.

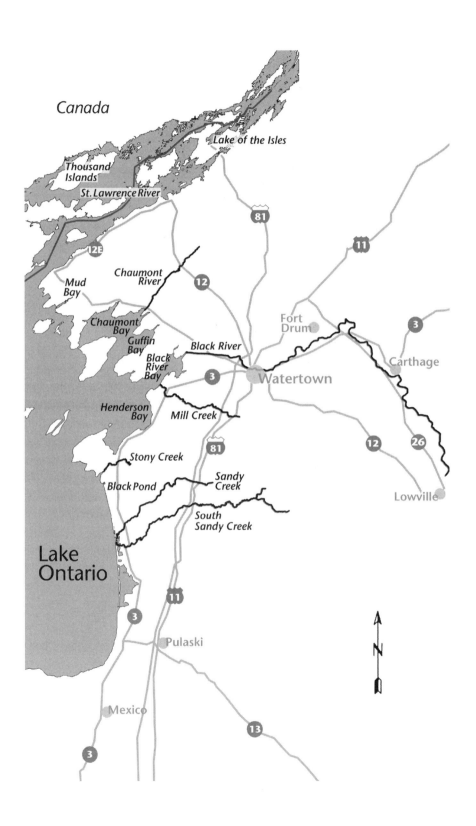

49A. Southwick Beach State Park

DESCRIPTION: Covering roughly 500 acres, this fee area borders the northern boundary of the Lakeview Marsh Wildlife Management Area. It offers numerous campsites (40 with electricity), hot showers, playgrounds, a sand beach, and a launch for hand-carried craft. The campground is open mid-May through mid-October. A day-use fee is charged from mid-June through Labor Day.

DIRECTIONS: Head south out of Henderson Harbor on NY 3 for about 7 miles.

49B. Lakeview Pond Public Access

DESCRIPTION: This site has a beach launch and parking for 15 rigs.

DIRECTIONS: Head south on NY 3 from site 49A for about 1 mile, turn west onto Pierrepont Place, and travel 0.5 mile.

ADDITIONAL INFORMATION: Motors greater than 10 horsepower are prohibited.

49C. Public Access

DESCRIPTION: This site has a launch for handheld craft on South Sandy Creek, upstream of the channel connecting Goose and Floodwood Ponds, parking for about 20 cars, picnic tables, handicapped-accessible shore-fishing access, a groomed hiking trail, and a Johnny-on-the-spot.

DIRECTIONS: On NY 3, a little over 2 miles south of Pierrepont Place (see site 49B).

ADDITIONAL INFORMATION: A short, steep drop prevents launching trailered craft. You'll have to paddle roughly a mile of scenic flat water, lazily winding through bottomland forest and marsh, to get to the ponds.

49D. South Colwell Pond Public Access

DESCRIPTION: This site has a beach launch and parking for 10 rigs.

THE FISHING: The launch area is a good spot for spring bullheads.

DIRECTIONS: Head south about 1 mile on NY 3 from site 49C, turn west onto Montario Point Road, and continue for about 0.8 mile to the WILD-LIFE MANAGEMENT AREA sign at the dirt road on the right.

50. SOUTH SANDY CREEK

KEY SPECIES: Chinook salmon and steelhead.

DESCRIPTION: This stream has it all—undercut banks, deep pools, fast runs, pocket water, even a slow, quiet, mile-long channel ending in the Lakeview Marsh Wildlife Management Area ponds.

Professional Guide Pat Miura preparing to release a steelie he took on a glo bug in South Sandy Creek.

TIPS: South Sandy Creek is the most popular alternative among purist white-water anglers when the nearby Salmon River is too high or overcrowded.

THE FISHING: Annually, the state stocks this stream with roughly 28,750 yearling steelhead and about 80,000 fingerling chinooks. From mid-September through October, mature kings in the 5- to 25-pound range rush the stream. Steelhead up to 15 pounds follow to feast on salmon eggs, staying until ice starts forming. Both species will take streamers and egg sacs. Steelies return immediately after ice-out and stick around into April, water levels permitting. Their stomachs full of spawn, they're not into large meals but ravenously snack on dime-sized egg sacs and $\frac{1}{16}$- to $\frac{1}{8}$-ounce white in-line spinners.

DIRECTIONS: From I-81 exit 40 (Pierrepont Manor), head west on NY 193 for about 4 miles to Ellisburg.

ADDITIONAL INFORMATION: Considered the heart of the stream, the hamlet of Ellisburg boasts a little under 0.5 mile of public fishing rights easements upstream of the NY 193 bridge, and virtually all the way downstream to the NY 3 bridge. Limited shoulder parking is available in the village; and during peak salmon season, a fee is charged to park in the large lot at the bridge.

CONTACT: New York State Department of Environmental Conservation Region 6.

50A. Public Access

DESCRIPTION: Located at the first waterfall impassable to lake-run fish, this site offers parking for 25 cars and about 0.25 mile of public access downstream of the bridge.

DIRECTIONS: From Ellisburg, travel north on NY 289 (west side of creek) for about a mile to Monitor Mill Road, turn right, and travel a few hundred yards to the bridge.

50B. Public Access

DESCRIPTION: This site leads to almost 2 miles of fast-flowing water loaded with pools, boulder-strewn runs, and undercut banks; parking for five cars.

DIRECTIONS: From its intersection with NY 193 on the west side of Ellisburg, head south on Main Street (turns into South Landing Road) for about a mile.

ADDITIONAL INFORMATION: A groomed trail, several hundred feet long and fenced on both sides, leads to the creek.

50C. Public Access

DESCRIPTION: Parking for about 5 cars.

DIRECTIONS: From site 50B, continue west on South Landing Road for 1.3 miles.

ADDITIONAL INFORMATION: From this site forward, the creek reaches the same level as the lake and slows down to a crawl.

50D. Public Access

DESCRIPTION: This site offers parking for about 30 cars, a beach launch for car-top craft, a handicapped fishing platform, creekside benches, and a groomed nature trail.

DIRECTIONS: From site 49C, continue west on South Landing Road for 0.5 mile, turn left onto NY 3, and travel 0.3 mile.

50E. Public Access

DESCRIPTION: Parking for 10 cars.

DIRECTIONS: From its intersection with CR 193 on the east side of the bridge in Ellisburg, head south on CR 121 for about 1.5 miles, bear right onto Nash Road (the dirt road), and continue 0.8 mile to the parking area at the end of the field.

ADDITIONAL INFORMATION: You'll have to hike several hundred paces due north, through a field, to get to the creek.

51. SANDY CREEK (JEFFERSON COUNTY)

KEY SPECIES: Chinook salmon, steelhead, and brown trout.

DESCRIPTION: This medium-sized creek has multiple personalities, flowing through a pastoral setting from Adams (I-81 exit 41) to Belleville, entering a low gorge above Woodville and sliding down a fractured slope at the bridge, leveling off and flowing over a fractured creekbed punctuated in violent backwashes, slicks, shallow pools, and runs, and eventually ironing out into a gently flowing channel before feeding Lakeview Marsh Wildlife Management Area's Floodwood Pond.

TIPS: Wear traction devices like Korkers while wading.

THE FISHING: Each year the state stocks this place with about 3,000 brown trout ranging from 8 to 14 inches. Quite a few stick around all summer and take worms during high water and nymphs when it's low. The creek's major draw is seasonal runs of chinook salmon reaching 25 pounds and steelhead up to 15 pounds. While they're known to reach as far as Adams during years of heavy rainfall, on average they normally don't get too far past Woodville. In autumn both species react violently to Egg-Sucking Leeches and Woolly Buggers. Come spring, spawning steelies move in and take glo bugs, single plastic eggs, and egg sacs chuck-n-ducked in pockets; and streamers swung through runs.

DIRECTIONS: NY 178 and CR 75 parallel the stream.

ADDITIONAL INFORMATION: Also called North Sandy Creek, this stream weaves in and out of view of the highway from Adams to Belleville, a distance of about 7 miles. This is all private property, but most owners don't seem to mind anglers fishing in stretches they haven't posted. However, if you're challenged, be polite and leave if asked to.

CONTACT: New York State Department of Environmental Conservation Region 6 and Thousand Islands International Tourism Council.

51A. Public Access

DESCRIPTION: Informal access, shoulder parking, and public fishing rights for about a mile upstream of the bridge, and downstream for about 2 miles.

Anglers fishing Sandy Creek in Woodville.

DIRECTIONS: From 1-81 exit 40 (Pierrepont Manor), head west on NY 193 for about 6 miles (you'll cross South Sandy Creek along the way) to Woodville, a hamlet that sits in the center of public fishing rights territory—and the creek's best salmonid fishing.

51B. Public Access

DESCRIPTION: This site offers parking for about 20 cars and public fishing rights easements upstream to Woodville, and downstream to just shy of the NY 3 bridge.

DIRECTIONS: From site 51A, take CR 120 (North Landing Road) south for about 0.4 mile; the site is on the right. You'll have to walk through a field for about 250 paces to the creek.

51C. Public Access

DESCRIPTION: This site has parking for about 30 cars and 1.5 miles of PFR upstream of the bridge.

DIRECTIONS: From site 51B, continue south on CR 120 for 0.8 mile, turn right onto NY 3, and travel 0.4 mile to the parking lot on the northwestern side of the bridge.

52. BLACK POND

KEY SPECIES: Northern pike, largemouth bass, sunfish, and bowfin.

DESCRIPTION: Situated at the north end of the Eastern Lake Ontario Dune and Wetland Area, a 17-mile-long barrier system boasting the tallest sand dunes between Lake Michigan and Cape Cod, this tiny (it only covers about 25 acres during wet summers) pond's south shore is part of the 526-acre Black Pond Wildlife Management Area. Fed by a small creek that's quickly absorbed by the surrounding marsh, its outlet is very runoff-sensitive, pouring into the lake when the pond is swollen with spring runoff and after heavy rains; but reduced to a trickle in typical summers. Lake winds easily fill in the outlet with sand and zebra mussel shells, raising the pond, but heavy summer rains pack enough runoff to punch a hole in the barrier, just about draining the pond. The fish have adapted to the feast-or-famine water conditions, and hide out in pockets, waiting for heavy westerlies to plug the hole in the barrier, usually within a matter of days.

TIPS: Gently jig a Berkley Atomic Teaser tipped with a Power Honey Worm a couple of feet below a tiny bobber.

THE FISHING: Northern pike averaging 22 inches are the most voracious predator. They respond violently to spinnerbaits and jerkbaits worked

Beach Scene, Black Pond WMA.

through the channel. Largemouth bass run anywhere from 1 to 3 pounds and take the same baits as northerns, but also have a taste for jig-n-pigs pitched into heavy cover. Sunfish ranging from 4 to 7 inches are plentiful and like worms, tiny jigs, and poppers. Bowfin running from 2 to 3 pounds thrive in this backwater and have a habit of taking baits targeting the other species when you least expect it.

DIRECTIONS: From I-81 exit 41 (Adams), head west on NY 178 for 6.5 miles, turn left onto CR 152, travel 2.4 miles and turn left onto NY 3, continue for 1.1 miles, turn right onto Bolton Road, and follow it to the WMA parking lot at the end.

ADDITIONAL INFORMATION: The Nature Conservancy's El Dorado Beach Preserve runs north of the WMA and includes the beach access to the pond. Its waterfront is off limits to humans July 1 to September 30 so that waterfowl can raise their young and get a break from people. The pond marks the end of the Eastern Lake Ontario Dune and Wetland Area. Dunes tower over the sandy beach that runs south, while the shoreline running north consists of bedrock littered with erratics, boulders strewn all over the place by retreating glaciers during the last ice age. Another natural feature marking the end of the dune barrier system is a relatively calm stretch of water the pond outlet's plume cuts into the surf.

CONTACT: New York State Department of Environmental Conservation Region 6 and The Nature Conservancy.

53. STONY CREEK

KEY SPECIES: Chinook salmon, steelhead, black bass, pickerel, and northern pike.

DESCRIPTION: This small creek flows through a tight gorge before feeding Lake Ontario on the east side of Sawyer Point.

TIPS: Chuck-n-duck egg-pattern flies in early spring for steelhead.

THE FISHING: Roughly 21,000 yearling steelhead are stocked into this creek annually. From mid-September through October, chinook salmon up to 20 pounds enter the creek during high water and strike gobs of fresh salmon roe or egg sacs. Steelhead up to 15 pounds enter the stream from October through first ice, and again from ice-out through mid-April, hitting egg sacs, egg-pattern flies, and worms. Waves of lake-run smallmouth bass pour into the lower reaches to spawn and many remain until July, eagerly hitting any crayfish, stickworm, or spinnerbait that comes within striking distance.

Resident largemouth bass up to 6 pounds, some northern pike averaging 28 inches, and pickerel ranging from 2 to 5 pounds thrive in the marshy habitat upstream of the mouth and take large minnows, fat-bodied crankbaits, and buzzbaits.

DIRECTIONS: NY 3 crosses the creek about 0.5 mile south of Aspinwall Corners, a major crossroads about 0.5 mile southeast of Henderson Harbor.

ADDITIONAL INFORMATION: The fishing access site on NY 3 offers parking for five cars and public fishing rights easements for about 1 mile upstream and downstream.

CONTACT: New York State Department of Environmental Conservation Region 6.

53A. Public Access

DESCRIPTION: A popular area with locals is the small park in the village of Henderson. Located at the dam next to the post office, the plunge pool often holds a salmonid or two in the morning; it's handicapped-accessible with shoulder parking.

DIRECTIONS: From its intersection with NY 3 in Aspinwall Corners, take NY 178 east for about 1 mile.

53B. Public Access

DESCRIPTION: Parking for five cars.

DIRECTIONS: From its intersection with NY 3 at Aspinwall Corners, take CR 152 (Danley Road) west for 1 mile.

ADDITIONAL INFORMATION: You'll have to hike 320 paces down a groomed gravel path ending in a relatively steep, 10-foot drop at the creek.

53C. Stony Creek Public Access

DESCRIPTION: This relatively large fishing access site has a triple-wide paved ramp, parking for at least 100 rigs, picnic tables, grills, shore fishing with a handicapped-friendly platform, and toilets.

THE FISHING: Although this site sees heavy boat traffic, it's all concentrated on the west end, from the ramp to the lake. Flattening out about 100 yards upstream of the ramp, the creek is lined on both sides with reeds and cattails, and its gently flowing waters hold resident and, during spawning time, lake-run populations of warm-water species.

DIRECTIONS: From site 53B, continue west on CR 152 for almost a mile to the stop sign, turn right onto Nutting Street Road, and travel for 0.2 mile.

54. HENDERSON BAY

KEY SPECIES: Black bass, northern pike, walleye, and yellow perch.

DESCRIPTION: Averaging 30 feet deep and dropping to a maximum of 40 feet, this is the southernmost bay in the group of embayments cut out of the east bank of the Golden Crescent like a moose antler.

TIPS: Drift large minnows over the deep weeds in the northeastern corner of Hoveys Island for pikeasaurus up to 20 pounds.

THE FISHING: In spring and fall, huge northern pike running anywhere from 8 to 20 pounds prowl the shallows along the entire bay. While a few trophy seekers go for them specifically, they're mostly targeted by guys fleeing bad weather that snuck up on them while on the lake, who enter the sheltered waters to flatline crankbaits like Bomber A's in 10 to 20 feet of water. Come summer, pike move deeper and respond to large minnows drifted a couple of feet off bottom, and to soft plastic minnows like Berkley's Power Jerk Shad worked violently above breaklines. The water is super clear and each strike highly visible. When a pike the size of a log darts out of the depths and slams your lure, it's a visual feast that'll send your blood pressure boiling into the cheap-seat section of your brain. The harbor's close proximity to the road makes it a favorite ice-fishing spot for yellow perch; and most anglers free-line large minnows or fish them on bottom, in about 20 feet of water, off tip-ups for trophy northerns.

Back about 20 years ago, signs on NY 3, at both ends of town, proclaimed WELCOME TO HENDERSON HARBOR: BLACK BASS CAPITAL OF NY. Rumor has it the wording was changed when town elders finally got fed up with pranksters continually offending the community's morality by removing the B in BASS; the fish didn't seem to mind, though. Henderson Bay has a good population of hawg bucketmouths and bronzebacks. Largemouths ranging from 1.5 to 6 pounds thrive in the weed beds on the south end, particularly in Henderson Harbor, and Whites and Snowshoe Bays. They like minnows dropped into openings, buzzbaits worked through emergent vegetation, and jig-n-pigs pitched under docks, or into windfalls and mats of debris. Smallmouth bass between 1 and 3 pounds hang out on the rocky drop-offs around the islands and shoals and respond to live crayfish, fat-bodied crankbaits, and jigs fished plain or tipped with a worm, minnow, or scented grub.

After spawning in the Black River, walleyes head back to the lake. Most of May finds them taking advantage of the river's warm plume by hanging around the entrance to Henderson Bay, where they climb onto Lime Barrel Shoal and the rocky shallows to the west and south of Bass

Island during low light to feed. They can be taken on everything from bladebaits and worms on spinner-rigged harnesses to crankbaits and bucktail jigs.

DIRECTIONS: CR 123 parallels the bay's east bank.

ADDITIONAL INFORMATION: As you come in from the lake, the entrance to the bay is loaded with shallow shoals. A couple of safe ways to get in are through the cut between the mainland and Hoveys Island and the channel between Bass and Horse Islands. The town of Henderson offers a paved, four-lane launch ramp, with parking for 85 rigs, on the south end of Henderson Harbor, off Military Road (CR 178). At press time, black bass season in Jefferson County runs from the third Saturday in June through November 30; catch-and-release fishing for them during the closed season is prohibited. Asked how anglers without GPS systems are supposed to figure out the boundary between Jefferson and Onondaga County, state fisheries biologist Frank Flack answers: "Don't fish north of Sandy Pond's outlet for post- or pre-season bass."

CONTACT: New York State Department of Environmental Conservation Region 6 and Henderson Harbor Chamber of Commerce.

54A. Westcott Beach State Park

DESCRIPTION: This 318-acre fee area offers 168 campsites without hookups and 83 with electricity, a paved launch ramp, parking for 10 rigs, fishing access on a couple of jetties, hot showers, a swimming beach, and hiking trails.

THE FISHING: The harbor and bay sides of the jetties see runs of white perch, bullheads, and yellow perch in spring, and a few post-spawn smallmouth bass hang out around the rip-rap through June. By summer, low water levels run everything back into the lake.

DIRECTIONS: On NY 3, about 4 miles north of Henderson Harbor.

55. MILL CREEK (JEFFERSON COUNTY)

KEY SPECIES: Coho salmon, chinook salmon, and steelhead.

DESCRIPTION: Possessing a relatively small volume of water, this creek slides over wide, relatively flat and clean bedrock, and all but dries up in summer. However, snowmelt and autumn rains inject it with bursts of life.

TIPS: Fish glo bugs in the pockets around the mouth for spring steelhead.

THE FISHING: Chinook salmon up to 35 pounds try running the creek each fall. Often frustrated by the low water, they mill around for a while in the pools and pockets up to the Military Road Bridge, a few hundred yards upstream of the mouth, viciously attacking crankbaits and streamers that get in their way. Winter thaws and spring runoff attract steelhead ranging from 3 to 10 pounds. Egg sacs and Rooster Tails are effective baits.

DIRECTIONS: On the north side of the village of Sackets Harbor.

ADDITIONAL INFORMATION: Mill Creek flows along the north edge of Madison Barracks, one of America's oldest army forts.

CONTACT: New York State Department of Environmental Conservation Region 6 and Thousand Islands International Tourism Council.

56. BLACK RIVER BAY

KEY SPECIES: Walleye, northern pike, pickerel, black bass, channel catfish, burbot, carp, yellow perch, black crappies, bullheads, white perch, and sheepshead.

DESCRIPTION: Five miles long and up to 3 miles wide, this bay is one of the lake's most productive fisheries. You name the habitat and it's here: islands, shoals, sprawling weed beds, steep drops, deep holes, channels, mudflats, stands of reeds and cattail mats.

TIPS: In May, flatline minnowbaits like Smithwick Rogues along the north shore for walleyes averaging 8 pounds.

THE FISHING: Many local guides consider walleye the bay's top bread-and-butter fish. Trophies running from 8 to 12 pounds are taken in the opening weeks of the season by trolling diving crankbaits off planer boards along the north shore in 12 to 18 feet of water. Purists use lead-core or wire line to get their baits deep, but less dedicated walleye enthusiasts find a monofilament line weighed down with a keel sinker works just fine. Jigging bladebaits or bucktails tipped with worms or minnows along drop-offs, current edges, and breaklines is also effective. By the end of June, most of the keeper walleyes move back to the lake but some remain, hanging out in 20 to 40 feet of water off Bull Rock and Everleigh Point. They'll hit jigs tipped with worms or minnows, vertically jigged bladebaits, and deep-diving minnowbaits. On cloudy days and at night, they come up pretty shallow and take crankbaits like Thundersticks and Challengers cast parallel to shore in 8 to 15 feet of water.

Coming in at a close second are smallmouth bass ranging from 1 to 3 pounds. They'll take a juicy crayfish or minnow drifted on bottom almost anytime, particularly along the breaks, drop-offs, and rocky bottoms found along the bay's north shore and off its points.

Bucketmouths rule the weeds and reeds off the mouth of the Perch River and in Muskellunge Bay. Go for them by tossing YUM Dingers rigged wacky-style into weed openings, working spinnerbaits and flat-billed crankbaits along the edges of vegetation, and tossing Texas-rigged 4-inch tubes into reeds.

Northern pike and pickerel share habitat with the bucketmouths. Surprisingly, average pickerel are almost as large and broad as the typical northern, probably because they're a little more reckless, engulfing anything that moves at first sight and worrying about the consequences later. Both respond to minnows, spinnerbaits, buzzbaits, and crankbaits.

Monster channel catfish, some over 20 pounds, are present in deep holes. While they're available anytime, they're fattest during the salmon run and can be caught on salmon parts: bellies, skein, even strips of milt.

This place is famed for panfish. Although a resident population of bullheads provides good fishing all summer long, lake-run bullheads, along with some yellow perch, white perch, and bay crappies, carpet the shallow, muddy flats at the mouths of the Perch and Muskellunge Rivers from ice-out through mid-May, gobbling up night crawlers still-fished on bottom. The perch will take worms too, but don't seem to develop a taste for them until April. In the meantime, they, and the crappies, like minnows, small tube jigs, Beetle Spins, and curly-tail grubs.

Burbot (the 16-pound, 12-ounce state record was caught here) averaging 3 pounds can be taken in deep water year-round but are mostly taken incidentally through the ice on minnows targeting perch and pike.

Sheepshead running from 3 to over 20 pounds thrive in the bay. These feisty scrappers respond best to crayfish, but also like worms and minnows, and are notorious for striking crankbaits intended for bass, northerns, and walleyes. Carp ranging from 10 to 40 pounds find the weed beds and mudflats to their liking and strike bread balls, corn, and commercial carp baits.

DIRECTIONS: NY 3 parallels the south shore, NY 180 runs along the east bank, and CR 59 skirts the north side.

ADDITIONAL INFORMATION: Large motorized craft can be launched at the village of Dexter's free site (two paved ramps, parking for about 25 rigs, Johnny-on-the-spot, B&J Bait Shop) on Liberty Street (off Water Street) at the northwestern corner of the NY 180 bridge. If you're going to use this launch to fish the mouths of the Perch and Muskellunge Rivers, be very careful; dangerous sandbars line the edges of the Black River's plume for quite a way downstream of its mouth, and you should motor well below the buoys before turning in, then stick close to the shoreline to the mouths.

CONTACT: New York State Department of Environmental Conservation Region 6 and Thousand Islands International Tourism Council.

56A. Dexter Marsh Public Access

DESCRIPTION: This site offers a beach launch suitable for small trailered craft, parking for 10 cars, and several hundred feet of bank-fishing access.

THE FISHING: After ice-out the Perch River submerges this marsh in 2 to 3 feet of water, drawing the lake's greatest runs of spring bullheads, making it the most important bullhead nursery on the lake. (Indeed, some locals claim—without anything to back it up—that in the old days locals filled their rowboats with 'em, ruining their boots in the slime, and Dexter Shoes were originally manufactured upstream, in the hamlet of the same name, to provide high-quality replacements.) Ranging from 10 to 16 inches, they hit worms, especially at night and on overcast days. Northern pike, pickerel, and black bass hang out in the weeds lining the river channel from the CR 59 bridge to the mouth.

DIRECTIONS: From Dexter, take Lakeview Drive (the sign says PILLAR POINT) for about 0.5 mile, turn left onto Doane Road (CR 59), and travel for about 1 mile.

56B. Muskellunge Bay Public Access

DESCRIPTION: This site offers a beach launch, parking for about 15 rigs, and bank fishing.

THE FISHING: Located across the bay from site 56A, this marshy area is part of the Dexter Marsh Wildlife Management Area and also gets great runs of spring bullheads. It holds post-spawn northerns, and pickerel and largemouth bass all summer long.

DIRECTIONS: On NY 180, about 1.5 miles south of Dexter.

56C. Black River Bay Public Access

DESCRIPTION: This site offers a small-craft launch and parking for about 30 rigs.

THE FISHING: This is another hot spot for spring bullheads, panfish, and early-season northerns and pickerel.

DIRECTIONS: Take NY 180 for about 2 miles south of Dexter, turn west onto Military Road, and continue for a little over 1 mile.

56D. Sackets Harbor

DESCRIPTION: Tucked into the south shore at the entrance to Black River Bay, the variety of habitats around this historic village is home to all the warm-water species.

THE FISHING: The drop-off running along Black Bay's south shore, from Gillmore to Storrs Point, is a northern pike and pickerel hot spot. From spring through fall, cast tube/minnow combinations, swimbaits, and fat-bodied crankbaits into the weeds on the shelves and work them back into deep water for pike averaging 26 inches and pickerel only a couple of inches smaller. In winter, fish shiners on bottom and be prepared to tangle with pike up to 15 pounds. Rounding Navy Point, the hook-like formation that protects the harbor, you'll find lots of cookie-cutter bucketmouths in the 1- to 2-pound range, with a smattering of larger ones. The outside of the harbor rip-rap at the marina off Madison Barracks draws lake-run smallmouths in early summer and holds largemouths all the time. They take free-lined minnows, crayfish, and swimbaits during pleasant and slightly stormy weather, finesse baits like Berkley's Atomic teasers, and 4-inch worms on drop-shot rigs when cold fronts and other meteorological extremes are moving in.

ADDITIONAL INFORMATION: It's said the first shot of the War of 1812 was fired here by the British. American colonists, boasting a gun but no cannonballs, located the British ordnance, wrapped rags around it so it would fit the barrel, fired, and knocked the mast off the flagship, sending it limping for Toronto while the fife and drum hilariously played "Yankee Doodle" on shore. The fence around the graveyard once circled Buckingham Palace and was given to America in compensation for British forces burning down the White House during the war. Brigadier General Zebulon Pike, discoverer of Pikes Peak, is buried in the cemetery. This was Ulysses S. Grant's first duty station upon graduating from West Point, and his quarters are now a country inn. Though some of the old buildings are in a terrible state of disrepair, many have been restored and turned into apartments by a private developer, making this historic ground one of the country's greatest living museums of military architecture.

DIRECTIONS: From I-81 exit 44, head west on CR 62 for about 7 miles.

57. BLACK RIVER

KEY SPECIES: Black bass, walleye, northern pike, pickerel, chinook salmon, coho salmon, landlocked Atlantic salmon, brown trout, steelhead, channel catfish, panfish, and suckers.

DESCRIPTION: From Watertown downstream to its mouth, this river only rests twice, both times above dams. Its raging personality results in highly oxygenated water ideal for supporting every fish native to New York . . . and some that aren't. The last leg of this 120-something-mile stream boasts habitats ranging from shallow ripples, raging rapids, and long sections of deep, fast water running through a spectacular gorge, to slow-flowing stretches punctuated with shoals, islands, marsh edges, drop-offs, gentle slopes, weed beds, lily pads—you name it. Fish ladders in the hamlets of Dexter and Glen Park give salmon and steelhead access up to the Great Falls/Mill Street Dam in Watertown, a distance of roughly 9 miles from the mouth.

TIPS: Bottom-fish the holes downstream of the village of Dexter with cut-bait for some of the biggest channel cats in the state.

THE FISHING: The stretch below Dexter is one of Lake Ontario's most productive cold-water fisheries. The reason: massive intervention by the state. Each year DEC stocks about 159,000 three-inch chinook salmon, 100,000 steelhead and domestic rainbow trout ranging from 3 to 4.5 inches long, and thousands of browns running from 7.5 to 13.5 inches long. Summer temperatures force them out into the lake where they remain until it's time to spawn.

"We no longer stock coho salmon but the lake produces wild ones and they're the first to show up in the river each autumn," says Frank Flack, senior fisheries biologist with DEC's Region 6. "They run like sheep, all at the same time, and they're done in a matter of days." They respond to skein, streamers, and minnowbaits.

Kings come next. Ranging anywhere from 6 (precocious fish called jacks and jennies) to 40 pounds, they pour in from October through mid-November. They're mostly targeted by shore anglers fishing raw skein on bottom. However, many are also taken on Long A's and Lazy Ikes back-trolled over their spawning beds: the gravel floors found just upstream of the northeastern corner of the NY 180 bridge and along the south side of the retaining wall separating the middle channel from the southern arm of the dam.

"We started stocking browns recently and the returns are growing larger each year," says Flack. Reaching anywhere from 5 to 15 pounds, they begin showing up about the same time the kings do and continue coming into December. They'll take glo bugs, Berkley 3-inch floating trout worms, and egg sacs worked in the current below floats.

Chromers running up to 20 pounds follow in their wakes to feed on the eggs. Many remain all winter long and are joined in the spring by schools of their kin looking to spawn. They'll take egg sacs, sponge, Rooster Tails, and crankbaits like Smithwick Rogues, Rapalas, and Lazy Ikes.

Although landlocked Atlantic salmon are no longer stocked, they can show up anytime from June through November. Dick McDonald, a state fisheries biologist, explains: "It's been demonstrated that Atlantics have a higher colonization and straying rate than any other salmon, and up to 10 percent run streams other than their natal waters." These fish trace their origins to one of two sources: the Salmon River Hatchery or, better still, natural reproduction.

Warm-water species thrive in the river year-round. For the first week or two of the season, post-spawn female walleyes up to 12 pounds can be caught in the channels, holes, and rapids below the Dexter Dam. Although much smaller, generally stretching from 16 to 21 inches, males are available until June and some return to the rapids in the fall. These fish respond to worms, minnows, jigs, and crankbaits like Bass Pro XPS Minnows and XPS Speed Lures.

Smallmouth bass range from too small to 3 pounds. They're the most prevalent species in the fast water between Watertown and Dexter; there are so many short ones the minimum length in this section is 10 inches. Downstream of the dam in Dexter the bronzebacks are larger. They respond to worms, crayfish, and minnows, but you can avoid the smallest ones by casting crankbaits, 3-inch tubes, and curly-tail grubs. Scrappy resident largemouths ranging from 1½ to 4 pounds flourish in the relatively quiet waters between Brownville and Dexter. They viciously attack jig-n-pigs, Texas-rigged worms, and spinnerbaits violating their space.

Pickerel and northern pike (the pickerel outnumber the northerns 10 to 1; 30 years ago it was the other way around) averaging 22 inches are available in the quiet water above the Dexter dam. In addition, northerns up to 40 inches and stocky pickerel (they're broader than the pike) running from 22 inches to 30 inches rule the lower river. McDonald suggests the reason they're so big is that "pike and pickerel are eating gobies—they're like snacks on the bottom—and we've experienced an increase in their growth rates." They take large minnows drifted or fished below bobbers; jerkbaits ripped violently and rapidly throughout the water column; buzzbaits ripped across the surface, over weed edges, and around windfalls; and Bass Pro Nitro Square Bill crankbaits worked along outcrops.

Huge catfish up to 25 pounds hang out in the deep holes below Dexter. "These fish are so big," according to cousin Staash Rybaak, who's been fishing for them for 40 years, "you can almost jump on their backs and ride 'em." They're especially hungry and big in the fall and hit raw skein, strips of milt, and pieces of salmon belly still-fished or control-drifted very slowly on bottom, particularly along seams in the current.

Late March through mid-May sees the rapids in Dexter teem with spawning suckers of every type. Some locals consider them a delicacy, while most other anglers simply accept the runs as "they are what they are" and take the spectacle in stride. However, a few sour grapes targeting steelhead and walleye take out their frustration on the "French trout" by snagging them, then throwing them on shore to die. Not only is this atrocious behavior unsportsman-like, it's illegal (no dead fish or parts can be discarded on shore), it offends innocent anglers and bystanders alike by stinking up the place, and it hurts the fishery by reducing the number of adults (bottom feeders, they're the lake's most efficient vacuum cleaners) and baby suckers (a primary forage base). Indeed, cousin Staash, no fan of suckers, scratches his head and wonders out loud: "What's wrong with these guys? They throw bait—you know, food!—into the water or run lures and flies through it and get pissed off when they catch or snag a sucker. Go figure."

From mid-May through the first week of June, massive schools of spawn-minded panfish—everything from white perch, white bass, and sunfish to bullheads, yellow perch, and rock bass—mill around the dams in Dexter in such quantities, locals drop everything and stand shoulder-to-shoulder fishing for them with worms, minnows, and small jigs tipped with everything from insect larvae or pieces of worms to Berkley Power Wigglers and Honey Worms.

DIRECTIONS: NY 12F parallels the river from Watertown to Dexter.

ADDITIONAL INFORMATION: Above the dam in Dexter, the minimum size for black bass is 10 inches; walleye fall under the state's regular regulations (minimum length of 15 inches; daily limit of 5). The village of Dexter offers ample shore-fishing access and a paved, two-lane boat launch with parking for 30 rigs on Liberty Street, just off the northwestern corner of the NY 180 bridge. Informal shore-fishing access with shoulder parking is on Lee Road (south side of the river, at the foot of the dam) and off Lock Street (off Water Street) on the north bank. Fishing is prohibited at the fish ladder in the center channel.

CONTACT: New York State Department of Environmental Conservation Region 6 and Thousand Islands International Tourism Council.

57A. Fish Island Public Access

DESCRIPTION: Located just above the dam in Dexter, on flat water locals call Turkey Hollow, this site has a paved ramp, parking for 100 rigs, and shore-fishing access. Slow and wide, the river brushes against swamps and marshes and is punctuated with islands.

THE FISHING: This stretch is warm-water habitat and has resident populations of pickerel up to 30 inches, northern pike running from 22 to 26 inches, largemouth bass ranging from 1 to 4 pounds, smallies averaging a little less than a pound, and walleyes up to 25 inches. Pacific salmon and browns run through here in the fall; and steelhead run in autumn and spring.

DIRECTIONS: Off Canal Street in Dexter.

57B. Public Access

DESCRIPTION: Situated below the Glen Park Power Project Dam, this site has parking for 10 cars.

THE FISHING: This stretch is loaded with smallmouths, a few browns and walleyes, and gets seasonal runs of salmon.

DIRECTIONS: About 2 miles east of Brownville on NY 12E. From the lot, cross the power canal, walk the edge on the other side, and follow the arrows down to the river.

ADDITIONAL INFORMATION: Glen Park—more specifically, Jim Woods Falls at the base of the power plant's dam—is recognized as the gateway to the Black River gorge. One of the most spectacularly scenic areas of the state, its sheer, 20-foot-high limestone cliffs drop straight into the

Professional whitewater guide Alex Atchie fishing a druidic setting in the Black River Gorge.

raging river without benefit of the talus slopes found in most gorges. "There's a couple goat paths you can take to the river, but walking and fishing is extremely difficult, requiring rock climbing skills to get around some of the drops; besides, both sides are privately owned and largely posted," says Alex Atchie, a white-water rafting guide for Adirondack River Outfitters, headquartered in Watertown. Doubling as a fishing guide, he specializes in adventurous fishing trips aboard a rubber raft to white-water sites bearing names like the Knife's Edge, Wailing Wall and Rocket Ride; past fossils and deposits of petrified primordial soup peeking out of cuts and gaps gouged out of the limestone over the millennium by white water. Besides being an amateur paleontologist, he dabbles in local history and enthralls clients between rapids and fishing spots with his rapid-fire knowledge of the industrial ruins along the river. The rapids he covers are loaded with feisty smallmouths ranging from 8 to 12 inches long; and trophy steelhead, browns, and kings, in season.

There is a fish ladder at Glen Park, and fishing is prohibited within 100 yards of the device.

57C. Public Access

DESCRIPTION: Located in the heart of the Watertown, this spot's fast water gets a lot of fishing pressure in spring and fall. Flack calls this the river's best and safest fishing spot between the city and Dexter.

THE FISHING: The DEC stocks about 5,800 browns ranging from 8 to 15 inches into this stretch annually. By May, the vast majority are harvested by locals fishing with worms, salted minnows, and lures like Challenger Minnows and Rooster Tail spinners. Most of the survivors migrate to Lake Ontario, but a few manage to hold on in spring holes year-round. Undersized smallmouths thrive in the pools and pockets, but fish up to 2 pounds are available.

DIRECTIONS: At the Vanduzee Street Bridge in Watertown.

ADDITIONAL INFORMATION: This site has parking for 10 cars and shore-fishing access on both sides of the river. Rafters and kayakers consider the rapids from here to Brownville the state's only year-round adventure-class white water.

58. GUFFIN BAY

KEY SPECIES: Walleye, black bass, northern pike, pickerel, yellow perch, black crappies, bullheads, and whitefish.

DESCRIPTION: Opening directly onto Lake Ontario via the channel running between Pillar Point and Point Peninsula (many folks consider this channel part of the bay, and it'll be treated as such here), the lake-run fish heading for the spawning grounds in Chaumont Bay and the Chaumont River pass through here. Cherry Island on the bay's north edge is the largest island in the Golden Crescent's bays.

TIPS: In May, flatline crankbaits like Bass Pro XPS Minnows about 15 feet down, along the drop-off on the southern half of Point Peninsula for trophy walleyes.

THE FISHING: Big walleyes are the bay's main draw. Most are taken by flatlining crankbaits from opening day through early June, and again in October and November. Bladebaits and bucktail jigs tipped with minnows and worms also catch "eyes," especially over humps and shoals in the outlet channel. Post-spawn smallmouths roam the mouth of Guffin Creek and the drop-offs around Cherry Island into mid-July. Work crayfish, minnows, scented tubes and curly-tail grubs, and fat-bodied crankbaits in 7 to 15 feet of water. Largemouth bass up to 5 pounds occupy the weed beds at bay's end and cotton to stickworms tossed into openings, as well as 4-inch finesse worms on Charlie Brewer Slider Heads worked in vegetation. Post-spawn northerns averaging 28 inches rule inshore weed edges until about mid-July, then split for deeper water. They hit spinnerbaits and minnows while in shallow; bucktail jigs, 3- to 4-inch tubes, and minnows in deep water. Chain pickerel share spring range with the northerns, and claim it as their own for the rest of the season. They'll take swimbaits, wide-bodied plugs like Bass Pro XPS Square Bills, and night crawlers swimmed on spinner harnesses. October sees schools of lake-run perch ranging from 10 to 13 inches enter the bay in such numbers they support dozens of locals who sell them to Harv's Fishery, a local fishmonger operating out of the village of Chaumont (315-408-6125). Sticking around until spring, they take minnows fished on bottom in 15 to 30 feet of water. Bullheads from 10 to 16 inches, yellow perch, and black crappies up to 1½ pounds move into the shallows near the islands off the tip of Point Salubrious immediately after ice-out. Fish worms on bottom for bullheads, and suspend minnows on tiny bobbers, 3 inches to 1 foot off bottom, in 3 to 6 feet of water for crappies and perch. While their numbers aren't great enough to attract a dedicated following, whitefish in the 18- to 25-inch range are plentiful enough to send anglers into reveries of catching one. They're usually taken incidentally on minnows targeting perch.

DIRECTIONS: Set between Black River Bay and Chaumont Bay.

CONTACT: New York State Department of Environmental Conservation Region 6 and Thousand Islands International Tourism Council.

59. CHAUMONT BAY

KEY SPECIES: Northern pike, walleye, black bass, sheepshead, yellow perch, crappies, rock bass, and bullheads.

DESCRIPTION: Covering 9,000 acres, this bay is the biggest in the Golden Crescent—it's so huge, in fact, locals like to think it's the biggest freshwater bay in the world. The isthmus connecting Point Peninsula to the mainland on the southwestern corner is so low and narrow, some folks won't drive over it on windy days for fear their cars will be swept into the bay.

TIPS: Cast wacky-rigged stickworms onto shoals, around windfalls, along weed edges, and into openings in the weeds for black bass.

THE FISHING: Ideal spawning habitat for warm-water species, the bay is a magnet for gamefish. Largemouth bass, some over 6 pounds, and northern pike averaging 8 pounds hang out year-round on the weedy shelves clinging to much of the shoreline, the massive weed bed in the gently sloping southwestern basin, and in the weeds crowning shallow shoals. Both species viciously attack loud crankbaits like Rat-L-Traps and Thundersticks, spoons like Johnson's Shutters and Sprites, spinnerbaits, and soft jerkbaits like Berkley's Power Jerk Shads. For most of May, walleyes from 6 to 12 pounds can be picked up by flatlining crankbaits like Bass Pro XPS Minnows and Bomber Long A's along the drop-off paralleling the south shore around Long Point State Park. When the walleyes move out in June, post-spawn smallmouth bass ranging from 1 to 3 pounds move in and stick around until mid-July. Additionally, post-spawn bronzebacks, the most plentiful black bass in the bay, can be found on the rock beds off the south shore of Three Mile Point and along the drop-offs at the entrances to Sawmill and Three Mile Bays where they take minnows, suspending minnowbaits jerked over deep weeds, and Berkley Gulp! 3-inch minnows on drop-shot rigs; keep an extra rod loaded with a Fluke on hand to throw into the weedy shelves along the shore. Come summer, they move onto Herrick Shoal, about a mile northeast of Long Point State Park, and the area around the mouth of the Chaumont River, and respond to spinnerbaits, wacky-rigged stickworms, and crayfish. Sheepshead, some up to 15 pounds, are numerous and strike worms and crayfish fished on bottom. From mid-autumn through spring, so many 8- to 13-inch lake-run perch enter the bay, they support commercial operations grandfathered to a few families that have been netting them for generations. They hit 2-inch scented grubs and minnows fished on bottom, and tiny jigs tipped with minnows and insect larvae like spikes through the ice. Crappies running from 10 to 13 inches thrive in the massive weed bed in the southwestern corner and can be taken year-round on minnows, Beetle Spins, and Johnson's Beetle Spin 'R Bait; and on dot jigs tipped with insect larvae through the ice. Bullheads storm into the area around the NY 12E bridge after ice-out, and they're joined by waves of rock bass in April and May. Both respond to worms fished on bottom. The bay's numerous weed beds are thick with sunfish up to a pound. They'll take night crawlers, Berkley Honey Worms, and wet flies.

DIRECTIONS: From Dexter, head north on NY 180 for about 2 miles. Turn left onto NY 12E and travel about 4 miles.

ADDITIONAL INFORMATION: The state launch on NY 12E, a little west of the village of Chaumont, offers a paved ramp and parking for 100 rigs.

CONTACT: New York State Department of Environmental Conservation Region 6 and Thousand Islands International Tourism Council.

59A. Three Mile Bay Waterway Access Site

DESCRIPTION: Located on a small bay tucked into the northeastern corner of Chaumont Bay, this site has a beach launch for car-top craft, shore access, and parking for about 25 cars.

THE FISHING: The mouth of Three Mile Creek offers good bullhead and crappie fishing from ice-out through mid-May, and some northerns into mid-June. Around the bass opener, the water warms up enough to run the northerns out to the cooler depths at the bay's entrance. They hit live minnows fished below bobbers, along with minnowbaits and jerkbaits worked along weed edges. Smallies come into the creek's mouth to spawn and some stick around until the end of June, responding to silver spoons and 3-inch curly-tail grubs. Largemouths find the creek mouth and estuary to their liking all summer long and hit big baits like jig-n-pigs and Texas-rigged 4-inch tubes, in watermelon or black, worked along the edges of emergent vegetation. By August, the water gets very shallow and warm, the province of round gobies and small panfish. Come October, chinooks and browns enter the creek, offering good sport to local kids fishing from the 12E bridge.

DIRECTIONS: From Chaumont, head north on NY 12E for about 2.5 miles.

59B. Long Point State Park

DESCRIPTION: This 22-acre fee area offers 86 tent and trailer sites (16 with electricity), a paved launch and marina, shore-fishing access on Chaumont Bay, showers, picnic areas, and playgrounds. Open May through September; a day-use fee is charged to noncampers in season.

DIRECTIONS: From the hamlet of Three Mile Bay, head north on NY 12E for about 2 miles. Turn left onto CR 57 (North Shore Road), cross the isthmus about 5 miles later, and head straight on State Park Road when CR 57 bears right.

60. CHAUMONT RIVER

KEY SPECIES: Largemouth bass, smallmouth bass, northern pike, channel catfish, gar, brown bullhead, panfish, and chinook salmon.

DESCRIPTION: Spawned by the convergence of several small tributaries west of La Fargeville, the Chaumont River runs in a relatively straight path, largely lined with emergent vegetation, for a little over 15 miles before feeding Chaumont Bay. The dam in Depauville limits lake-run fish to the river's lower 7 miles.

Author holding a monster smallie he caught in the Chaumont River on a Berkley Atomic Teaser tipped with a red Berkley Honey Worm.

TIPS: From late September through mid-November, small runs of chinook salmon rush the river up to Depauville, offering exciting white-water trophy fishing in the small stretch of rapids below the dam.

THE FISHING: This midsized stream's wealth of shallow habitats makes it one of Lake Ontario's most productive nurseries, and holding areas for young-of-the-year of every warm-water species in the lake. Its plentiful cover and food support an extraordinary trophy fishery. Largemouth bass in the 2- to 5-pound range thrive among the lower river's thick cattails, reeds, and weeds. They respond to floating worms worked rapidly over holes in the grass, poppers worked through clusters of lily pads, spinnerbaits cast onto flats and worked into deep water, and Texas-rigged 7- to 10-inch worms and 3- to 4-inch tubes dragged along weed edges, drop-offs, and breaks, or pitched into windfalls and under docks. Smallmouths averaging 2 pounds are numerous on the drop-offs of deep channels and around bridge abutments near the mouth, taking bucktail jigs, tubes, and crayfish worked on bottom. Ranked as one of the state's top waters for trophy channel cats, primarily because they have a relatively unhindered 7-mile run to Depauville, without many bank-fishing spots along the way, they provide big-game fishing thrills on cut bait, chicken livers, large shiners, and commercially pre-pared baits like Berkley's Catfish Bait Chunks control-drifted slowly just off the floor or fished right on bottom. Northern pike are plen-tiful in the river's gentle currents and have a taste for large minnows and spinnerbaits. All the emergent vegetation draws great quantities of 18- to 30-inch gar each spring to spawn. Go for them by casting rope lures onto mudflats and along the edges of emergent vegetation. Massive schools of bullheads ranging from 10 to 14 inches move in to spawn in the spring. On warm spring evenings, locals come out in such numbers to bottom-fish for them with worms around the NY 180 bridge that the riverfront turns carnival-like, set ablaze by Coleman Lanterns and headlamp beams. Lake-run rock bass up to a couple of pounds swarm in from late April through May and respond to small minnows and lures.

DIRECTIONS: From I-81 exit 46 in Watertown, take NY 12F west 5.2 miles to Dexter and turn right onto NY 180 north. Two miles later turn left onto 12E and follow it for about 7 miles to the north end of the village of Chaumont.

ADDITIONAL INFORMATION: Informal shore-fishing access with parking for about 10 cars is available on the northeastern corner of the NY 12E bridge. Additional bank access is available on the southeastern corner of the bridge, but parking is very limited. Informal access to the white-water stretch is available on private property in Depauville.

CONTACT: New York State Department of Environmental Conservation Region 6 and Thousand Islands International Tourism Council.

61. MUD BAY

KEY SPECIES: Walleyes, channel catfish, bullheads, and black crappies.

DESCRIPTION: The third bay south of the source of the St. Lawrence River, Mud Bay is long and narrow, and fed by Kents Creek, the largest tributary north of the Chaumont River.

TIPS: During the last week of walleye season, tip a Swedish Pimple with a minnow or two and work it slowly and gently on bottom—leaving it completely still at times.

THE FISHING: Located in an area notorious for monster walleyes, Mud Bay is the best spot on eastern Lake Ontario for trophy walleye through the ice. The fishing improves as March moves along, with most of the biggest fish taken within the last few hours of the season. Local anglers claim the bite is only good after dark. In warmer weather, huge channel cats roam the floor around the bay's entrance and respond to cutbait and shrimp fished on bottom. Massive quantities of bullheads move in after ice-out and take worms fished on bottom. Crappies are spurred into feeding a couple of weeks after ice-out and remain insatiable all of April. They hit minnows and small tubes.

DIRECTIONS: From the Three Mile Bay Waterway Access Site (site 59A), head north on NY 12E for 4.7 miles, turn left onto Bates Road, travel 2.9 miles to the FISHING ACCESS SITE sign, turn left, and travel 0.3 mile down the gravel road to the water.

ADDITIONAL INFORMATION: The Bates Road fishing access site has parking for 20 cars on the beach and an additional 20 cars at the road. Although designed primarily for ice-fishing access, it has a gravel ramp suitable for launching small trailered craft.

CONTACT: New York State Department of Environmental Conservation Region 6.

62. THOUSAND ISLANDS (ST. LAWRENCE RIVER)

KEY SPECIES: Muskellunge, black bass, northern pike, walleye, carp, yellow perch, black crappies, sunfish, rock bass, and brown bullheads.

DESCRIPTION: Draining the entire Great Lakes system (the world's greatest freshwater reservoirs, combined they cover fully 1 percent of the planet), the St. Lawrence is the world's 14th largest river. Its Thousand Islands section stretches for roughly 40 miles, from Tibbetts Point to Chippewa Bay.

TIPS: Muskies are biggest and hungriest in autumn.

THE FISHING: This is trophy water. Arthur Lawton's 69-pound, 15-ounce muskie—a fish that held the world record until being dethroned in the 1990s on a technicality (by an only slightly less controversial fish, incidentally)—came out of here. Their numbers nose-dived in the 1960s and 1970s, but catch-and-release practices, along with increased minimum lengths, allowed them to bounce back. Currently 20-pounders are common, 40-pounders are very possible, and 50-pounders are caught each year. Most are taken by trolling large crankbaits like Swim Whizzes and Buchertail Depth Raiders; and a good number also responds to top-water lures like Jitterbugs and buzzbaits. Muskies usually spend summer out in the lake and migrate into the river in autumn to prepare for spawning.

Northern pike average 4 pounds, but there are enough in the 10- to 15-pound range to make targeting them reasonable. While a skillful guide

Capt. Bob Walters, Water Wolf Charters, instructing his client on how to release a trophy musky unharmed.

can still get his clients 25 pike a day, their numbers are down significantly from 20 years ago. Some scientists trace the problem to the construction of the Seaway Trail, whose flow regime prevents extreme fluctuations in river levels, destroying marshes northerns need for spawning. Others blame the drop in pike numbers on shrinking weed beds, the result of strict antipollution laws that reduce nutrients discharged into the river by municipalities and industry. The remaining pike are larger, healthier, and a lot more challenging to catch. Captain Myrle Bauer—the dean of St. Lawrence River muskie and northern pike guides, famed for leading clients to trophy muskies in the morning, followed by 20 or more northerns in the afternoon—says enhanced water clarity "requires you fish farther from the boat." The largest pikeasauruses are most successfully targeted with large live minnows. However, scrappy northerns in the 22- to 26-inch range love minnowbaits like Bomber A's, buzzbaits, spinnerbaits, swimbaits, bucktail jigs tipped with minnows or scented plastic worms, and jig-rigged tubes tipped with minnows.

There's a great population of largemouth bass in the 3- to 6-pound range, but they're hard to locate in the river itself. Mostly they hang out in creek mouths and in reeds found in backwaters of bays where they strike crayfish, minnows, stickworms fished wacky-style, Texas-rigged worms tossed into windfalls, docks, and other structure, and loud surface offerings like poppers, darters, and prop baits on calm days. One of the most exciting techniques in fishingdom is fly fishing with a popper in lily pads. Cast it onto a pad, let it sit for a few seconds, and jump it from pad to pad. If you're lucky, a bass will explode through the vegetation to nail it, or, better still, swim out to the edge of the pads to see what's jumping around on its roof, and hit the popper as it jumps off the vegetation.

The smallmouth is the river's bread-and-butter bass. Although Captain Matt Heath leads clients to 5-something-pounders annually, typical bronzebacks go about 1½ pounds. Find a school and you can catch them till your arms hurt. In spring and fall, they respond best to minnows. Come summer, they like crayfish and Carolina-rigged worms dragged on bottom over rock fields, 3-inch plastic minnows and leeches drop-shotted along breaklines, and spinnerbaits and crankbaits worked along weed edges. They're also suckers for darters like Zara Spooks worked walk-the-dog-style on calm days.

Walleyes weighing 10 pounds are caught so frequently, they rarely raise an eyebrow anymore. Early and late in the season, when the water is cold, they come up on shoals to take advantage of warmer tempera-tures—and the bait basking there—and respond to crankbaits and swim-baits. In summer, they hang out in deeper water and hit flatlined diving crankbaits like Flicker Shads, Reef Runners, and Wally Divers; spoons like Krocodiles trolled off downriggers; and jigs tipped with worms, minnows, or 3-inch YUM Walleye Grubs and bounced on bottom, es-pecially on the steep slopes of drop-offs, wherever there's current.

The state's greatest concentration of really huge carp, ranging from 20 to 50 pounds, is found here. Most are taken by bow fishing. However, anglers are learning the thrill of monster carp on light tackle and are increasingly going after them with kernel corn, bread balls, and baked potato.

Yellow perch ranging from 7 to 12 inches, sunfish running from 5 to 7 inches, and rock bass up to a pound can be found anywhere, anytime. Black crappies up to 1½ pounds roam the bays. Perch, crappies, and rock bass love small minnows, wet flies, and 2-inch curly-tail grubs and Berkley PowerBait Atomic Teasers tipped with Honey Worms or Power Wigglers; all but the crappies have a taste for worms. Also, sunfish, crap-pies, and rock bass provide explosive summertime action on tiny pop-pers worked over weedy and rocky shallows. In spring bullheads ranging from 8 to 16 inches congregate on shallow, muddy flats and take worms still-fished on bottom.

DIRECTIONS: NY 12 and NY 37 parallel the eastern half of the river, and NY 12, NY 12E, and CR 6 parallel its western half.

ADDITIONAL INFORMATION: "For every one of the 1,800 islands that is visible year-round, there are three just below the surface," says Captain Matt Heath, "and anyone foolish enough to go out on the river for the first time without a guide, or at least charts, is risking serious prop damage . . . or worse." At press time, black bass season in Jefferson and St. Lawrence Counties runs from the third Saturday in June through November 30 and fishing for them during the closed season, even catch-and-release, is prohibited. All river villages offer municipal docks and boat launches. The north side of the river is Canadian, and you need a Province of Ontario license to fish there. Many fishing derbies are held here annu-ally, including qualifying events for major tournaments (check tourism offices for details).

CONTACT: Thousand Islands International Tourism Council and New York State Department of Environmental Conservation Region 6.

62A. Cape Vincent Fisheries Research Station Aquarium and Visitor Center

DESCRIPTION: Located about 3 miles east of the source of the St. Lawrence River, this state facility is open from mid-May to October and offers free transient docking for up to two nights in a sheltered harbor, picnic tables, a gazebo, shore-fishing access, an aquarium, toilets, and showers.

THE FISHING: Large muskies prowl the outside edges of deep weeds and hug rock beds from late summer until season's end, responding to large crankbaits flatlined with lead core or trolled behind keel sinkers so they'll run 15 to 30 feet deep. Walleyes averaging 7 pounds can be taken along drop-offs and on rocky flats by flatlining diving lures like Wally Divers or trolling Smithwick Rogues off divers in 10 to 25 feet of water; use planer boards to keep the lure out of the motor's wake. The weed bed out front holds year-round populations of northern pike ranging from 3 to 5 pounds (try drifting large minnows), 6- to 13-inch yellow perch (anchor in anywhere from 10 to 20 feet of water and bottom-fish with minnows), and smallmouth bass averaging 1½ pounds (they love crayfish drifted over rock fields, and jigs tipped with worms or scented plastic baits and worked along drop-offs).

DIRECTIONS: From Watertown, head north on NY 12 for 18 miles into Clayton and turn west onto NY 12E. Travel for 14 miles into the village of Cape Vincent. The facility is at 541 East Broadway.

62B. Cape Vincent Village Park

DESCRIPTION: This no-fee riverside municipal facility offers picnic tables, toilets, parking for 25 cars, a launch with two paved ramps, and parking for about 20 rigs.

THE FISHING: Occupying several hundred feet of riverbank, this park's railing and benches make it the ideal spot for safe, leisurely fishing. Dropping off quickly, its relatively deep water is visited by every species of fish in the river in spring and fall. It's a local hot spot for bottom-fishing with worms for catfish, bullheads, perch, sunnies, and round gobies; crayfish for smallies; and bouncing bucktail jigs tipped with worms or minnows for walleyes, bronzebacks, and northerns. Farther out, in a diagonal line from the launch to the head of Carlton Island, runs the main shipping channel. This is one of the spots on the river that hosts respectable numbers of resident muskies year-round, and enjoys a spike in the population each autumn. They respond to Berger King Rigs trolled at 2 to 4 mph, 15 to 30 feet down, over the drop-offs and deep weed lines of Featherbed Shoal (south side of the channel), Hinkley Flats Shoal (just a hair off the Canadian border), and Carlton Island. Smallmouths can be taken over shoals and drop-offs all season long with minnows, crayfish, jig-ribbed tubes, and Carolina-rigged 4-inch scented worms. Walleyes thrive on deep rocky flats and along drop-offs, where they respond to swimbaits, night crawlers trolled or drifted just off bottom on spinner-rigged harnesses, and bucktail jigs tipped with minnows or worms and bounced or dragged on bottom; at night they come up on the shoals and take minnowbaits.

DIRECTIONS: Off NY 12E, on the east side of Cape Vincent.

ADDITIONAL INFORMATION: Wolfe Island is Canadian territory and the border runs just off Hinkley Point. Anglers packing only a New York State fishing license risk getting busted for fishing illegally if they stray onto Hinkley Flats shoal.

62C. Burnham Point State Park

DESCRIPTION: This 12-acre fee area offers 48 campsites (18 with electric hookups), showers, a picnic area, swing sets, a gravel launch ramp with parking for 10 rigs, and dockage. The campground is open mid-May through mid-September. Free day use is permitted off-season.

THE FISHING: From Peos Bay (0.75 mile east of the park) to Dodge Bay (two bays farther downstream), the shoreline drops off quickly to a shelf that is 20 feet deep. Northern pike and smallmouth bass hold here year-round and readily hit minnows and diving crankbaits. Carlton Island, due north, is an internationally famous hot spot for walleyes. They range from 4 to 10 pounds and take bucktail jigs tipped with minnows or night crawlers. Many are also taken in daytime by trolling spoons like Krocodiles 15 to 30 feet deep off downriggers and at night by flatlining suspending and deep-diving crankbaits.

DIRECTIONS: About 4 miles east of Cape Vincent, on NY 12E.

62D. Cedar Point State Park

DESCRIPTION: One of the oldest parks in the state system, this fee area offers 172 campsites (55 with electric and 33 with full hookups), hot showers, a single-lane, hard-surface boat launch, and a marina with docks, gas, and boating supplies. In addition, this family-oriented place boasts a kids' playground, a ball field, horseshoe pits, a sheltered swimming beach, and fishing access from shore and a pier. The campground is open from early May through Columbus Day weekend, and free day use is allowed off season.

THE FISHING: The park offers the only shallow water for miles around. Steep drop-offs hug the shoreline for miles in both directions. Smallmouth bass are plentiful on the deep shelves west of the park and on the sharp drop-offs to the east where they take crayfish and Carolina-rigged finesse worms. Northern pike and an occasional muskie prowl the steep drop-off east of Linda Island and have a reputation for savagely striking large shiners.

DIRECTIONS: On NY 12E, 6 miles west of Clayton.

62E. Clayton Launch Ramp and Village Dock

DESCRIPTION: This fee area offers a paved ramp and parking for about 40 rigs.

THE FISHING: Nestled deep in the Thousand Islands, the village of Clayton has been launching memorable angling adventures ever since fishing crossed from subsistence to sport, earning the picturesque hamlet the distinction of being the gateway to the world's hottest trophy muskie spots. While these toothy "water wolves" occupy the canyons between the nearby shoals and islands year-round, the vast majority of truly great fish appear in autumn to take advantage of the river's relatively plentiful bait (defined by Captain Bob Walters as any species that isn't a muskie) and warmer temperatures, as well as to prepare for spawning. Just about every angler who specializes in the species agrees the Clayton area holds more trophies, including the next world record, than any other part of the Great Lakes system. Popular local spots for the brutes include the steep drops on the south side of Grindstone Island, the Trench (the entrance to 40-acre shoals from the shipping channel), Picton Channel (Captain Bob Walters suggests trolling it during a west wind), and along the drop-off between Round Island and Reed Point. Troll for them with large offerings like Believers and Berger King Rigs. You don't have to get up for them at the crack of dawn, either; Captain Walters claims his most productive time is between 10 a.m. and 2 p.m.

French Creek and its bay are ranked as one of the hottest largemouth bass and northern pike spots on the river. Both species can be found prowling its diverse habitats year-round. In addition, walleyes and smallmouths hang out on steep drop-offs at the entrances to area bays, around islands and shoals, coming up on shoals in the evening to feed. Large shiners free-lined in weed openings, along their edges, and around structure like windfalls and docks; Flukes ripped over submerged vegetation; and stickworms fished wacky-style along breaklines will draw strikes from northerns and largemouths. Bronzebacks and walleyes hit bucktail jigs fished plain or tipped with minnows, worms, or Power Grubs, and worked deep along drop-offs. Smallmouths also have a taste for Carolina-rigged 4-inch scented worms and 3-inch Berkley Twitchtail minnows worked on drop-shot rigs.

The Clayton area has always been famed for monster yellow perch. Partial to weed beds, schools of 'em hang out all summer along the drops and on the weedy flats west of Bartlett Point. Come summer, Harv VanDewalker, a fishmonger operating out of Chaumont Bay, abandons his home waters in the bays of the Golden Crescent in favor of this area, and bottom-fishes for them with minnows. Still, perch can be found just about anywhere from shallow mud- and rock flats to deep humps and shoals and even in 100 feet of water in the main shipping channel, where they'll suspend or hug bottom. They hit worms, minnows, small in-line spinners, and minnowbaits. Massive quantities of rock bass inhabit the shoals and rocky shallows, responding to the same baits the perch hit. Black crappies load up in French Creek from ice-out until around mid-April and strike minnows and lures like Beetle Spins and Berkley PowerBait Atomic Teasers tipped with a red Berkley Honey Worm. Bullheads swarm in around the same time and pig out on worms. Sunfish follow from late May through June and love worms, tiny lures like Berkley's Atomic Mites, and poppers on calm days.

DIRECTIONS: Located at the end of Mary Street, right on French Creek Bay.

62F. Frink Park

DESCRIPTION: Downtown Clayton occupies the head of a squared point. Frink Park sits on the eastern edge of the waterfront's business district, on a slab of granite that held the old railroad station and coal docks; the water at the base of the former coal dock is 20 feet deep and quickly drops another 50 feet by the time it reaches the edge of the main shipping channel. The Riverwalk, a paved path, runs east in front of the 1000 Islands Harbor Hotel along abandoned cribs and decaying concrete remains, standing in silent testimony to the hamlet's former timber days; as the path wraps around the point, the river bottom rises into shallow mud flats spotted with weed beds.

THE FISHING: Just about every species in the drink comes to the park at one time or another. Safe, scenic, easily accessible, punctuated with benches, this spot is popular spring through fall with family groups dunking worms and crayfish for everything from perch, rock bass, and smallmouth bass to catfish, carp, and round gobies. Walleyes have been known to come to shore to feed at night and have been taken by anglers targeting smallmouths by vertically jigging Sonars off the dock wall or working Challenger and XBS minnows over the cribs. A few largemouth bass claim the shallow weeds on the east side of the point and respond to scented, plastic worms rigged on Charlie Brewer Slider Heads and worked in the weeds, as well as wacky-rigged stickworms dropped into openings and around structure. Northern pike rule the deep weeds on the drop-off running from the point's northeastern tip through the channel between Round Island and the mainland, and hit jig-rigged tubes and bucktail jigs tipped with minnows in deep water, red and white Dardevles swimmed or jigged along the drop-off, and Mepps Aglia spinners worked along the outside edges of grass lines.

DIRECTIONS: Located on Riverside Drive in Clayton.

62G. Grass Point State Park

DESCRIPTION: This 60-plus-acre fee area offers 77 campsites (21 with electric hookups), hot showers, dockage with 32 slips, a paved double-wide ramp, parking for 10 rigs, swimming on a sandy beach (lifeguard on duty), playgrounds, and picnic areas. The campground is open from mid-May through mid-September. Free day use is allowed off season.

THE FISHING: The weedy shallows along the mainland from Round Island to the Thousand Islands Bridge hold massive numbers of northern pike ranging from 22 to 24 inches, with a smattering of 30- to 40-inchers to keep things interesting. They hit minnows drifted or free-lined along weed edges and drop-offs, spinnerbaits cast over weed beds and parallel to drop-offs, and suspending crankbaits jerked over deep vegetation. The area's lush cover also boasts a few largemouth bass ranging from 2 to 6 pounds. They're especially fond of 7-inch Texas-rigged scented worms and huge baits like jig-n-pigs worked in vegetation. Swarms of sunfish and perch thrive in the grass and love worms and small scented plastic baits like 1- and 2-inch tubes and curly-tail grubs. The weed lines on the outside edges of nearby islands hold larger northern pike ranging from 24 to 28 inches, and smallmouth bass averaging 1½ pounds. Both take minnows drifted a foot or so off bottom and over the tops of deep weeds; and Rat-L-Traps and swimbaits worked throughout the water column. In addition, in summer the bronzebacks can't resist crayfish fished deep, or worms worked over rock fields after a heavy rain. Approaching the American Narrows, forced into a bottleneck and cut by numerous small islands and shoals, the river's current accelerates noticeably. Catfish averaging about 8 pounds love the rapid flow and roam the shelves skirting the outside edges of the islands, in anywhere from 18 to 30 feet of water. They'll take gobs of worms, large minnows, and cutbait still-fished or control-drifted on bottom. Walleyes also love the structure-rich currents in the area and have recently come into their own. Fish up to 10 pounds are possible and respond to flatlined diving crankbaits, worms trolled with the current on spinner-rigged harnesses, vertically jigged bladebaits and bucktail jigs tipped with worms, and minnowbaits and swimbaits cast over shoals around dawn and early evening. Mid-October sees muskies cruising the drop-off stretching from Reed Point to Round Island. They are generally targeted by trolling large crankbaits in 15 to 30 feet of water.

DIRECTIONS: From Clayton, take NY 12 east for 5 miles.

62H. Wellesley Island State Park

DESCRIPTION: Covering 2,636 acres, this park contains the largest parcel of undeveloped land in the Thousand Islands. Its campground, open from the last Friday in April through mid-October, offers hundreds of campsites, including trailer sites with electricity and full hookups, showers, a sandy beach, picnic facilities, three beach launches for car-toppers, a marina with two paved ramps, dockage, parking for 100 rigs, and shore-fishing access. In addition, there are 10 cabins and 12 cottages available year-round. The park's free, 600-acre Minna Anthony Common Nature Center offers hiking trails through a forested peninsula, past striking wetlands, old-growth forest, sheer granite outcrops, and some of the most scenic shoreline in the Thousand Islands. The park is open all year, but the day-use fee is only charged from May through mid-October.

THE FISHING: Boasting several miles of shoreline, this park offers loads of bank-fishing access. The marina area on the north shore and Eel Bay are especially popular with family groups bank-fishing for perch, bullheads, and rock bass with worms. Northern pike ranging from 22 to 36 inches prowl weed patches, boulder fields, windfalls, boat docks, ruins, and other structure within casting distance of shore and respond to large shiners fished below bobbers, red and white spoons jigged or retrieved steadily over and around cover, and spinnerbaits, jerkbaits, and crankbaits ripped through the water column, especially along weed edges. Largemouths running from 1½ to 6 pounds can be found in the windfalls, forest litter, and reeds on Eel Bay's marshy east end. Go for them by dropping soft stickworms into branches of windfalls and under submerged timber; working Texas-rigged 4-inch tubes along the edges of reeds and in their pockets; and by casting jig-n-pigs into slop clinging to shore. Post-spawn smallmouths hang out on the flats below the granite outcrops looming over the park's Minna Anthony Common Nature Center until about the first week of July, responding to 3-inch tubes slowly dragged on bottom. They spend the rest of summer on the drop-offs along the park's north shore, the trench on the western edge of Eel Bay, and in the Narrows, the natural cut between Wellesley Island and Murray Isle. They hit crayfish, minnows, bucktail jigs, and fat-bodied crankbaits.

South Bay, a short distance down from the Narrows, gets swarms of bullheads April through May. They can't resist worms still-fished on bottom. Panfish hold in this bay year-round. They all respond to worms, while the perch and rock bass also like minnows, small crayfish, and jigs. Northerns, largemouths, and a few crappies also occupy the bay. The pike and bucketmouths respond to minnows, crankbaits, and bucktail jigs tipped with soft stickworms and yo-yoed in weed pockets, deep grass, and drop-offs. The strawberry bass love minnows and small lures like Beetle Spins and bucktail jigs tipped with scented plastic baits.

In deep summer, the narrow American strip of water on the south edge of the Canadian Middle Channel is a refuge for smallmouths and some walleyes. Go for the bronzebacks by drifting crayfish on bottom in 20 to 50 feet of water; and for walleyes by slow-trolling worms on spinner-rigged harnesses in the same depths. Both will also take bucktail jigs (plain or tipped with worms or minnows) bounced or dragged on bottom. On cloudy days and at night, these gamefish come up on the American shelf and take crankbaits and bucktail jigs.

DIRECTIONS: Cross the American Narrows on the Thousand Islands Bridge (I-81), and take exit 51. Turn right onto CR 191, then right again about 0.25 mile later onto CR 100. Travel for a few hundred yards, take the next right onto Cross Island Road, and continue for about a mile to the park.

ADDITIONAL INFORMATION: A $2.75 toll is charged to cross the Thousand Islands Bridge. Discount books are available at the tollbooths. The Canadian border skirts the park's north shore. If you cast from the bank, you'll be all right; but if you go out in a boat without a GPS to let you know where the international boundary is, it's a good idea to carry a Canadian fishing license. From May to October, the author conducts monthly kids' fishing classes on Saturdays during holiday weekends and the second or third Saturday in June, August, and October; contact the Minna Anthony Nature Center (315-482-2479) for dates and times.

62I. Canoe Point State Park

DESCRIPTION: Nestled in the northeastern tip of Grindstone Island, this fee area overlooks the Canadian channel and is accessible by boat only. It offers 35 campsites, six cabins, a shelter, potable water, and toilets. Open from Memorial Day through Labor Day.

THE FISHING: While the shallow waters off the park keep campers happy with their abundant yellow perch, the place is generally used as a staging area for angling Grindstone Island's habitats, ranging from massive weed beds to deep rifts. The channels off its east bank are loaded with northerns and smallmouths. Pike are plentiful along Grindstone's entire south shore year-round and rule the flats and shallow bays up until July. As summer progresses they move into deeper water off the mouths of bays, along shoals and drop-offs. Schools of smallmouths compete with the northerns in these habitats. In mid-October muskies move into the channel between Picton Island and Eel Bay for the winter, and are known to slam large minnows, in-line spinners, spinnerbaits, Bomber A's, Smithwick Rogues, and tubes targeting northern pike.

DIRECTIONS: On the northeastern tip of Grindstone Island, due west from the northwestern point of Wellesley Island.

62J. Keewaydin State Park

DESCRIPTION: This 241-acre fee area offers 41 campsites, a marina with a paved ramp and 110 slips, parking for 50 rigs, picnic facilities, a swimming pool, and shore-fishing access on paved paths skirting the park's steep slopes. Camping is allowed from mid-May through Labor Day. Free day use is permitted off season.

THE FISHING: One of the most scenic spots on the river, the American Narrows boasts some of the heaviest boat traffic in the Thousand Islands. Still, according to Captain Matt Heath, the smallmouths and northerns are there: "You just have to time your trip to avoid the congestion, like at dawn and dusk." The drop-offs along the main channel and off the countless nearby islands are loaded with smallmouths. Effective techniques for taking these scrappers include drifting crayfish on bottom, drop-shotting 3-inch plastic minnows and leeches, and casting wide-bodied crankbaits like Bass Pro XPS Square Bill. Northerns thrive in the narrow weed lines clinging to the shelves near shore. They can be taken by jigging a red and white Dardevle spoon so it darts and flutters. The park's marina is a popular ice-fishing spot for perch, northerns, and an occasional walleye. The perch respond to ice jigs tipped with insect larvae like spikes or mousies, and the northerns and walleyes like large minnows. Although the majority of anglers surround themselves with tip-ups loaded with large minnows and sit in the center of their sets whiling away the time between hits by jigging for panfish, a select few targets pikeasauruses and walleye exclusively, jigging for them with Swedish Pimples or other jigging spoons tipped with minnows.

DIRECTIONS: Take NY 12 west out of Alexandria Bay for about 2 miles.

ADDITIONAL INFORMATION: Part of this park is atop a granite outcrop towering over the American Narrows. A couple of antique gazebos are on the cliff, offering spectacular views of river traffic, including surrealistic scenes of monstrous freighters seemingly emerging from Comfort Island.

62K. Mary Island State Park

DESCRIPTION: Accessible by boat only, this fee area is perched atop a high, heavily wooded 12-acre island overlooking the Canadian Middle Channel. It offers 12 campsites, picnic facilities, potable water, and toilets during camping season, mid-May through Labor Day. Free day use is permitted off season.

THE FISHING: The island's north shore quickly drops 50 feet. Smallmouths and northerns are drawn here by the cool, safe depths in close proximity to the productive shallows on the island's other three sides. Target them by casting crankbaits over shallow areas at dawn and dusk, and cover deeper water as the day gets brighter, hotter.

The international boundary is only a few hundred feet north.

DIRECTIONS: Cross the American Narrows from Keewaydin State Park and head east along Wellesley Island. Mary Island sits on its eastern tip, separated from the larger landmass by a channel that's only a few yards wide.

62L. Kring Point State Park

DESCRIPTION: This 56-acre fee area is on a peninsula and offers eight cabins, 58 tent sites without hookups, 28 sites with electricity, a paved boat launch, parking for 10 rigs, two docks, a swimming beach, shore-fishing access, hot showers, and microwave oven rentals for use in the cabins. The campground is open the first Saturday in May through Columbus Day. A day-use fee is charged from Memorial Day through Labor Day.

THE FISHING: Northern pike ranging from 22 to 36 inches can be found in the mouths of bays, in channels, and over the sprawling weed beds, where they respond to minnows and spinnerbaits. Smallmouth bass up to 3 pounds prowl the drop-offs in search of succulent crayfish, or any other bite-sized object that appears to be alive. They're especially fond of jig-rigged scented plastics like tubes and curly-tail grubs jigged or dragged on bottom. Goose Bay, on the peninsula's south side, loads up with bullheads in the spring. They'll take any worm they come across. Come summer, its weed beds are a magnet for largemouth bass, yellow perch, and sunfish. The bigmouths like large baits like jig-n-pigs and Texas-rigged 7-inch scented worms tossed into heavy cover. The little guys like worms and tiny lures like Berkley's Power Mites and Atomic Teasers. When water temperatures reach the upper 40s in autumn, the weeds lay down and northerns move into the bay to over-winter. Urged on by the dropping temperatures to fatten up before the cold sets in, they enthusiastically hit stickbaits, soft and hard jerkbaits, spinnerbaits, bucktail jigs, you name it.

DIRECTIONS: Head north out of Alexandria Bay on NY 12 for about 5 miles, turn west onto Kring Point Road, and continue for about 1.5 miles.

62M. Cedar Island State Park

DESCRIPTION: Located at the entrance of Chippewa Bay, this park is on an island that is half private and half state-owned. The public property has been made into a fee area offering day-use and camping sections. The day-use area offers a pavilion, picnic facilities, hiking trails, and shore fishing. The campground has 18 lightly wooded sites, toilets, and two floating docks.

THE FISHING: Chippewa Bay is a traditional hot spot for northern pike ranging from 22 to 36 inches. They can be found virtually anywhere in the bay from September through spring, around tributaries in May, and at the drop-offs around Cedar Island all summer long. They hit large minnows and their imitations. The river channel outside of the bay is a productive trolling area for muskies in autumn. Troll large crankbaits and Berger King Rigs about 2 mph, 15 to 30 feet deep. Largemouth bass up to 6 pounds thrive in the bay's massive weed beds and hit everything from plastic snakes and frogs to hair bugs worked on the surface. Smallmouth bass averaging 1½ pounds always mill around the rock beds and drop-offs around Chippewa Point and the bay's entrance. They'll take swimbaits and hard suspending crankbaits jerked through the water column. Brown bullheads up to 14 inches literally invade the bay to spawn from April through May and hit worms. Yellow perch ranging from 7 to 11 inches, black crappies up to 14 inches, and rock bass, pumpkinseeds, and bluegills from 5 to 10 inches live in the bay year-round and respond to 3-inch plastic worms and small, spinner-rigged plastic baits ranging from tubes to curly-tail grubs. For a change of pace, try fly fishing with a Mickey Finn streamer.

DIRECTIONS: Launch at the public ramp off Denner Road in the hamlet of Chippewa Bay and head northwest for about a mile. Cedar Island is the relatively large island on the edge of the river's main channel, between Oak Island and Chippewa Point.

63. LAKE OF THE ISLES

KEY SPECIES: Largemouth bass, northern pike, yellow perch, black crappies, and sunfish.

DESCRIPTION: Set into the east end of Wellesley Island, this 2,500-acre lake averages 8 feet deep and has a maximum depth of 20 feet. Two navigable channels connect it to the St. Lawrence River: the Rift, located on the northeastern end, and the unnamed channel running out of the eastern tip. The international border runs down the middle of the channels, and separates Wellesley Island from Canada's Hill Island.

TIPS: Fish the deep pools and channel of the Rift with wet flies on a sinking line for huge bluegills and pumpkinseeds.

THE FISHING: This is considered the best spot in the Thousand Islands for bucketmouths. The average size is 3 pounds, but many tipping the scale at more than 5 pounds are caught regularly. They respond to soft plastic baits like Berkley's Power Jerk Shad ripped over submerged weeds, Texas-rigged 7- and 10-inch worms dragged slowly along breaklines, jig-n-pigs pitched into vegetation and shoreline slop, and walking-the-dog with darters and floating minnowbaits twitched over calm surfaces at dusk and dawn. Northern pike averaging 24 inches are plentiful. Captain Matt Heath says the best time to get them is in May, and suggests casting spoons like Dardevles over emerging weeds. The rest of the year, they respond enthusiastically to free-lined minnows, and bucktail- and rubber-skirted jigs tipped with trailers like umYUM Shakin' Worms, and worked along deep weed edges. From spring through fall, crappies and perch, some up to 13 inches long, hit minnows fished below bobbers or on bottom, and curly-tailed grubs and Beetle Spins retrieved steadily through the water column. Sunfish up to ½ pound are plentiful and respond to worms and flies; try float-fishing a Gulp! Pinched Crawler in the narrow channels between shoreline outcrops and weeds. Heath says this is one of the most popular ice-fishing spots on the river. "There's no current, so ice forms early and stays late," he explains. Northern pike like big minnows fished below tip-ups; the yellow perch and crappies take dot jigs and Swedish Pimples tipped with mousies, spikes, and minnows; sunfish respond to tiny jigs tipped with insect larvae and gently jigged just below the surface.

DIRECTIONS: Head east out of Clayton on NY 12 for about 5 miles. Get on I-81 north, cross the Thousand Islands Bridge ($2.75 toll), and get off at exit 51. Turn left onto CR 191 and travel for about 2 miles.

ADDITIONAL INFORMATION: Covering 12 acres of choice waterfront, DeWolf Point State Park (a fee area located on CR 191) offers campsites, 14 cabins, a paved launch, parking for 10 rigs, and hot showers. The campground is open from mid-May through Labor Day; free day use off season. A Canadian license is required to fish in that nation's waters. The Canadians are extremely protective of their territory, so if you don't have a chart or GPS showing the location of the international boundary, avoid fishing in the lake's northeastern corner and the channels leading to the river.

CONTACT: New York State Department of Environmental Conservation Region 6 and Thousand Islands International Tourism Council.

APPENDIX

IN MOST CASES, fishing information can be obtained toll-free by contacting county tourism offices or regional councils such as the Thousand Islands International Tourism Council. If that doesn't work or if you require detailed, site-specific information like stocking reports and future management plans, contact the fisheries office in the regional New York State Department of Environmental Conservation office.

Visitor Bureaus, Visitor Associations, and County Tourism Offices

Buffalo Niagara Convention & Visitors Bureau
617 Main Street, Suite 200
Buffalo, NY 14203-1496
888-228-3369
www.visitbuffaloniagara.com

Cayuga County Tourism
131 Genesee Street
Auburn, NY 13021
800-499-9615
315-947-6348 (fishing hotline)
www.tourcayuga.com

Chautauqua County Visitors Bureau
P.O. Box 1441
Chautauqua, NY 14722
800-242-4569
www.tourchautauqua.com

Clayton Chamber of Commerce
517 Riverside Drive
Clayton, NY 13624
800-252-9806
www.1000islands-clayton.com

Henderson Harbor Area Chamber of Commerce
P.O. Box 468
Henderson Harbor, NY 13651
888-938-5568

Niagara Tourism and Convention Corporation
10 Rainbow Boulevard
Niagara Falls, NY 14303
800-338-7890
www.niagara-usa.com

Orleans County Tourism
14016 Route 31 West
Albion, NY 14411
800-724-0314
585-589-3220 (fishing hotline)
www.orleanscountytourism.com

Oswego County Tourism
46 East Bridge Street
Oswego, NY 13126
315-349-8322
800-248-4386 (Fish-n-Fun line)
www.visitoswegocounty.com

Visit Rochester
45 East Avenue
Rochester, NY 14604
800-677-7282
www.visitrochester.com

Wayne County Tourism
9 Pearl Street
Suite 3
Lyons, NY 14489
800-527-6510
315-946-5466 (fishing hotline)
www.waynecountytourism.com

Regional Councils, Associations, and Commissions

Seaway Trail, Inc.
401 West Main Street
Sackets Harbor, NY 13685
800-732-9298
www.seawaytrail.com

Thousand Islands International Tourism Council
P.O. Box 709
Wellesley Island, NY 13640
800-847-5263
www.visit1000islands.com

New York State Department of Environmental Conservation

Website: www.dec.ny.gov

Fisheries Office
NYSDEC Region 6
State Office Building
317 Washington Street
Watertown, NY 13601-3787
315-785-2261

Fisheries Office
NYSDEC Region 7
1285 Fisher Avenue
Cortland, NY 13045-1090
607-753-3095

Fisheries Office
NYSDEC Region 8
6274 East Avon-Lima Road
Avon, NY 14414-9519
585-226-2466

Fisheries Office
NYSDEC Region 9, Lake Erie Unit
178 Point Drive North
Dunkirk, NY 14048
716-366-0228
www.dec.ny.gov/outdoor/9217.html (Lake Erie Fishing Hotline report)

State Parks

State parks generally charge a day-use fee from Memorial Day through Labor Day.
Reservations for camping can be made by calling the NY State Parks Reservation
Center at 800-456-2267 or online: www.reserveamerica.com.

Burnham Point State Park
34075 Route 12E
Cape Vincent, NY 13618
315-654-2324

Cedar Island State Park
County Route 93
Hammond, NY 13646
315-482-3331

Cedar Point State Park
36661 Cedar Point State Park Drive
Clayton, NY 13624
315-654-2522

DeWolf Point State Park
45920 County Route 191
Fineview, NY 13640
315-482-2722
Summer: 315-482-2012

Evangola State Park
10191 Old Lake Shore Road
Irving, NY 14081
716-549-1802

Fair Haven Beach State Park
14985 State Park Road
P.O. Box 16
Fair Haven, NY 13604
315-947-5205

Four Mile Creek State Park
1055 Lake Road
Youngstown, NY 14174
716-745-3802

Golden Hill State Park
9691 Lower Lake Road
Barker, NY 14012
716-795-3885 or 795-3117

Grass Point State Park
42247 Grassy Point Road
Alexandria Bay, NY 13607
315-686-4472

Hamlin Beach State Park
1 Camp Road
Hamlin, NY 14464
585-964-2462

Keewaydin State Park
45165 NYS Route 12
Alexandria Bay, NY 13607
315-482-3331

Kring Point State Park
25950 Kring Point Road
Redwood, NY 13679
315-482-2444

Lakeside Beach State Park
Route 18
Waterport, NY 14571
716-682-4888

Long Point State Park (Lake Ontario)
7495 State Park Road
Three Mile Bay, NY 13693
315-649-5258

Mary Island State Park
36661 Cedar Point State Park Drive
Clayton, NY 13624
315-654-2522

Sandy Island Beach State Park
3387 County Route 15
Pulaski, NY 13145
315-387-2657

Selkirk Shores State Park
7101 State Route 3
Pulaski, NY 13142
315-298-5737

Southwick Beach State Park
8119 Southwicks Place
Henderson, NY 13650
315-846-5338

Wellesley Island State Park
44927 Cross Island Road
Fineview, NY 13640
315-482-2722

Westcott Beach State Park
Route 3
Henderson, NY 13650
315-938-5083

Wilson-Tuscarora State Park
3371 Lake Road
P.O. Box 324
Wilson, NY 14172
716-751-6361

County and Town Parks

Monroe County Parks Department
171 Reservoir Avenue
Rochester, NY 14620
585-753-7275
www.monroecounty.gov/parks

Indian Territories

Cattaraugus Indian Reservation
Seneca Nation of Indians
Route 438
Irving, NY 14081
716-532-4900
sni@localnt.com

Guides, Captains, Bait Shops, and Other Sources Mentioned in the Text

Marc Arena
Red October Baits
32 Cornelia Street
Buffalo, NY 14210
www.redoctoberbaits.com
716-997-8970

Alex Atchie
315-782-3904

Bait Shop
5444 Ridge Road West
Spencerport, NY 14559
585-402-8609
www.tackle-prices.com

Captain Frank Campbell
Niagara Region Charters
914 Morley Avenue
Niagara Falls, NY 14305
www.niagaracharter.com
frank@niagaracharter.com
716-284-8546

Captain Myrle Bauer
Net Results Charters
604 James Street
Clayton, NY 13624
315-686-2122

Ron Bierstine
Orleans Outdoor
1764 Oak Orchard Road
Albion, NY 14411
www.orleansoutdoor.com
info@orleansoutdoor.com
585-682-4546

Captain Ryan "Tiny" Gilbert
One More Fish Guide Service
315-529-6427
onemorefish@twcny.rr.com

Captain Matt Heath
Seaway Charters
Thousand Islands
Alexandria Bay, NY
www.seawaycharters.com
captainmatt@seawaycharters.com
315-408-6798

Captain Tom Marks
GR8 Lakes Fishing Adventures, LLC
www.gr8lakesfishing.com
716-997-6919

Captain Rick Miick
Dream Catcher Charters and Guide Service
247 Hadley Road
Sandy Creek, NY 13145
315-387-5920
www.trophydreamcatcher.com

Pat Miura
Pat's Guide Service
106 Park Street
Glen Park, NY 13601
pmiura@aol.com
315-777-3570

Mark Moskal
Summit to Stream Adventures
mark@summittostream.com
607-535-2701

Larry Muroski
Larry's Oswego Salmon Shop
357 West 1st Street
Oswego, NY 13126
315-342-2778
oswegonybait@yahoo.com

Captain Darryl Raate
Water Wolf Charters
315-529-8279
www.stlawrencemuskiefishing.com

Captain Richard Stanton
Stanton Charter Service
7495 County Line Road
Auburn, NY 13021
315-246-4767
www.stantoncharters.com
Fishmrtex@aol.com

Tony Scime
Scime's Tackle and Variety
2815 River Road
Buffalo, NY 14207
716-444-1704

Harv VanDewalker
Harv's Fishery
harv'sfishery@tds.net
315-408-6125

Captain Bob Walters
Water Wolf Charters
P.O. Box 33
Skaneateles Falls, NY 13153
www.waterwolfcharters.com
315-529-2697

More Contacts

Brookfield Renewable Energy Group
U.S. Operations
200 Donald Lynch Boulevard
Marlborough, MA 01752
www.brookfieldrenewable.com

The Nature Conservancy
Central & Western Chapter
1048 University Avenue
Rochester, NY 14607
585-546-8030

INDEX

ABOUT THE AUTHOR

Born in a renovated concentration camp in post-war Germany, to slave laborers deported from Ukraine by the Nazis during the conflict, Spider learned early in life the spiritual, emotional and practical benefits of fishing. A freelance writer and photographer since the early 1980s, Spider has published numerous features in magazines, ranging from *In-Fisherman*, *Outdoor Life*, and *Great Lakes Angler* to *The American Legion Magazine*, *Log Home Living*, and *Boating Life*. He is also the author of *Fishing Eastern New York* and *Fishing Western New York* (both from Falcon Guide), and writes a blog for Oswego County Tourism: huntingandfishinginoswego .blogspot.com.